Indulgences

ALSO BY LORA BRODY

Growing Up on The Chocolate Diet

Indulgences

ONE COOK'S QUEST
FOR THE DELICIOUS THINGS IN LIFE

by Lora Brody

LITTLE, BROWN AND COMPANY · BOSTON · TORONTO

FIRST EDITION

"Commander's Palace Milk Punch" from *The Commander's Palace New Orleans Cookbook* by Ella and Dick Brennan. Copyright © 1984 by Commander's Palace, Inc. Used by permission of Clarkson N. Potter, Inc., and the authors.

"Roast Duck with Apples and Calvados" from *The Seasonal Kitchen* by Perla Meyers, Copyright © 1973 by Perla Meyers. Reprinted by permission of Henry Holt and Company, Inc.

Grateful thanks to Paola Starace of the Hotel Cipriani and Mary Homi, International Public Relations, Inc., for permission to use "Chocolate Soufflé Nerone Hotel Cipriani," "Chocolate Almond Cake Hotel Cipriani," "Bitter Chocolate Ice Cream Hotel Cipriani" and "Chocolate Sauce Hotel Cipriani."

LIBRARY OF CONGRESS CATALOGING-IN-PUBLICATION DATA

BRODY, LORA, 1945–
  INDULGENCES : ONE COOK'S QUEST FOR THE DELICIOUS THINGS IN LIFE.

  INCLUDES INDEX.
  1. COOKERY.   I. TITLE.
TX715.B849132 1987   641.5   87-3396
ISBN 0-316-10906-1

DESIGNED BY JEANNE ABBOUD

ILLUSTRATIONS BY MARY F. RHINELANDER

*Published simultaneously in Canada
by Little, Brown & Company (Canada) Limited*

PRINTED IN THE UNITED STATES OF AMERICA

Contents

Indulgences

Introduction

*L*ife is just a bowl of cherries. Your life, maybe. My life is a dish of raspberries, a spoonful of caviar, a sip of champagne and a pat of sweet butter melting into a hot biscuit. Not only is my bowl oversized, it runneth over with a wonderful and diverse assortment of foods, flavors and textures — from foie gras to red chile peppers, mangos to mushrooms. These are foods I have grown up with, gone in search of and (in some cases) had to learn to love. Some are costly and tend to intimidate the uninitiated cook; some can be grown in your own backyard and eaten right out of your hand. Most of all, these are foods with which to indulge your eyes, your nose, your taste buds: yourself.

What makes these particular foods even more special to me are the adventures (and misadventures) I have had in the discovery, quest and preparation of them. In sharing these stories with you, I hope the message that comes across is that it's all right to have fun with food, and that cooking can and should be a loving, giving act that is enjoyed not only by those eating, but by the cook as well. In a time when so many people tend to take food too seriously, it's important to remember that a sense of humor is an essential ingredient to any successful dish.

In 1959 my idea of a great indulgence was to spend a hot July day at Ocean Beach in New London, Connecticut, and drive home, sunburned to a crisp (no one ever went into the water — your teased and sprayed bouffant hairdo wouldn't stand up to the surf), via Higgie's, a hamburger stand in Colchester, Connecticut, where the perfect hamburger was made. These were the burgers dreams are made of — barbecued right before your eyes by cynical, tourist-tired teenagers who never got to go to Ocean Beach on a weekend. Fortunately, the cooks didn't take their hostility out on the food; the hamburgers were divine. Totally unlike the flat, greasy fast-food disks of today, these plump juicy burgers were hand-formed and had insides that were rare (the new ones don't even have insides). They were served on small, soft egg rolls with lots of relish and a side of fries. I would eat at least three and, if I had skipped both breakfast and lunch in my rush to get to the beach, sometimes even four of these tasty treasures. Higgie's chocolate milk shakes were made with real chocolate syrup, chocolate ice cream and ice-cold milk. This was before fast-food chains discovered that seaweed makes milk shakes thicker (and impossible to suck through a straw without permanently straining your cheek muscles). It was a wonderful and deliciously satisfying meal.

But this was in 1959, when I was a freshman in high school. My standards of indulgences had changed by the time I got to college. By then I was into apple pie. Now, my mom makes a great apple pie, but since she can't always be persuaded to come across, I found a place that would cater to my indulgence anytime I felt like it. Located on the Berlin Turnpike in Berlin, Connecticut, was a diner called the Puritan. They served a slice of deep-dish, hot apple pie that came in an ovenproof, oval-shaped, brown-speckled ceramic dish. On top of the flaky crust was a scoop of the richest vanilla ice cream — already in a state of meltdown as it was whisked to the table. On the side came a little pitcher of steamy hot syrup that smelled of cinnamon, nutmeg and cloves. In the days when I thought I would always have a waist without working for it, I could eat two servings of this apple heaven.

This indulging came in the days before I had learned how to cook, before I had learned that special and delicious dishes are made up of special and delicious ingredients. Then I married and went to live in New York City and began to travel. I began to learn about more magic ingredients than I had ever dreamed existed. I learned real fast that no matter how fancy you made those black olive slices, they never took the place of truffles; and even though it filled the bill during grammar school, Reddi-Wip was not even in the same stratosphere as homemade whipped cream or crème fraîche. Suddenly my list of indulgences — foods that were so special that they transcended everyday eating — began to grow to include things I had never even heard about when I was eating spiced hot apple pie. Some of these things were expensive or hard to come by, but that made them even more special. They deserved to be treated with tender loving care both when served in the "native" state and when used as ingredients. I spent hours researching recipes before I began to cook, and days dreaming up new and wonderful ways to use these foods, to justify their expense.

Like novice jewelers who use silver and copper instead of gold, some of you might hesitate to use expensive ingredients for fear of ruining them in the preparation process. Fortunately, in the case of most of these foods, the less done to them the better. I have included simple recipes that respect the innate virtues of the food. For the time when the reader feels more comfortable experimenting, there are slightly more complicated recipes.

Part of the excitement, at least for me, of serving these indulgences comes from the fact that they are oftimes not easy to find. There is a certain thrill in anticipating the boxes and bundles from Oregon and upstate New York. I have attempted to include foods that are available by mail order during some part of the year, along with the mail-order sources.

Finally, this list of indulgences is totally subjective. These are, simply, my favorite foods. You may not find some of your favorites and may well be surprised at mine. Calorie-wise, I know that those of you who have read my first book, *Growing Up on The Chocolate Diet*, won't be surprised to find that *Indulgences* isn't a book about spa food. I do hope, though, that you chuckle at and/or relate to my stories and are inspired to try (and retry) some of these very special and delicious foods.

Apricots

No doubt about it, my mother makes the best *hamantaschen* in the world. These three-cornered, fruit-puree-filled pastries that are served at Purim come in a multitude of versions from yeasted dough to strudel, but my mother's kind, with their cookielike pastry, tops them all. Purim is the great Jewish feminist holiday that honors brave Queen Esther, who exposed a plot by the wicked Haman that would have wiped out the Jews of Persia. Modern-day celebrations involve children dressing up as the beautiful queen, her formidable husband, King Ahasuerus, Esther's supportive Uncle Mordecai or the despicable villain, Haman. During the reading of the megillah, or the story of Purim, the congregation twirls noisemakers (*greggers*) every time Haman's name is spoken — to blot out the sound of it. The three-cornered shape of the hamantaschen comes from the configuration of Haman's hat. *Tzedakah* (giving of charity), especially in the form of *shalachmanos* (gifts of food), is also an important part of this holiday. In my family this meant making packages of hamantaschen that my brother and I would deliver to friends and neighbors. My mother's hamantaschen came with three fillings: poppy seed (which my father loved), prune (which all the kids hated, but all the grown-ups loved) and apricot (which all the kids fought over). My father bought the two fruit fillings in New York City at a store called Paprikas Weiss, which specialized in Hungarian foods. There thick purees, called lekvar, were spooned out of large containers into smaller jars. I could never wait until we got home to stick my fingers into the apricot lekvar. The tart/sweet taste was always a shock to my mouth. Even a tiny taste made my mouth pucker with pleasure.

I would sit at the kitchen table watching my mother making the dough (she never measured) and rolling it out. I would help her cut the squares and carefully place a dab of poppy seed paste or prune or apricot lekvar on the center of each.

"Not too much," she would warn, "or the filling will leak out all over the place and I'll have to clean the oven." Together we would pinch the edges closed to form the traditional shape.

The smell of those cookies baking was almost too much to bear. I would watch through the little glass door of the oven while the dough browned and the fillings bubbled up through the seams. As soon as they were out, we transferred them onto a rack to cool, but I could never wait until they were completely cool to try one. How many times I burned my mouth on hot apricots in my haste to eat one.

To this day, whenever I taste that delicious flavor of hot apricots, whether it is inside strudel or in a soufflé or even in the hamantaschen I make for my children every Purim, like Proust and his madeleine, I am transported back to the comfort and warmth of my mother's kitchen.

⚜ Apricots ⚜

FRESH apricots have a short season, the peak of which is mid-June. Since the best apricots are tree-ripened, they should be ready to eat when you buy them. The mealy quality some store-bought apricots (and other fruits like peaches and nectarines) have is a result of their having been picked too early and held in cold storage. Look for plump, dull orange, blemish-free, firm but not hard fruit. The flesh should be tender and sweet-tasting. This fragile fruit, a member of the rose family, bruises easily, so if you plan to store it, do so carefully, packed in tissue, in the refrigerator.

As far as dried apricots are concerned, my favorites are the jumbo-sized sold in health food stores and available from some mail-order sources (see list in back of book). They are a wonderful source of iron. The brownish unsulfured apricots taste great but are not as aesthetically pleasing as their plump, bright-colored kin. Like most dried fruit, dried apricots will keep for months in a tightly covered glass jar stored out of direct sunlight.

COLD CREAM OF APRICOT SOUP

This velvety-smooth concoction is the creation of my recipe tester, Beverly Jones. It makes a memorable first course.

*1 11-ounce box (approximately 2½ cups) dried
    apricots
2 tablespoons Amaretto
2½ cups water
1 cinnamon stick
1 cup orange juice
2 tablespoons cornstarch
1½ teaspoons lemon rind, finely grated
¼ cup honey
½ teaspoon mace
¼ teaspoon salt
2 cups champagne or fruity white wine
1 cup light cream
sour cream for garnish*

Measure ½ cup apricots, cut them into slivers, sprinkle with the Amaretto and reserve. Place the remaining apricots, water and cinnamon stick in a large saucepan and bring to a boil. Reduce heat and simmer, covered, for 30 minutes. Remove the cinnamon stick and puree the mixture in a food processor or blender. Return the mixture to the saucepan. Mix the orange juice and cornstarch in a small bowl. Bring the apricot mixture to a boil and whisk in the orange juice/cornstarch mixture, the lemon rind, honey, mace and salt. Lower the heat and simmer for several minutes, until the mixture has thickened. Cool the soup completely. Stir in the champagne or wine and finally the cream. Keep cold until ready to serve. Garnish with a dollop of sour cream and the reserved slivers of apricots.

Serves 8

IVY'S TURKEY BREAST

There are two teenagers, one finicky five-year-old and two adults in our family. It's not too often that I find an entree that all of us go nuts over. My good friend Ivy Feuerstadt not only provided a delicious solution to our diverse dining requirements, but a simple one as well. This sweet-and-sour-style dish is served almost every Friday night in our home — and in Ivy's too.

> *1 fresh, uncooked turkey breast*
> *⅓ cup butter*
> *2 teaspoons Kosher salt*
> *freshly ground pepper*
> *4 large onions, peeled and sliced*
> *3 large carrots, peeled and sliced*
> *1 cup dried apricots*
> *¾ cup golden raisins*
> *1 6-ounce container partially defrosted frozen*
>   *orange juice concentrate*
> *1 10- to 12-ounce jar apricot preserves*
> *1½ cups white wine*

Preheat the oven to 350 degrees with the rack in the center position. Rinse the turkey breast and dry it very well. Place it in a large roasting pan. Rub the butter over the top of the breast and sprinkle it with the salt and pepper. Place the vegetables and the apricots and raisins around the turkey. Combine the orange juice, the preserves and the wine and add the mixture to the pan. Add a little water if necessary to make sure there is a 2-inch layer of liquid in the bottom of the pan. Insert a roasting thermometer into the thickest part of the breast and cook the turkey until it has an internal temperature of 185 degrees. If, halfway through the cooking, the top begins to get too brown, cover it loosely with greased foil.

Let the turkey cool slightly in the pan and then slice it, layering the meat back into the vegetables and sauce in the pan. Serve with rice or noodles. This makes delicious cold sandwiches.

Serves about 8, depending upon the size of the turkey breast

SUE SMALL'S HAZELNUT AND APRICOT DACQUOISE

It's eight o'clock on a Saturday night. My husband looks at me with that familiar gleam in his eye. What could he possibly want?

"I'm dying for a piece of Sue Small's apricot dacquoise," he says, smacking his lips.

"It's Saturday night, the busiest restaurant night of the week. The Peacock is always jammed. What makes you think we could get a reservation?" I'm so supportive of his cravings. He disappears for a moment. I hear him on the phone. He reappears and announces, "As a special favor, Sue can give us a table at ten thirty." Ten thirty? I'm starving now. I can't possibly wait two and a half hours for dinner. Two and a half hours later we are in Cambridge, Massachusetts, eagerly devouring chicken liver mousse, duck breast with cranberries and finally — the dessert that my husband would kill for — the divine hazelnut and apricot dacquoise, Sue's specialty.

FOR THE MERINGUE:

8 extra-large egg whites
pinch of salt
2 cups granulated sugar
2 teaspoons vanilla extract
1 teaspoon white vinegar
*2 cups hazelnuts, toasted, peeled and finely
    ground (see about toasting hazelnuts on p.
    153), plus 1 dozen whole, toasted, peeled
    hazelnuts for garnishing*

Preheat the oven to 325 degrees with the rack in the center position. Butter two 9 x 3-inch springform pans, line the bottoms with parchment or wax paper, then butter the paper. Dust the pans with flour, shaking out the excess.

In the bowl of an electric mixer, beat the egg whites and the salt until they hold stiff peaks. Add the sugar 2 teaspoons at a time, beating well after each addition. Beat in the vanilla extract and vinegar. Using a large rubber spatula, fold in the ground hazelnuts.

Divide the batter between the 2 pans and smooth the tops. Bake the layers for 40 minutes. At the end of that time, carefully remove the sides of the pans (you may have to release the cakes with a sharp knife) and continue baking another 10–12 minutes or until the outside of the layers is crisp. Cool the layers on racks, then remove the bottoms of the springform pans and parchment or wax paper. Reverse the layers so they are upright.

FOR THE APRICOT FILLING:

6 ounces (1⅓ cups) dried apricots
1 cup water
2 tablespoons granulated sugar
strip of lemon rind
2 cups chilled heavy cream
2 tablespoons Kirsch or Amaretto
confectioners' sugar

Soak the apricots in the water for 2 hours. Place the mixture in a small saucepan, add the granulated sugar and the lemon rind. Cover the pan and simmer the apricots until they are soft (about 15 minutes). Strain the apricots, reserving 2 tablespoons of the cooking liquid. Discard the lemon rind. Puree the fruit and reserved liquid in a food processor or blender. Refrigerate until cold.

Beat the cream until it holds stiff peaks and reserve half for decoration. Fold the apricot puree into the remaining half. Mix in the Kirsch or Amaretto.

TO ASSEMBLE:

Set 1 layer right side up on a large flat plate. Cover the layer with the apricot/cream filling. Place the other layer right side up on top of the filling. Sift some confectioners' sugar on top. Place the rest of the whipped cream into a pastry bag fitted with a large star tube. Pipe 12 rosettes around the edge of the top of the cake and garnish each rosette with a whole hazelnut. Let the cake sit in the refrigerator for several hours before cutting.

Serves 1 hungry husband or 10 normal people

$\mathscr{H}$AMANTASCHEN

These freeze well.

1 1/3 cups sweet (unsalted) butter at room
    temperature
1 cup granulated sugar
2 extra-large eggs
1 teaspoon vanilla extract
6 tablespoons water
4 cups flour

Cream the butter and sugar until light and fluffy. Add the eggs one at a time and continue beating until the mixture is light. Mix in the vanilla extract and water. Gradually add the flour until a soft ball is formed. Wrap well and refrigerate overnight.

FOR THE FILLING:

14 ounces (approximately 2 2/3 cups) dried
    apricots
1 cup orange juice
2 tablespoons lemon juice
1/3 cup granulated sugar

In a small saucepan combine apricots, orange juice, lemon juice and sugar. Bring mixture to a boil over high heat. Reduce heat and simmer uncovered for 15 minutes or until most of the liquid is absorbed. Cool to room temperature. Puree in food processor or blender until smooth.

TO FORM THE COOKIES:

Set the oven at 375 degrees with the rack in the center position. Line a heavy-duty baking sheet with foil. On a lightly floured work surface, roll the chilled dough to a thickness of 1/8 of an inch. Use a glass or round cookie cutter to cut the dough into 2 1/2-inch circles.

Place a generous teaspoon of filling in the center of each circle. Lift the edges and pinch them together to form a 3-cornered triangle. Bake the cookies for about 15 minutes or until they are lightly browned.

Makes about 2 dozen

Brandy

The evening before Mardi Gras last year I stood in the New Orleans kitchen of Ralph and Susan Brennan, helping them to get organized for a brunch they were throwing for a hundred guests the next day. Ralph had brought cases of dishes and stacks of linens from his fine French Quarter bistro, Mr. B's. Susan had been busy shopping, cooking and decorating the house with purple and yellow balloons, streamers and multicolored Mardi Gras beads.

"I think we have everything," said Susan, surveying the counter piled high with silver trays and chafing dishes that would hold the crayfish étouffée and gumbo. I mentally checked off items that from years of catering I knew would be essential. Yes, there were cocktail napkins, silverware and candlesticks. Ice was stockpiled in the freezer in the garage. The refrigerator bulged with fresh fruit and several enormous plastic jugs filled with what looked like milk. Beer and liquor bottles were piled in every other available space. There were enough dishes to serve all of the French Quarter should they decide to stop by.

"Susan, you've forgotten coffee cups and a coffee maker!" I said, relieved to have thought of these items then instead of the next day, when driving across the city to the restaurant would have been impossible.

"We don't need to serve coffee; we have milk punch," said Ralph, pointing to the jugs in the refrigerator.

"You mean you're inviting a hundred people to your house for brunch and you're not going to give them coffee?" My caffeine center was put on red alert.

"Lora, we could make gallons of coffee, but no one would drink it — this is Mardi Gras. Who would waste time drinking coffee when you could have milk punch?" Well, I thought, this milk punch must really be some big deal to be able to take the place of my drink of drinks.

In the middle of that night I felt someone tugging at my shoulder.

"Lora, want to get up and see Pete Fountain and his marching band?" It was Susan, wide-awake and dressed.

"It's the middle of the night," I mumbled into my pillow. Next to me, David, my husband, slept the good sleep — the kind that comes from an evening of moderation.

"No, it's six A.M. It only feels like it's the middle of the night because of all those Ramos gin fizzes you drank last night."

I felt like the guy in that old Shelley Berman skit who is so hung over that his teeth itch.

"Come on," she urged. "They only do it once a year, on Mardi Gras morning. They leave from Commander's Palace, right around the corner. You shouldn't miss it." I dragged my protesting body out of bed and into some clothes and followed her outside. My head followed reluctantly. The weather woke me up instantly. What was a balmy, seventy-degree day just yesterday had turned into a dark and bone-chilling Boston special. I had left a nice warm bed for this? Susan assured me that this kind of change was typical for New Orleans, although she did admit it was colder than usual. We walked quickly around the corner to Ella Brennan's restaurant, Commander's Palace, the famous, stately teal-hued shrine to the best of New Orleans cookery. The guard at the courtyard, recognizing Susan as a member of the clan, ushered us into the garden. Mardi Gras already carried with it a certain unreality (especially at this hour of the morning, when we had already seen one large blue rabbit and a cast of women dressed up as Peanut M & M's roaming the street), but this was a scene out of pure fantasy. In the courtyard stood perhaps forty middle-aged and very prosperous-looking gentlemen. Each wore a sparkling silver gray morning coat with pants and vest to match. Around their middles were silver lamé cummerbunds and set upon their heads were silver and gray top hats. Dozens of necklaces of silver beads hung around silver lapels, and shiny silver spats were the finishing touches on already extraordinary masterpieces. Some of the gentlemen sported white or red roses on their coats. All were sipping a white drink from a short glass and none of them looked as cold as I felt.

"Come on," urged Susan, "you'll warm up once you drink some milk punch."

"Coffee . . ." I pleaded as she steered me into the bar area, where a jolly bartender poured some of the white mixture over a glassful of ice, grated some nutmeg on it and handed it to me. The last thing I wanted was something with ice in it. I wanted a cup of hot black coffee — actually two cups, one to drink and the other to pour over my freezing hands. I looked around. Everyone who was drinking milk punch (and that was everyone but me at this point) looked warm — or at least looked as if the cold wasn't bothering them. What the heck, I figured, as I took a sip. It's amazing that something that could look so insipid and benign could taste so potent and affect my insides so quickly. I felt a little like I had swallowed a very gentle furnace. A velvet fist is what crossed my mind as I drained the glass and held it out for a refill.

"This is the smoothest drink I've ever tasted. What's the secret?" I asked the bartender.

"That's the brandy, ma'am," he replied. "Makes it go down real easy, doesn't it?"

I was thinking about getting another refill when Susan pulled me outside to see the parade assemble. She pointed out Pete Fountain, the legendary jazz clarinetist who along with his band would lead the parade. The other silver-attired gentlemen were important New Orleanians who felt deservedly proud to have a coveted spot in the parade. We waved to John Brennan, Ralph's uncle, as he took his place in the line. The musicians picked up their instruments and the marchers fell in line behind them. To the strains of "When the Saints Go Marching In," the line of silver men shuffled toward the gate to the street. Outside, the mob eagerly called to them, "Hey, mister! Throw me some beads!" and the silver necklaces flew through the air toward outstretched hands.

I fortified myself with another milk punch to warm my way home and reflected fleetingly on how easy it would be to give up coffee if every day could be Mardi Gras.

⋟ Brandy ⋞

QUITE simply, brandy is the liquor distilled from wine or the fermented juices of fruits such as cherries, peaches, plums and the like. The second distillation (the first being the process that resulted in the wine) is done in aged wood, which creates a smooth and sophisticated flavor. Armagnac and cognac are two of the best-known brandies. Cognac, which of the two has a lower alcohol content, has caramel coloring added to it as well as a small amount of sugar. Armagnac is drier with a slightly higher alcohol level that results from a less complete distillation than cognac. Hundreds of fruit brandies are made all over the world, some of a better quality than others. It is possible to make your own flavored liqueurs using brandy as a base (see the recipe for Kahlúa on p. 302).

BRANDIED CHERRIES JUBILEE

This was the very first flambéed dessert I ever tried. It's pretty straightforward if you remember to have the sauce hot when it goes on top of the cherries and the ice cream. If your hair or sleeves are long and flowing, get them far out of the way before you light the match.

> *1 1-pound jar sweet cherries in syrup*
> *½ cup granulated sugar*
> *½ cup water*
> *½ cup Kirschwasser or other cherry brandy*
> *1½ pints best-quality vanilla ice cream*

Strain the cherries and reserve the syrup. Combine the cherry syrup, the sugar and the water in a small saucepan and cook over moderate heat until the mixture reduces by about half. There should be slightly more than 1 cup of liquid. Add the brandy to the sauce and cook for 2 or 3 more minutes. Meanwhile divide the ice cream among 6 glasses and place a spoonful of cherries on top of the ice cream in each. If you want to show off at the table, bring the dishes out at this point. Hold a match over the hot sauce in the pan — it should ignite right away — and pour the flaming sauce over the ice cream.

Serves 6

CAFÉ BRÛLOT

The combination of brandy and strong hot coffee can't be beat. This is another New Orleans recipe. It also makes wonderful iced coffee, garnished with sweetened and brandy-flavored whipped cream.

> *1 orange*
> *2 lemons*
> *2 cinnamon sticks, broken in half*
> *1 tablespoon whole cloves*
> *¼ cup dark brown sugar, firmly packed*
> *4 jiggers brandy*
> *4 cups strong coffee with chickory*

Peel the orange and the lemons so that you have the widest strips of peel possible. Combine the peels, the cinnamon sticks, the cloves, the sugar and the brandy in a medium-sized, heavy pot. Add the hot coffee and stir briefly over moderate heat. Divide among 4 cups, leaving the solids in the pan.

Serves 4

ARMAGNAC SEMIFREDDO

This creamy-smooth Italian ice cream dish has the surprise of tiny pieces of dried apple in it.

> *⅓ cup plus 2 tablespoons Armagnac*
> *¾ cup dried apples, diced*
> *1 cup light brown sugar, firmly packed*
> *¾ cup water*
> *6 extra-large egg yolks*
> *3 cups heavy cream*

Heat the Armagnac in a small pan and add the diced apples. Turn off the heat and let the apples soak for 20 minutes. Combine the sugar and water in a small pan and bring to a boil, stirring until the sugar dissolves. Boil without stirring for 5 minutes. Beat the egg yolks in an electric mixer (with a whip attachment if possible) until they are thick and light-colored. With the machine on medium speed, pour the hot sugar syrup in, in a slow, thin stream. Place the mixer on high speed and continue beating until the mixture is cool to the touch. This will take 15–20 minutes. On slow speed add the Armagnac and apples. Whip the cream in a separate bowl and fold the mixtures together. Spoon the mixture into stemmed glasses, cover with plastic wrap and freeze overnight (or at least 10 hours) before serving. Allow to soften for a few minutes before serving.

Serves 8

$\mathcal{C}$OMMANDER'S PALACE MILK PUNCH

This recipe comes from *The Commander's Palace New Orleans Cookbook* by Ella and Dick Brennan.

TO MAKE 1 DRINK:

1½ ounces (3 tablespoons) brandy
1 teaspoon vanilla extract
½ ounce (1 tablespoon) simple syrup (see recipe below)
1 ounce (2 tablespoons) half-and-half
2 ounces (4 tablespoons) milk
freshly grated nutmeg

Half fill a cocktail shaker with ice cubes. Add the liquor, vanilla extract, syrup, half-and-half and milk. Cover and shake vigorously. Strain into a 9-ounce old-fashioned glass. Top with nutmeg.

TO MAKE SIMPLE SYRUP:

1 cup water
2 cups granulated sugar

Combine the water and sugar in a small saucepan. Place over high heat and stir until the sugar dissolves. Simmer for 5 minutes. Cool. Store extra syrup in a covered jar in the refrigerator for future use.

Sweet Butter

I am lying on the cold, hard linoleum floor thinking about butter. Actually, I am not lying still. I am doing leg lifts. Fifty of them. To Strauss's "Blue Danube Waltz." I am surrounded by eighteen other women of various ages and shapes, most dressed like me in wild-colored leotards, lying on their backs sweating and panting as they raise and lower their left legs, slowly and deliberately, stopping their turned-out foot inches above the floor before returning it, with precise deliberation, toward the ceiling, with knee unbent, to the count of eight.

This is the twelve o'clock class at that Cambridge, Massachusetts, institution known simply as "Erna's." This is Studio Sporer, an unassuming whitewashed one-story building with a brown wooden entry located just the other side of fashionable Harvard Square. For decades it has been THE place to exercise, not, mind you, à la Jane Fonda — who was in utero when Erna had been teaching for a decade — but the Erna way, with grace and dignity and respect for your body. When I started at Erna's twelve years ago my posture was dreadful and my tummy getting flabby. Erna was close to seventy then. Her posture was perfect and her stomach flat as a board. This diminutive, sparkling, white-haired Viennese dynamo took on the job of whipping my poor body into shape. Not an easy task.

In Boston there are only two seasons, winter and August, so my thin but out-of-shape body was hidden from view most of the time. You see, I needed more motivation than just the promise of firm thighs and a straight back to get me sweating. I needed something else to drive me to lie on Erna's spotless floor viewing the white-painted tin ceiling and white hanging globes and do hundreds of leg lifts, or stand in formation with the other "Sporer Girls," arms flapping while we did jumping jacks, or run ("Hup, hup, hup," Erna would call) around and around the perimeter of the room for four minutes to polka tempo of "Who Stole the Kishka." That's where the butter came in.

I love butter. I crave it. There is something about the deliciously satisfying taste it gives even the lowliest piece of toast that makes me reach for that old butter dish. You may like your green vegetables parboiled and sprinkled with a little lemon juice and freshly ground pepper. Not me — I prefer a big pat of sweet butter tossed into my broccoli or zucchini. Your idea of a great breakfast may be a bowl of granola with a scoop of yogurt or cottage cheese. Yuck. Give me a stack of pancakes any day — a chunk of butter sitting on top of the pile, melting down into the puddle of maple syrup on the plate.

I used to be a moderate butter freak until I discovered the joys of sweet butter. First of all, in its fancy silver foil wrapping it looks a damn sight classier than the saltier version. And it tastes so much better. I guess because there is no salt to hide that rich butter taste. To my mind, there is nothing more delicious than a thick slice of hot-from-the-oven French bread with a hunk of cold sweet butter tucked inside. If I thought something this mundane was great, imagine the ecstasy I felt when I tasted my first beurre blanc, a sauce that's mostly butter with a few other things thrown in. Well, as with any good news, the bad news soon followed when I realized that butter, whether directly or indirectly, was responsible for all those unsightly lumps on my upper thighs and the love handles on my waist. Not only that, our men of medicine were heard decrying my favorite fat: clogs the arteries, makes your heart go gaga. What could I do? I didn't want to do in my circulatory system or turn my heart into blubber. My beloved butter was banished.

I like to operate on the reward system. After lying on the floor of Erna's studio doing leg lifts and sit-ups for a few weeks I realized that a streamlined body was not enough reward for all this work. That's when I started thinking about butter again. I made a deal with myself. If I was faithful and conscientious in the exercise department (no bent knees during leg lifts, touching the floor with my palms — not fingers — during toe touches, really running instead of gabbing during the four-minute marathon), then I would reward myself with butter in some form or another. After this decision, exercise at Erna's took on a whole new dimension. During leg lifts and tummy curls I would fantasize about the shape my butter fix would take: melting into a corn muffin hot from the oven, nestled into the steaming slit in the top of a hot baked potato, sliding down an ear of sweet corn, or simply tucked into a hunk of French bread. I was inspired — a woman with a mission. I stationed myself in the front of the class, directly in front of Erna, where no slipups would be missed. Her sharp blue eyes never missed a trick. I was driven by butter. Frenzied toe touches, sit-ups until my stomach screamed. And my four-minute run became more like the four-minute mile. One class a week quickly escalated to three, and before I knew it, I was spending more time in Cambridge exercising than I was doing anything else. My leotard wardrobe expanded to meet my expanded activity. Vividly attired in chartreuse tights and iridescent pink tank top I dipped and turned. In shiny black and egg-yolk yellow I grunted inches off my torso — all the while indulging in my butter fantasies. Erna never guessed what was fueling this frenzied dedication.

For as many years as I exercised I suspect no one knew what fueled my dedication. Yes, I adored beautiful and wise Erna, who made the prospect of growing old with grace, style and a straight back one I could entertain without too much angst. Yes, I loved my friends from the studio and looked forward to seeing them and getting the latest gossip. Yes, I was thrilled to death with the change in my body. But it was the thrill of being able to slather my morning bagel, my afternoon scone and my evening potato with — you guessed it — BUTTER! that kept me at it all those years. Well, now the secret can be told. Thanks to Erna the exercise ethic has been instilled so strongly in me that I no longer feel driven to use butter as my whip. But, I offer this story to those of you looking for inspiration. Just think, you could run for roast beef, swim laps for

Löwenbräu or do push-ups for pasta just like my friend who loves to say, "I hate to eat and run, but I have to run to eat."

⊱ Sweet Butter ⊰

WHEN you agitate, or churn, heavy cream so that the liquid portion (the buttermilk) separates out, you are left with sweet butter. You can do this at home, but to supply your household with butter made from heavy cream would be expensive and wasteful unless you made use of the resultant buttermilk. The butter that you buy in the store is inspected by state-licensed butter graders who are supervised by the U.S. Department of Agriculture. The butter is graded on flavor, color and salt content. Grade AA butter has a delicate taste, sweet flavor and no discernible odor. It has a smooth, creamy texture and is not overly salty. Unsalted AA butter (of the unsalted butters this is the kind most available in supermarkets) tends to have a lower water content than salted butter and no salt taste whatsoever. It has a shorter shelf life (salt acts as a preservative as well as masking other flavors that might be absorbed) and should be kept, double-wrapped in foil, in the freezer until ready to use.

The color and flavor of butter vary from season to season according to the diet of the cow. High-quality butter should be firm and solid, devoid of little holes. It should not ooze water or buttermilk. When butter is spoiled, it will taste rancid and should be thrown away. Storing butter at room temperature will cause it to turn rancid faster than storing it in the refrigerator. Like milk and cream, butter will easily absorb the smells of things around it, so keep it well covered.

Butter is chosen over other fats for its flavor. When you want a neutral taste, use vegetable oil instead. In baking, chilled butter, when cut into flour, creates a flaky crust. Vegetable shortening used in combination with butter creates an even flakier product with the added benefit of the butter flavor. Imported Danish and French butters have a delicate taste and higher butterfat content. They should be used for eating, not baking, to fully enjoy their flavor.

To Clarify Butter

The milk solids in butter burn at a low temperature. So that you can cook with butter at a high temperature without having burned particles in it, you must first clarify the butter. There are several ways to do this: melt the butter and strain it through several layers of cheesecloth; or melt it and skim off the foam on top, then pour off the butter and discard the watery liquid on the bottom of the pan. This clarified butter will lack some of the buttery flavor since it is the milk solids that have the taste. Another solution is to use half unclarified butter and half vegetable oil when sautéing — the oil will keep the butter from burning and the butter's taste will be only partially diluted.

To Make Butter

While I would not suggest that you make your own sweet butter every time you need it, it is fun to see just how easily it can be done. Watch out, though, because the homemade kind will spoil you for the store-bought butter. You must use heavy cream with a high butterfat content and not the ultrapasteurized kind, which will leave your butter with a cooked taste. Naturally you will get the highest butter yield from the cream with the highest butterfat content. Try to get your cream from a dairy so that you can ask about the butterfat content. From two cups of heavy cream you will get about three quarters of a cup sweet butter and one cup buttermilk. Use the buttermilk to make pancakes or biscuits, or to drink and enjoy as a low-calorie treat.

While the butter can be made in a food processor, a blender or with an electric mixer, I've had the most success using a food processor fitted with the steel blade. The blender is very slow and the mixture splatters out of the mixer bowl.

TO MAKE HOMEMADE SWEET BUTTER:

2 cups (1 pint) heavy cream (preferably not
ultrapasteurized), very cold, available in
health food stores
8 ice cubes, crushed

Beat the cream either in a food processor fitted with a steel blade, in a blender or with an electric mixer (drape a towel over the top) until it separates or curdles. Pour off the liquid (buttermilk) and add the crushed ice to the remaining butterfat. Process (or beat) until the ice melts. Pour the mass into a large strainer lined with a double layer of cheesecloth. Gather up the edges of the cheesecloth and squeeze out as much of the remaining liquid as you can. Discard this liquid. Break up the butter and place it in a large bowl. Cover it with very cold water, and knead with your fingers to remove any traces of milk. (Milk will cause the butter to turn rancid very fast.) Again pour the mass into a strainer lined with clean cheesecloth and squeeze out the liquid. Shape the butter into a flat round and wrap it in cheesecloth to absorb any remaining liquid, then cover with plastic wrap and refrigerate. The flavor of the butter will improve after a day or so and will keep up to a week under refrigeration, or it can be frozen.

Makes ¾ cup sweet butter

$\mathcal{H}$OLLANDAISE SAUCE

This classic butter-thickened, lemon-scented sauce belongs in the repertoire of any cook who has graduated from can opener to canard. Think of it as mayonnaise's "hot" cousin, since the principle is the same, but instead of the cold oil that is used to emulsify the egg yolks in mayonnaise, hot butter is used in hollandaise. Here is a foolproof recipe for making it in the blender or food processor. Use this delicate sauce on fish, chicken and egg dishes.

> *1 cup (½ pound) sweet (unsalted) butter*
> *3 extra-large egg yolks*
> *1 tablespoon strained lemon or lime juice*
> *2 tablespoons hot water*
> *pinch of powdered mustard*
> *salt and white pepper*

In a small saucepan heat the butter carefully so that it does not brown. Skim off the white foam. Place the egg yolks in the jar of the blender or work bowl of the food processor (use the steel blade) and blend or process for 1 minute. Add the lemon or lime juice, the hot water and the mustard. Blend or process for another 30 seconds. With the machine on, dribble in the hot butter in a very tiny stream at first, increasing it as the sauce begins to emulsify. Do not pour in the white solids at the bottom of the pan. Add enough butter to make the sauce creamy and thick. Correct the seasoning — you may want more lemon or lime juice and mustard — and add the salt and pepper to taste. Keep the sauce warm in a pot set over hot water and gently pour a thin film of melted butter on top to keep from forming a crust. If the sauce separates, beat in boiling water a teaspoon at a time.

Makes 1⅓ cups

HERB BUTTER

This easy-to-prepare condiment is delicious on fish and chicken and vegetables. I serve it with corn on the cob and sometimes on Sunday's bagels. I make several crocks of herb butter when I find myself overrun with herbs from the garden, and keep them in the freezer. This recipe can be doubled and tripled.

> *2 sticks (1 cup) sweet (unsalted) butter at*
> *room temperature*
> *½ cup loosely packed fresh herbs such as*
> *tarragon, chives, basil, thyme, rosemary,*
> *fennel, coriander, etc.*
> *2 teaspoons dried mustard*
> *2 tablespoons vinegar*
> *dash of Worcestershire sauce to taste*
> *dash of hot pepper sauce*

Cut the butter into chunks and place them in the work bowl of a food processor fitted with the metal blade. Process until very smooth. Wash and dry the herbs and remove the stems. Add the herbs, mustard, vinegar and sauces to the processor and process until well blended. Store in tightly covered containers in the refrigerator or freezer.

Makes 1½ cups

PRALINES

To my mind, there is nothing quite as heavenly as the buttered taste of a freshly made praline. My friend Joe Cahn, who runs the unique New Orleans School of Cooking, serves up a delectable, melt-in-your-mouth pecan praline — along with a brand of good old humor — that has won him raves from Maine to the Keys. It is important to use a candy thermometer.

> 1½ cups granulated sugar
> ¾ cup light brown sugar, firmly packed
> ½ cup whole milk
> ¾ stick (6 tablespoons) sweet (unsalted) butter
> 1½ cups toasted pecans (see note)
> 1 teaspoon vanilla extract

Spread 3 sheets of wax paper, foil or parchment with a thin coat of soft butter.

Combine all the ingredients except the vanilla extract in a medium-sized, heavy-bottomed pot and set it over moderate heat. Stir until the sugars melt, then increase the heat and cook, stirring constantly, until the mixture reaches 238–240 degrees on a candy thermometer — this is the soft ball stage. During the boiling process use a pastry brush dipped in water to wash down any sugar crystals that might form on the sides of the pan. Remove the pot from the heat and add the vanilla extract. Stir until the mixture begins to thicken and becomes creamy and cloudy and the pecans stay suspended in the mixture.

Quickly spoon the pralines out onto the buttered paper using two tablespoons. If the mixture becomes too hard to handle before you have formed all the candies, reheat it, stirring gently over low heat until it softens. Cool before indulging — if possible.

Makes about 50 pralines

NOTE: To toast pecans, place the pecans in 1 layer on a baking sheet and bake at 275 degrees for 20–25 minutes or until they are lightly browned and the kitchen smells wonderful.

APPLE STRUDEL

Filo or strudel dough can be intimidating the first time you work with it, but with a little practice and some determination you can turn out strudel just like grandma used to make (and remember, grandma used to make her own dough). Filo or strudel dough is available in the freezer department of most supermarkets. Keep it frozen until a few hours before you plan to use it, then remove it from the freezer and let it sit on the counter in its plastic bag.

FOR THE APPLE FILLING:

1 cup golden raisins
¼ cup brandy or cognac
4 large Granny Smith apples, peeled, cored
  and cut into chunks
⅔ cup walnuts, coarsely chopped
2 teaspoons cinnamon
⅔ cup dark brown sugar, firmly packed
1 teaspoon finely grated lemon rind
juice of 1 lemon

Place the raisins and brandy in a small saucepan and cook over moderate heat for several minutes. Cool slightly, then combine the raisins and any leftover liquid with the rest of the ingredients.

TO MAKE THE STRUDEL:

3 sheets of filo or strudel dough, defrosted if
  previously frozen
1 cup clarified butter (see p. 25)
bread crumbs

Spread a clean, dry dish towel on a heavy-duty baking sheet coated with butter. Open the filo and unfold the leaves, leaving them stacked. Cover the stack with a large piece of plastic wrap (this keeps the dough from drying out). Place 1 sheet of filo on the towel. Use a wide pastry brush to brush it with the butter. Sprinkle about 2 table-spoons bread crumbs on the dough and place another sheet on top of that. Brush with butter and sprinkle with more of the bread crumbs. Repeat one more time with the last sheet. Place the filling in a 2-inch strip, 2 inches up from the bottom (long) edge of the dough, extending to within 2 inches of the ends. Fold the side ends in and fold the bottom edge over the filling. Use the dish towel to flip the strudel over itself away from you to form a roll. Gently roll the strudel off the towel and onto the center of the baking sheet. You can freeze the strudel at this point (cover it well with plastic wrap and foil) or bake it.

TO BAKE:

3 tablespoons sweet (unsalted) butter, melted
¼ cup granulated sugar mixed with 1
tablespoon cinnamon

Preheat the oven to 400 degrees with the rack in the center position. Brush the strudel liberally with butter and sprinkle with cinnamon sugar. Bake for 15 minutes, then turn the oven down to 350 degrees and bake for another 15 minutes. If the strudel starts to get too brown, cover it loosely with foil. If the bottom starts to burn, slip another cookie sheet under the first one. Serve hot.

Serves 6–8

Caviar

My problem with eggs started one afternoon when I was in the fourth grade. I was walking home from school behind Mary Ann Lipshitz, who happened to be one of only three girls in the entire fifth grade who had talked her mother into buying her a bra. Mary Ann had this obnoxious habit of constantly adjusting her bra straps so that there could be no doubt about the fact that she had something that I didn't. My mother had told me that I could have a bra as soon as I had something to hold it down. This particular day Mary Ann and her friends were talking about a filmstrip they had seen in girls' gym. They spent a lot of time giggling and squealing about things they had seen in the film. Then they had this very serious discussion about eggs. I followed them more closely so I could hear what they were saying. I was only catching bits and pieces of the conversation but it sounded pretty weird to me. What did they mean about eggs inside a woman's body? I visualized chicken-sized eggs sitting in my stomach. Well, they really must not have been paying such good attention to the film-strip. Eggs in your body, for heaven's sake, who ever heard of anything so ridiculous?

When I got home I turned to my available sources of information, the *World Almanac* and the 1950 edition of the *World Book Encyclopedia*. Under "Egg" there was absolutely no mention of the human female anatomy. The image of those large, hard ovals in my stomach was beginning to fade. Just to make sure, I asked my mother. She gave me one of those knowing smiles (just like the one that years later I gave my son when he asked how my penis fell off) and began this elaborate explanation, the bottom line of which was that yes, indeed, eggs grew in a woman's body. My first inclination was to deny the whole sordid business, but the facts had been corroborated by busty Mary Ann and her pals. This was truly the most disgusting thing I had ever heard of. No way were any eggs going to grow in my body. I decided right then and there that (1) I would never become a woman and (2) I would never eat another egg as long as I lived.

"Aren't you going to include caviar?" asked my editor when I showed her the chapter list for this book. "I would think that caviar would be almost the ultimate indulgence." I was torn between agreeing with her and being true to my original premise for this book — that I would write only about those indulgences that were near and dear to my heart. Here I was, a grown woman who had come to terms with chicken eggs (I found out you couldn't have a chocolate soufflé without them). I had not, however, been able to develop an affinity for fish eggs. But I agreed to give caviar a chance. I called my friend John Boyajian, who runs a luxury food importing and distributing firm in Boston. Among the things he imports and has a great knowledge of is caviar. Could he help me learn to love caviar? I asked. Could he help me? He replied with a smile in his voice. He could introduce me to Mr. Caviar himself, Christian Petrossian.

The Petrossians are known worldwide as the first family of caviar. Fleeing Russia just before the revolution, they found themselves in Paris, where, as Mr. Petrossian put it, there was no reciprocity for the academic and business accomplishments they had developed in their native land. The family turned to their knowledge of caviar and within a short time had established themselves as world-class importers of premier-quality Russian caviar. Now, with a shop in Paris and a shop and restaurant in New York City, the Petrossians have the distinction of being the only company allowed actually to participate in the sturgeon catch on the Caspian Sea, where they insure the premium quality of their supply by personally choosing the caviar lot by lot and supervising the preparation and packaging of the eggs.

When John and I flew to New York to meet Christian Petrossian, I had no idea what lay in store for me. At best I thought I might learn to like caviar, at worst I supposed my original premise would be borne out — that chicken eggs were my limit. My first glimpse of the building that housed the shop and restaurant was enough to capture my interest. The historic Alwyn Court Building at the corner of Fifty-eighth Street and Seventh Avenue in Manhattan was in the classic Renaissance style of François I. Built in 1907, it was fairly dripping with nymphs, cherubs, dragons and gargoyles. There didn't seem to be a single plain spot on the entire facade, so ornately decorated was it with romantic goings-on.

A curved glass entry and marble steps led into the jewel of a shop. Immediately my eye was caught by the Petrossian trademark: an old-fashioned schooner in full sail, etched in an elegant rondelle on an inside glass wall. Done in an understated art deco motif, the elegant shop, with its richly lacquered burled walnut walls, curved glass cases with brass fittings and black and warm beige marble, was the perfect setting for the treasures displayed in the cases. In the small case closest to the entryway was the caviar, which was displayed in the beautiful round blue and gold tins with the Petrossian ship on the cover. In the lower part of the case was the caviar presentoir, the silver, gold and crystal implements for serving the caviar. The other, larger case held fillets of smoked wild Atlantic salmon, other fish, foie gras and truffles. The thick glass shelves behind the cases held the other Petrossian products, such as jars of *confit* (preserved goose or duck), duck breasts with wild mushrooms and red beans with sautéed goose. There were oblong tins of goose and duck foie gras with and without truffles, and ribbon-bedecked crocks of exotic preserved fruits. On top of the counter was a large basket full of whole glacéed oranges the size of baseballs and chocolate truffles wrapped in silvery paper. There was a magic in the air and I felt as if I had entered a secret treasure room. I couldn't wait to meet the king who presided over this splendid miniature palace.

John introduced me to a tall, very distinguished and very handsome man. At forty-three, Christian Petrossian was more the prince type than the king. He kissed my hand. Now, I ask you, when was the last time a young, rich and divinely handsome European gentleman kissed your hand? He could have represented the first family of tofu and I would have been hooked. He led John and me to our table in the small restaurant immediately adjacent to the shop. Here the art deco style was repeated in the stunning bar made of black granite with its chrome bar stools and reflected in the etched figures on the glass wall behind the bar. The table was stunning, covered with a pearl gray cloth and napkins echoing the Petrossian ship. The Limoges china created exclusively for the restaurant had a white center with five thick royal blue bands sandwiched between two thin gold bands on the rim. Heavy Christofle silver and delicately tall, narrow champagne flutes completed the setting. Lining the walls of the restaurant were delicate art deco bronze sculptures. The lighting was provided by opaque wall sconces made by Lalique. The splendid beauty of the restaurant and shop was a testimonial to Mr. Petrossian's personal philosophy that "the patron's eye must savor the visual experience to the same degree that his palate delights in the gourmet dining experience." Well, if the caviar was going to be anywhere near as wonderful as the setting, I was already won over.

Christian suggested that we begin with some champagne. John and I enthusiastically endorsed that suggestion. The waiter filled our flutes with pale golden wine, waiting until the bubbles subsided to fill them almost to the top. Since the glasses were so incredibly tall and thin it took a lot of concentration on my part to make sure mine didn't topple into my host's lap.

"Now, I suggest we have some caviar to start, since that is the purpose of your visit," said Christian. John and I were game. Even though John has constant access to caviar, he seems really to love it. I sure did hope I did too. Christian told the waiter what to bring and moments later a candelabralike affair that made me feel exactly like Liberace was set down in front of me. John and I faced our very own caviar presentoir on its own silver platter. This low, graceful, curving sterling silver, three-armed piece had shallow cups set upon its ornate stems. Into each cup was set a hand-cut crystal coupelle. Each coupelle was filled with fifty grams of caviar: beluga, ossetra and sevruga. We're talking thousands — and I do mean thousands — of eggs. I felt that old egg phobia creeping back. I looked around for some parsley, lemon and onion garnish so that I could fool myself into thinking that I was not eating what I really was. John informed me that "all that bologna" is used when people serve caviar that isn't the very best, to hide an inferior taste. Christian agreed that only an imbecile would try to adulterate the pure flavor of premium caviar.

He suggested that I start with the beluga since it has the most delicate taste, then have some champagne to clear my palate, move on to the sevruga, which has the strongest taste, and finally (after another sip of champagne) savor the ossetra (James Bond's favorite), which has a fruity flavor. I looked around for a fork, but instead lying next to my silver plate was a solid-gold caviar paddle; silver or any metal other than gold would create a metallic taste and ruin the caviar. Anything that should be eaten with a gold paddle must be great. Now I was game. I scooped my paddle into the large, shiny pearl gray grains of the beluga. Into my mouth it went. My mouth had a religious experience; it was born again, you might say. The sensation was almost indescribable (but since I'm a food writer, I've given it a shot). Sublime smoothness like liquid silk covered my tongue. Tiny sparks of vaguely salty/smoky impulses stirred around the roof of my mouth and the edges of my tongue. My mind was awakened to tastes and textures that until then I had never dreamed existed. I didn't want to swallow and give up the taste, but even when I did my mouth remained coated with that unbelievably satiny taste and texture.

More champagne and on to the sevruga, which has the most distinctive taste of the three. Its small glistening gray grains are, of the three, the only ones that taste vaguely as if they might be related to a fish. My little paddle dipped back and forth between the caviars while I sipped champagne between each kind.

"Drink a little champagne and try the ossetra. We save it for last because it has the most delicate perfume," urged my host. Who was I to argue? Into the grains, slightly smaller and a little lighter in color than the beluga, went my little golden paddle. The flavor, while still incredibly delicate, was slightly more pronounced and tasted a little fruity. The same magic feelings danced around my mouth as I savored what Christian terms the "delicacy that is more for the brain than for the stomach." Life is good.

After the last grain of caviar found its way into my appreciative mouth, Christian insisted that before the main course John and I should sample the pressed caviar. This product is made by pressing four pounds of caviar together to make one pound — a conserve of sorts. The result is a very intense flavor that is highly preferred by caviar connoisseurs. Now, you just don't use your regular old golden paddle for the pressed caviar. You eat it on blini, small, hot, yeasted buckwheat pancakes, dripping with melted butter and sour cream. A generous spoonful of pressed caviar goes on top of each one. The pressed caviar looks almost like black marmalade. It is thick and shiny and unbelievably rich — and that's just the way it tastes too. Here is the essence of the caviar flavor, multiplied a hundred times. The flavor is so wildly intense that it needs the cushion of blini to calm it down a bit.

It was three o'clock in the afternoon. The elegant couples who were sitting along the mink-lined banquettes had all left and we had the place to ourselves. John and I had together consumed the better part of two bottles of champagne and close to three hundred dollars' worth of the world's best caviar. Our host nibbled on melon balls and indicated to the waiter that we were ready for the main course. I was beginning to confuse fantasy with reality. The rest of the lunch was as breathtaking as the start and the cloudlike chocolate cake the pastry chef had created for dessert was sublime. We noticed that Christian passed on both the sauced luncheon entree and the dessert. Proclaiming himself "on a diet" (although I saw absolutely no need for one), he calmed his longing for dessert (he loves chocolate) by pulling from his pocket a string of solid-gold worry beads.

Over espresso John and I asked Christian about the aura of snobbism associated with caviar. We talked about how your average man or woman is intimidated by the whole idea, not to mention the cost. He replied that in Europe caviar is as enthusiastically appreciated as fine wine. Although it is expensive, you need only a very small amount to enjoy it, and of course it's not necessary to serve the caviar in silver dishes and spoon it up with golden paddles. He told us a story to illustrate his point:

"Our shop in Paris is located on the Boulevard de Latour Maubourge. It is a very old shop — it once was an antique store — and very unpretentious. Many kinds of people come there to buy caviar, smoked salmon and foie gras. Several years ago there was some construction going on in the street in front of the shop. For the better part of a week a group of workmen was digging with heavy equipment. At the end of the week two of these construction workers came into the shop. They were dressed in their overalls and heavy boots. My aunt, who was working in the shop at that time, thinking that perhaps they needed access to the basement, asked how she could help them. They replied that all week long they had watched people coming into the store and leaving with tins of caviar. Curious, they had decided to see what the attraction was. They wanted to buy some caviar for lunch. My aunt, delighted at their interest, gave them a good price. They took their caviar outside and sat on the curb in front of the shop, spread the caviar on their *baguettes* and thoroughly enjoyed their lunch."

It was a charming story, which Christian told to illustrate his family's dedication to the job of making sure everyone who is inclined to try it can enjoy one of the world's most extraordinary foods. Even me.

⤬ Caviar ⤬

THE landlocked Caspian Sea, bordered by Iran and Russia, provides a unique environment for three varieties of enormous and peculiar-looking fish known as sturgeon. After feasting on a diet of Caspian algae, crab and lobster, these slow-moving fish return to the delta of the Volga River to spawn. Here the female of the species becomes a wildly valued prize, yielding up to 10 percent of her body weight in a "black gold" that is more highly prized than oil: beluga, ossetra and sevruga caviar. While the appearance, flavor and texture of these three varieties differ slightly, the overall sublime experience of eating real caviar is hard to top.

By law, only eggs harvested from sturgeon can be called caviar. This includes keluga, the roe of Chinese sturgeon; American golden caviar from sturgeon caught off the coast of Oregon, Washington and Alaska; and the Caspian sturgeon mentioned above. Someday, as New York's Hudson River is returned to its unpolluted state, we can look forward to caviar from the sturgeon being grown there.

If it's the authentic Caspian caviar you want, it is essential to buy from a reputable source. For an item this expensive, you want the best. Try to buy a known brand such as Petrossian, Iron Gate, Cristal or Hansen-Sturm as opposed to a generic brand. The eggs should be glossy and clean-looking. There should be a faint but pleasant aroma. The eggs should be whole and the caviar shouldn't have a soupy consistency, and finally the flavor should remind you of the ocean but not be fishy.

CLASSIC CAVIAR PRESENTATION

To my mind there is only one way to enjoy the only true caviar, the eggs of the sturgeon raised in the Caspian Sea. Beluga, sevruga, and ossetra caviar should be served as simply as possible. My friend and caviar maven John Boyajian recommends serving it on thinly sliced, lightly toasted brioche (a more than acceptable substitute is Pepperidge Farm Thin Sliced White or Whole Wheat bread, lightly toasted). Cut the crusts off before you toast the bread. The thinnest coating of sweet butter is an option. The caviar should be removed from the refrigerator ten minutes before you plan to serve it. It is not essential to keep it on ice unless you plan to have it out for longer than a half hour. If you do serve it on ice, take care not to get any water on the caviar; the water will turn it milky. We always serve the caviar in the original container set out on a white linen napkin. The perfect accompaniment is a glass of fine dry champagne or, if you prefer, a glass of ice-cold vodka.

CAVIAR OMELET

3 extra-large eggs
2 tablespoons water
1 tablespoon fresh chives, finely sliced
½ teaspoon salt
freshly ground pepper
3 tablespoons butter
3 tablespoons sour cream
2 tablespoons caviar

Whisk the eggs and water in a small bowl. Add the chives and the salt and pepper. Melt the butter in a nonstick skillet with sloping sides or in an omelet pan. When the butter is sizzling, add the eggs. Cook the omelet over high heat, stirring it with a fork and shaking the pan briskly back and forth. When the omelet is set, turn off the heat and spread the sour cream in the center. Flip the sides of the omelet over the center and turn the omelet out onto a heated plate. Top with the caviar.

Serves 1

BLINI WITH CAVIAR

According to Christian Petrossian, only the strong-flavored pressed caviar, a conserve of sorts made by putting the eggs under pressure so that they rupture and become a thick and very flavorful paste, should be used in the preparation of blini. These blini contain both buckwheat and white flour. They can be made ahead and refrigerated until ready to use. Steam or microwave them to reheat.

FOR THE BLINI:

1½ cups milk
1 tablespoon granulated sugar
1 tablespoon active dry yeast
4 eggs, separated
½ teaspoon salt
1 cup sifted all-purpose flour
1 cup buckwheat flour
3 tablespoons melted butter
additional butter for cooking

Scald the milk in a small saucepan and stir in the sugar. Cool to room temperature and add the yeast, stirring until it dissolves. Beat the egg yolks until thick, and fold into the batter. Add the salt. Mix in the flours and melted butter. Place this mixture in a bowl, cover it with plastic wrap and a towel and let it sit in a warm place or in a pan of warm water (90 degrees) for about 1 hour or until the batter has doubled in bulk. Beat the egg whites until they hold firm peaks and fold them into the batter. Butter a heavy-duty griddle or nonstick skillet and set it over moderate heat. Use a scantly filled ¼-cup measure to measure out 3-inch pancakes, turning them when they get lightly browned. Regrease pan as necessary to keep the blini from sticking.

Makes about 20 blini

blini
melted clarified butter
sour cream or crème fraîche
pressed caviar at room temperature or other
    caviar of your choice

Place the blini on a warm plate and drizzle a little butter over them. Spread with sour cream or crème fraîche. Spoon some caviar on top. I am of the nonrolling school, but you may wish to roll your blini, crepe-style, before enjoying them.

$\mathcal{O}$EUF AU CAVIAR

The following recipe, created by world-renowned chef Louis Outhier, is one of the showstoppers in his U.S. restaurant, Le Marquis, located in the Lafayette Hotel in Boston. Fresh quail eggs can be found in specialty markets and at some poultry farms. In a pinch you could substitute two chicken eggs. This recipe makes one caviar egg.

1 jumbo chicken egg
2 fresh quail eggs
1 tablespoon sweet (unsalted) butter
2 tablespoons heavy cream
salt, pepper and cayenne to taste
1 teaspoon fresh lemon juice
1 tablespoon vodka
⅓ ounce beluga caviar
2 tablespoons freshly whipped heavy cream for
    garnish

Use either a small, very sharp knife or one of those special egg gadgets to slice the top third off the chicken egg, leaving the edge as smooth as possible. Pour out the egg and reserve it. Wash the eggshell and drain it well. Place the reserved egg and the 2 quail eggs in the top of a double boiler set over gently simmering water. Whisk the eggs until they have just begun to set. You want them very soft and moist. Remove from heat and whisk in the butter.

Whip the cream (the easiest way is to place the cream in a small metal bowl set over a larger metal bowl filled with ice and whisk until it is thick). Season with salt, pepper and cayenne. Whisk in the lemon juice and vodka. Place the eggshell in a doily-lined eggcup and use a demitasse spoon to fill it three-quarters full with the egg mixture. Use a pastry bag fitted with a medium star tip to pipe a rosette of whipped cream on top. Top with the caviar. Serve immediately.

Makes 1 caviar egg

Champagne

My father appreciates champagne and usually let me have a sip from his glass when I was a child. I learned just how strongly he felt about serving it the correct way when he opened a special bottle to celebrate my engagement. Among the celebrants were my mother, my husband-to-be, his best man and my maid of honor. Dad chilled the champagne to just the right temperature, lined up the crystal flutes and expertly removed the cork. He had carefully filled almost all the glasses when the best man grabbed his glass and said he wanted to show us something really terrific. He scooped some of the strawberry ice cream we had for dessert and plopped it into the bottom of the flute. He then proudly held the glass out to my horrified father and indicated that if Dad would now fill his glass the resulting concoction would be a million times better than a plain old glass of French champagne — a champagne float! To his everlasting credit, my father, envisioning me with a fractured wedding party, poured. But the look he gave this guy should have injected champagne bubbles into his bloodstream. The moral is, I guess, if you want to make champagne floats, use cheap champagne.

My dad taught me well — I love good champagne. The price being what it is, I can't afford to drink it as often as I would like. One place I did manage to get more than my share of great champagne was aboard the *Queen Elizabeth II* during a cruise to the Caribbean. I teach and lecture about chocolate once or twice a year aboard the *Queen*. It is a wonderful and completely hedonistic experience. During this particular cruise, my husband, David, and I had the good fortune to be seated in the Queen's Grill, the most elegant dining room on the ship. The room, lined with pale paneling made of rare wood, is a study in luxury. Shimmering crystal chandeliers and sparkling silverware sit on table linens so fine that touching them makes you feel as if you have arrived. Fresh flowers and service so attentive that I was tempted to indulge in one continuous all-day meal. The sky was the limit in this dining room. Anything my little palate craved could be had for the asking. Caviar, foie gras, beef Wellington, crown roast of lamb, rare duck breast with kumquats, soufflé Rothschild — you name it and it appeared. The final evening our meal began with beluga caviar and ended with banana splits.

It was clear that there were three kinds of people who ate in this dining room: the very rich, who never traveled any other way; the just-retired, who had waited all their lives for this and now were going to do it right; and us — the freeloaders, as it were. We were lucky enough to be seated next to a couple who were in the second group. They were in their mid-fifties and about to retire from demanding jobs — he in the construction business and she as a teacher. In a room full of excruciatingly dressed men in black ties and women in long gowns and serious jewelry, our tablemates were a breath of fresh air — he in his sport coat and she in her sundress. It seems this was a new relationship, full of newfound love and brimming over with romance. Neither one of them had ever taken a trip like this and they were having the time of their lives until the sommelier threw a glitch into their works. The first night at dinner he glided up to our table and asked the retired couple if they had chosen from the wine list. Overwhelmed with the choices on the list, the former teacher replied that she just wanted a glass of white wine. The sommelier looked visibly shaken — like someone had goosed him from behind — and replied, "Madame, on board the *Queen Elizabeth*, we don't 'do' a glass of white wine." Her escort said, "Well, then just bring us a carafe of house white." He had the sommelier's number and was dialing like crazy. The sommelier was apoplectic.

We quickly ordered wine just to reduce the tension. Our companions decided then and there that they would do without wine during the cruise — that's how offended they were at the wine steward's behavior. I agreed with them wholeheartedly, but didn't volunteer to join them in their protest (what, and give up wine? I would rather have made a large cash donation to their cause, which, it turns out, is exactly what happened).

Several nights later we arrived at dinner after the other couple had already been seated. To our great surprise, we saw, placed next to their side of the table, a silver ice bucket with a bottle sticking out of it. One thing I can recognize a mile away with my eyes closed is a bottle of Dom Pérignon. In their ice bucket was a bottle of Dom Pérignon. I was marveling at how fast the tastes of our new friends had changed when they informed me that the travel agency they had booked their first-class tickets through had sent them this bottle of bubbly. I guess our dinner companions could tell from the way my eyes were bugging out (even though my husband slammed me with the side of his foot several times) that I wanted some.

"Would you like to share this with us?" they asked. How I love people who can read my mind. The sommelier, nose held high, uncorked the bottle. Flutes filled with the pale golden magic. We toasted to the good life. The bubbles filled my mouth and my head. I felt beautiful and supremely happy. We drank that bottle with the first two courses of the meal and when the sommelier poured the last drop, my husband said, "Oh, dear, it's all gone. I'll order another bottle to finish the meal with." The sommelier gave an evil grin. I couldn't believe David had done it, and then I realized that he, unlike me, had not looked at the champagne prices. Since I love champagne so much, I automatically check it out first on the wine lists in case there is something good we can afford. There was nothing good that we could afford on this menu — especially the Dom Pérignon. I wanted to drink as much as I could before David got the check. To his credit he turned only a little pink and pressed his lips together sort of thoughtfully when the bad news came. It's amazing how much a little taste of the good life can cost. He signed the tab like a gentleman and then said he needed to lie down for a little while. The other couple would never know . . . so we thought.

To our utter amazement, the next night when we arrived at our table, there was yet another bottle of Dom Pérignon. David, thinking that the sommelier was playing a nasty trick, was about to clutch his heart (and wallet) when our friends said that they had enjoyed the two bottles at dinner last night so much that they wanted to have more tonight. Now, remember that these folks had not seen a wine list since the first night, and I strongly suspected they did not spend that night perusing the list for expensive champagne. I was not looking forward to the moment when the bill arrived. If David, who at times in his life has laid out megabucks for my indulgences, had a hard time with it, this guy was going to lose it completely. When the meal was over I kept watch for the sommelier's approach so I could take the chicken's way out. When I saw him, check in hand, head for our table, I made a quick dash for the ladies' room. I could hear the roar as the door closed behind me.

Three bottles of Dom Pérignon in two nights — heaven. It's been a few years since then, but as with all marvelous experiences, the taste lingers on.

❧ Champagne ❧

CHAMPAGNE is the sparkling wine made from both the red and white grapes grown in France in the vineyards on both sides of the River Marne, between Reims and Épernay, west of Châlons-sur-Marne. Only wine made from grapes grown in this region can be called champagne. Unlike still wines, champagne is partly fermented in its securely corked bottle. This means that the carbonic acid gas generated by fermentation cannot escape, and it remains in solution until the cork is removed and the wine poured. The gas then rushes out of the wine and makes the bubbles for which champagne is famous. When wines from different champagne vineyards and different years are blended together, the result is nonvintage champagne; when the wine made in any one year is good enough not to need the backing of older reserves of better wines, it is known as vintage champagne. Most champagne is pale gold in color. Then there is pink or delicately salmon-colored champagne made by mixing red and white wine before the secondary fermentation or by performing a secondary fermentation on red wine.*

The price range for champagne — real champagne, not sparkling wine from Spain, the United States or regions of France other than the Champagne district — goes from twelve dollars a bottle up to hundreds of dollars. You should buy champagne in a reputable wine store, where an informed salesperson can make recommendations in your price range.

To serve: If you really want to do it right, throw out those saucer-shaped champagne glasses or use them for ice cream. These glasses, rumored to be modeled on the shape of Marie Antoinette's breasts, allow the wonderful bubbles to escape too quickly. Tall, thinly ta-pered champagne flutes are the best way to serve champagne, which should be served chilled but not freezing cold. Pour so that you can see the label — people like to know what they're drinking.

Storing: Always keep at least one bottle in the refrigerator. Keep the others in a cool, dark place where the temperature range is between 50 and 70 degrees. Unless you have excellent wine storage facilities, don't keep champagne for more than a year, since it doesn't improve in the bottle.

How to tell if it's good: As Art Buchwald says, it should feel the way your arm does when it falls asleep. If it's wildly bubbly and tastes like Alka-Seltzer, then you've got a clunker. The wine should taste sharp and sweetish and not too yeasty.

To open a bottle of champagne: Place a napkin over the cork and grasp the cork (underneath the napkin) securely with one hand. Hold the bottom of the bottle with the other hand, with your fingers in the well. Slowly turn the bottom hand — you are turning the bottle, not the cork. The object is to remove the cork without a loud pop and without the bubbles streaming out of the bottle. Be very careful not to open a bottle with the cork either uncovered or pointed toward your (or anyone else's) eyes.

*In part from *Dictionary of Gastronomy* by Andre L. Simon and Robin Howe.

BELLINI COCKTAIL

This elegant concoction was invented by Harry Cipriani and served at the famous Harry's bar in Venice. The original recipe calls for white peach puree, but don't let the lack of this elusive fruit prevent you from trying this recipe. Use any kind of fresh peach, just make sure it's fully ripe.

>   *1 large, ripe peach (a white peach is*
>   *traditional but not mandatory)*
>   *⅔ cup Italian champagne*

Peel and chop the peach. Puree the pulp in a food processor or blender and then force the puree through a fine sieve (you should have approximately ⅓ cup puree).

Mix the puree and champagne well with a long spoon (not in a blender) and pour into 2 wine glasses or champagne flutes. The acid of the fruit will form a bubbly head on the champagne.

Serves 2

STRAWBERRIES IN CHAMPAGNE

One of the most delightfully decadent, impromptu dessert experiences I ever had took place on the wide front porch of a friend's Victorian home on a country road just outside Stockbridge, Massachusetts. We had spent the morning picking strawberries in a nearby field. We sat on that porch, sheltered from the midday heat, debating how to serve the plump, sweet berries that were piled high in an old basket on the table in front of us. One person insisted that nothing short of strawberry shortcake would do justice to the fruit. Another person opted for something with meringue and custard. A very wise third person, who had no desire to spend a moment inside cooking on such a gorgeous summer day, went to the kitchen and returned with a bottle of chilled champagne and four wine glasses. She opened the bottle and poured us each a glass. She plucked a fat berry from the basket, dunked it into the champagne, swished it around and popped it into her mouth. The look of supreme pleasure on her face prompted us to follow suit — and we were glad we did.

$\mathcal{P}$INK CHAMPAGNE SAUCE

While pink champagne, at least the inexpensive version, is usually too sweet for my taste, I find it delicious in the following dessert sauce.

1½ cups light cream
4 extra-large egg yolks
⅓ cup granulated sugar
4 teaspoons cornstarch
3 tablespoons seedless raspberry jam
finely grated peel of 1 lime
1 cup pink champagne

Heat the cream in a 3-quart saucepan until small bubbles appear around the edge. Beat the egg yolks together with the sugar and cornstarch until pale and thickened. Beat in the raspberry jam and half of the champagne. Add the hot cream in a steady stream, beating constantly, and return the entire mixture to the pan. Cook over moderate heat, whisking constantly, just until the mixture thickens and is smooth. Whisk for 1 minute off the heat before adding the additional champagne. Either serve warm, or cool to room temperature. This is wonderful served over fresh berries (while it is still warm) or over ice cream.

Makes about 3 cups

$\mathcal{F}$RESH PEAR AND CHAMPAGNE SORBET

This elegant recipe is the creation of Gunter Preuss, the chef/owner of the Versailles restaurant of New Orleans. A sweet dessert sorbet, it makes quite an impression and captures the essence of pears at their peak of ripeness.

> 2 cups granulated sugar
> 4 cups water
> 8 very ripe and flavorful pears
> ½ cup lemon juice
> 1½ cups champagne

Combine the sugar and water in a saucepan over moderate heat. Stir and cook only until the sugar completely dissolves. Remove from heat. Peel and core the pears and puree them. Add this mixture to the sugar syrup. Add the lemon juice. Process the mixture in an ice cream freezer.

Scoop the sorbet into a large, well-chilled silver (or other metal) bowl. Pour the champagne over it and blend. This should be done at the table! Serve in champagne glasses.

Serves 8–10

CHAMPAGNE AND MELON SOUP

> 1 ripe, medium-sized honeydew melon
> 1 ripe cantaloupe
> ¼ cup lime juice
> 1 cup sour cream
> ½ teaspoon cinnamon
> 2 teaspoons dried mint
> 2 tablespoons granulated sugar
> 1½ cups dry champagne
> fresh mint for garnish

Cut the melons into wedges. Scoop out the seeds and cut the fruit into 1-inch chunks. Use only the sweet ripe pulp, taking care not to use the harder pulp near the rind. Puree the melon in several batches in a food processor fitted with a metal blade. Add the lime juice, the sour cream, the cinnamon, the dried mint, the sugar and the champagne and process another 30 seconds to combine all the ingredients. Ladle into chilled bowls and garnish with the fresh mint.

Serves 8

Chestnuts

With the exception of my mother's sister, who has a beautiful soprano voice, everyone in my family is totally devoid of musical talent. What we lack in ability, however, we make up for in enthusiasm. You might say we come from a long line of professional audiences. We are world-class applauders.

When it became obvious to my parents that no matter how much they invested in piano lessons for us kids, there was no way that we would suddenly blossom into prodigies — hell, we couldn't even pound through "The Merry Farmer" without having it sound like a John Cage special — they regrouped. Faced with the prospect of yet another generation of children who would rather go to the dentist than practice the piano, my father wised up and decided to spend his hard-earned money on opera and symphony tickets instead of "throwing it out on the street" (which meant giving it to the piano teacher who came every week and then complained to our parents that we hadn't even touched the piano since the last lesson).

The very first opera I ever saw was a performance of Richard Strauss's *Der Rosenkavalier*. I saw it with my parents at the old Metropolitan Opera House in New York City. This was on December 22, 1957, and I was twelve years old.

New York City at Christmastime is a magical place. Even to a gawky, bookish, preadolescent girl who, staring out at the world from glasses that kept slipping down her nose and wrestling with new braces that cut the inside of her mouth, couldn't decide to snarl or smile at her parents from one moment to the next, it was enticing. The city shimmered with thousands of colored lights and in almost every department store window were mechanical Santas and elves moving back and forth, up and down to the sound of Christmas carols and the insistent bells of the Salvation Army workers hovering around their black kettles. Added to this were the tinkling bells and the clip-clop of the horses carrying tourists in their carriages toward Central Park. There were the smells of the city: bus exhaust intermingling with the sweet smoky smell of chestnuts roasting on the carts on every corner.

My father stopped to buy a bag of these chestnuts and put it into the pocket of his overcoat. As we made our way to the Met, I walked next to my father while my mother and brother walked behind us. This way I could pretend they didn't exist — my brother because he was such a pain, and my mother because she was the competition. With them out of sight it was easier to pretend that I was wearing my own elegant furs and French perfume and was being taken to the opera by the handsomest man of all.

While the outside of the old Met was not as flashy as the new one, with its magnificent Chagall windows and fancy fountain, the inside had the new one beat by a mile. Even though by the time I first saw it, it was a little seedy and run-down, the interior still made a glorious impression on me. Mostly what I remember is gold and deep ruby red: the ornate balconies forming the famous horseshoe and the red velvet seats. It wasn't just the gilt and velvet that made it so special. There were the ladies in their swishing chiffon gowns and the men in formal evening dress standing so tall and looking so important. Ladies were bigger then, with real bosoms (demure cleavage was in then and my short stature gave me the best view), and corset-trimmed waists that accented generous hips. In the crooks of their white-gloved arms they carried jeweled evening bags, and tiny mother-of-pearl opera glasses dangled on gold chains from their wrists. I saw several women with fur pieces — like the kind my aunt Sarah had — made out of several foxes sewn together, biting their own tails to secure them around soft white shoulders. The smell of French perfume and Cuban cigars filled the crowded lobby.

At the sound of the chimes all the fancy people filed into the orchestra section and everyone else (my family, for example) climbed the curving staircase to the upper reaches of the house. My father had managed to get seats in the first row of the dress circle, which is the next to the highest balcony, and even though they were off to the side a bit, we had a splendid bird's-eye view of the whole stage and most of the audience below us.

Der Rosenkavalier is my father's very favorite opera. He loves it so well that I had to nudge him several times to keep him from singing along loud enough for the people in back of us to hear. The opera is a long one — almost three hours — and somewhat confusing, be-cause there is a role played by a woman pretending to be a man, who has this other woman fall in love with her. There is also this baron who is after her when she pretends, at one point, to be a man playing a woman. In the middle there is a stretch that has lots of singing (in German) and very little action to hold a child's attention. My brother and I, not quite the instant converts my dad had counted on, started to squirm. Dad reached into his pocket and pulled out a small brown paper bag. Opening it very slowly so that it wouldn't make too much noise, he pulled out two roasted chestnuts, peeled them and gave one each to me and my brother.

I had never had a chestnut before, but I remembered the cart and the wonderful warm smell of the roasting chestnuts and, while I was not an experimental eater, I figured that this golden misshapen orb was part of the total New York experience and therefore good. I nibbled off a piece. It was soft and mealy and pretty subtle — at first. Then, I took another bite and found the flavor, while still not terribly pronounced, certainly nonthreatening and almost agreeable. Before I knew it, my chestnut was gone and Daddy was peeling another one for me and then another. This got me through the "boring" part and right into the last act, where all hell breaks loose as illegitimate children pop in and out of windows crying "Papa, Papa" to the hapless baron and the music soars and swells in a way that won my heart and soul and inspired a lifelong love of opera. Like generations of my family before, I used my true talent and clapped until my hands were sore. I knew it pleased my father no end to see that I had inherited the family's one musical gift.

Outside, the city had been transformed by a flurry of fat white snowflakes. The crowd standing outside hailing taxis looked like figures inside one of those glass paperweights that snow when you shake them. As we walked toward the hotel (I had my program clutched in my hand), snow gathered in my eyelashes and frosted my hair. It muted the sounds of the city. We passed the chestnut man. The coals in his cart glowed red-hot and the snow hitting the fire made sparks that crackled out into the night. The sweet smell followed us down the snowy avenue along with the now-distant music, and lodged itself into my memory so firmly that every time I smell roasting chestnuts I can almost feel the snow and hear the music.

❧ To Prepare Fresh Chestnuts ❧

FALL is the time for fresh Italian chestnuts. Because of their high water content, they are quite perishable. When you shop, look for unblemished shells that do not reveal hollow spots when pressed. Keep fresh chestnuts refrigerated until ready to use. When you peel them, make sure there are no moldy or black spots.

To roast chestnuts, preheat the oven to 450 degrees with the rack in the center position. Use a small, very sharp knife (a surgeon's scalpel is perfect for this) to pierce the shell with an X on the flat side of each chestnut. Place the chestnuts, flat side up, in a single layer in a shallow roasting pan. Add about half an inch of hot water. Roast the chestnuts for about fifteen to twenty minutes. When cool enough to handle, pry off the shell. Roasted chestnuts are perfect to serve with drinks or a glass of wine before dinner. Set out a small bowl of coarse (Kosher) salt to dip the chestnuts in.

Chestnuts intended for pureeing should first be boiled. Cut the same X on the flat part of each one and place them in a pan of boiling water for about fifteen minutes. Drain well, cool and peel. If you plan to use the chestnuts in a savory dish, simmer them, when shelled, in chicken stock for about twenty minutes. If they are destined for a sweet dish, simmer them in milk and a tablespoon of vanilla extract. When they are cool, either mash them with a potato masher or puree them with the addition of a small amount of cream or stock (depending again upon their destination) in the food processor.

If you plan to peel fresh chestnuts for cooking, it is best to prepare many more than you'll need for that one recipe. The shelling can be a bit tedious, but once you've gotten into it you might as well make enough to freeze for the next time. I freeze mine in heavy-duty Ziploc plastic bags.

Another way to peel chestnuts is to make the same X with a knife (piercing the skin) and then plunge them into very hot oil for a minute or so. The shell will pop open. Take care to let them cool before you peel them.

Like the vendors on the streets of New York, you too can roast chestnuts over a fire. Cut an X in each one and hold it with tongs over hot coals until the shell begins to peel away.

It is possible to buy canned or glass-jarred chestnuts, chestnut puree (both sweetened and unsweetened) and whole glacéed chestnuts in syrup. These commercially prepared products are, for the most part, fine substitutions, but for me, there is nothing like the taste of a freshly roasted chestnut.

CHESTNUT-STILTON PASTA SAUCE

This hearty, rich sauce is the perfect thing for a cool fall evening. You can use either fresh chestnuts or the kind that comes in jars.

> *1 large onion, finely diced*
> *2 tablespoons butter*
> *4 cups heavy cream*
> *½ pound Stilton cheese*
> *1½ cups whole cooked and peeled chestnuts (see*
> *pp. 54–55, about preparing fresh chestnuts),*
> *or the canned variety*

Sauté the onion in the butter over medium heat until it has wilted and is transparent. Place the heavy cream in a large saucepan and simmer until it has reduced by half. This will take about 20 minutes. Take care not to let the cream come to a full boil or it will overflow the pan. Lower the heat, stir in the onion and cook 5 more minutes. Trim the rind from the Stilton and crumble the cheese. Stir it into the sauce. Cook on very low heat 5 more minutes. Break the chestnuts into large pieces and just before serving, stir them into the warm sauce. Serve over a wide-cut pasta, such as fettuccine.

Makes 4 cups

CHESTNUT AND STOUT STUFFING

> 2 loaves day-old bread
> 4 tablespoons butter
> 3 stalks celery
> 2 onions, chopped
> 2 large leeks (white part only), well rinsed
>   and thinly sliced
> 2 cloves garlic, minced
> 1 cup dark stout
> ½ cup chicken stock
> 2 cups roasted chestnuts, shelled and cut in
>   half (canned chestnuts can be substituted)
> salt and pepper to taste

Toast the bread, cut it into 1-inch cubes and place the cubes in a large bowl. Melt the butter in a large skillet and sauté the celery, onions and leeks until they are soft. Add the garlic and cook a few more minutes. Add the stout and chicken stock, raise the heat and simmer for 15 minutes. Pour the hot liquid over the bread cubes and mix. Mix in the chestnuts. Add salt and pepper to taste.

Makes enough to stuff a 10-pound capon or turkey

MONT BLANC

This classic French dessert, named after a snowcapped mountain, is made with sweetened chestnut puree. Make your own puree following these instructions, or use a high-quality canned preparation.

2½ pounds chestnuts
hot water
2½ cups milk
½ cup granulated sugar
1 vanilla bean
¼ teaspoon powdered ginger
½ teaspoon cinnamon
2 tablespoons sweet (unsalted) butter
¼ cup dark rum
1 cup heavy cream, whipped
confectioners' sugar

Use a sharp knife to make an *X* on the flat side of each chestnut. Place the chestnuts in a pan and cover with hot water. Boil for 15 minutes. Drain the water and when the chestnuts are cool enough to handle, peel them. Place the chestnuts, milk, granulated sugar and vanilla bean in a saucepan. Simmer over low heat until very tender — about 45 minutes to an hour. Drain the chestnuts, reserving the milk. Puree in a food processor, adding the ginger, cinnamon and butter and just enough of the reserved milk to make a smooth puree. The mixture will have the consistency of mashed potatoes. Let the mixture cool and then place a large-hole sieve over a serving plate and use a wooden spoon to press the puree through into a mound on the plate. Top with rosettes of whipped cream and then sift the confectioners' sugar over the dessert.

Serves 6–8

CANDIED CHESTNUT TOPPING

This is delicious over vanilla ice cream.

2 cups roasted chestnuts, shelled
3 cups water
½ cup dark brown sugar, firmly packed
½ cup maple syrup
½ cup light corn syrup
2 teaspoons vanilla extract
¼–⅓ cup dark rum

Break each chestnut into 4 pieces. In a saucepan combine the water, sugar, maple syrup and corn syrup. Bring the mixture to a boil, stirring once or twice, add the chestnuts and lower the heat. Continue to cook over low heat until the syrup has reduced by about half. When the mixture has cooled, add the vanilla extract and rum. Spoon into clean glass jars and refrigerate until ready to use.

Makes 2 cups

Chiles

*I*t was almost midnight when my husband, David, and I arrived at Sam Arnold's restaurant on the outskirts of Denver. Our quest for authentic cooking of the Southwest had brought us here. The Fort, a large, two-storied, rust-colored adobe building, looked like it could boast Kit Carson among its regulars. Sam and his daughter Holly greeted us at the entrance and gave us a tour of the marvelous building, which was a warren of low-ceilinged rooms filled with Western memorabilia. We felt as if we had stepped back in time to an enchanted place where men toted six-shooters instead of attaché cases and buffalo was something you ate instead of ogled at the zoo.

Sam is an expert on early Southwestern cookery. But this doesn't begin to describe the multifaceted and multitalented man who has with single-minded enthusiasm and determination built a mecca for those of us who love good food and great times. He has a twinkle in his eye and a joke at the ready. He is the consummate host and a world-class storyteller. His unstoppable curiosity and quest for the authentic leaves others breathless in his wake.

"Come sit down and have a drink," said Sam as he escorted us to a table on an enclosed veranda. The lights of Denver sparkled like so many pieces of silver in the valley far below. The people at the adjoining tables were a curious mixture of urban chic and country casual. Elegant designer-shop silks sat next to working denim and cowboy boots. The waiter brought a round of jelly glasses filled to the brim with a concoction that I assumed would have me under the table in about three seconds.

"That black stuff on the bottom is gunpowder — great source of iron," said Sam. Figuring that this was a test of some sort, I said a silent prayer and knocked back half the glass. I hoped that Sam was impressed.

"Here, try this," he said, waving a morsel on a toothpick in front of me.

"Ummm . . . good," I said, reaching for another before my husband had a chance to clean the plate.

"Critter fritters," Sam informed us.

"What exactly are critter fritters?" I asked, thinking that maybe the test wasn't quite over.

"Fried turkey balls. We call 'em Rocky Mountain oysters, too." Well, that was a first for me — and a tasty first at that.

Sam reached over and skewered a small green pepper from another plate. "Now," he said, "this is a real specialty of the Fort. Pickled jalapeño peppers stuffed with peanut butter. No nibbling. You have to pop the whole thing into your mouth at once and the peanut butter takes the heat out of the pepper." He looked at me expectantly, his twinkle radiating at five hundred watts. For this poor Easterner, used to eating Concord grape jelly with my peanut butter, here was the real test. I had flown two thousand miles to be tortured by a culinary historian brandishing fiery hot peppers? Perhaps I should consider a career change. Did interior decorators have to eat things that would incinerate their lips and leave holes in their tongues? Sam waved the pepper closer to my face.

"Come on, you'll love this, it's really quite tasty — in fact it's downright delicious." David, knowing his turn was next, was watching me very quietly, perhaps hoping that I'd love the little tidbits so much that I would eat his portion too. The heavenly smells of grilled steaks were wafting around our table. My stomach was screaming for attention. But clearly there would be no food until I bit the bullet, as it were. I popped the thing into my mouth and following Sam's coaching chewed fast. The result was remarkable and believe it or not, as Sam had promised, quite delicious. The fiery heat of the pepper was smothered to a large degree by the smoothness of the peanut butter; not so much that the resulting taste was bland — hardly — but it was certainly tolerable.

"Hey, this is really good," I said (or something that sort of sounded like that, because my mouth was still full of peanut butter). I reached for another. Sam looked proud of me and reached over to spear another pepper to hold in front of David.

From Denver we drove with Sam and his friend Jorg Fischer, an apprentice chef at the Intercontinental in Hamburg, Germany, south through the Rocky Mountains to Telluride, where Sam did a cooking demonstration at the annual wine festival. At every meal we had, Sam continued to introduce me to the fantastically versatile chile. From elegant sauces to down-home Mexican dishes — red and green, hot, smoked and mild — those chiles put the spark and soul into every mouthful. We began to speculate on how chiles could be used to liven up traditional dishes. I said I'd bet they could even be used to make matzoh balls. That sparked everyone's imagination and that is how I came to find myself in Sam's kitchen in his condominium in Santa Fe (the next stop after Telluride), whipping up some chicken soup and matzoh balls with jalapeño peppers. Even Jorg (who was in charge of grilling the Colorado trout) agreed that they were super. I wonder what my grandmother would say.

⍚ Chiles ⍚

In his book *Frying Pans West*, Sam Arnold, dean of chiles, says the following about chiles:

The first Americans coming to New Mexico were greeted with a shocking new culinary experience, the chile pepper. Although black pepper and red cayenne pepper were well known in European cultures, the red chile as found in the Southwest was a totally new experience. Then, as now, Americans usually found the initial meeting was a hot and unpleasant one. After re-

peated exposure to the chile pod, however, most people become virtual addicts. I am one of these chile addicts. I find most meals without chile in some form as bland as a meal without salt.

Chiles grow in many variations of size and type — from the tiny chile piquin and the miniature raisin chile to the larger two- or three-inch-long green jalapeño; and finally, in size to the big chile poblano, which is a seven- or eight-inch-long green or red pepper pod. The only difference between a red and green chile pod is that when allowed to fully ripen, the green pod turns red. There is, however, a different flavor to each. Pods may be used fresh, dried, canned or frozen.

The hotness of a chile comes from an oily substance called "capsaicin." It is generated in the little globules on the inside ribs of the chile. If these are undisturbed, even the hottest chile will be like a sweet pepper in its meat and seeds. However, bumping, picking, packing or just the act of pulling it off the plant will rupture some of these fine globules, allowing the burning hot oil to spread within the interior of the chile.

Remember, if you are using fresh chiles, WEAR GLOVES and don't rub your eyes or even touch your face with your hands. For novices, it is easier to use the canned or dried varieties.

JALAPEÑO SURPRISES, THE FORT RESTAURANT

12 or so pickled small jalapeño peppers
12 teaspoons natural peanut butter, chunky or
  smooth

Cut the peppers in half the long way and remove the seeds and inner membrane. Place a teaspoon of peanut butter in one half of each pepper and then place the other half on top. Serve with drinks.

Makes 1 dozen

HOT MATZOH BALLS

4 tablespoons chicken fat (see note)
4 eggs
1 medium onion, very finely diced
⅓ cup fresh cilantro (also called coriander or
  Chinese parsley), finely chopped
4 tablespoons diced, canned jalapeño peppers
½ cup water
1 teaspoon salt
freshly ground pepper
1 cup matzoh meal
3 quarts rich chicken soup (homemade or
  commercially prepared)
3 carrots, thickly sliced
cilantro for garnish

Melt the chicken fat and mix in the eggs, onion, cilantro, peppers, water, salt and pepper. Stir in the matzoh meal until it is well moistened. Cover the bowl and refrigerate for about 40 minutes. Bring the soup to a simmer in a large pot. Add the carrot slices. Use two teaspoons dipped in cold water, or one teaspoon and your hand to form the matzoh balls. Drop them into the simmering soup and cook covered for 40 minutes. Keep the soup at a low simmer and don't lift the lid during the cooking time.

To serve, ladle some soup, a few carrot slices and 2 or 3 matzoh balls into soup bowls. Garnish with fresh cilantro.

Serves 10

NOTE: The easiest way to get chicken fat is to skim it off the top of stock made with either fowl (which has more taste) or chicken. Alternatively you can buy chicken fat in most supermarkets or stores that carry Kosher products.

$\mathcal{S}$AM ARNOLD'S RED CHILE SAUCE

This delicious and easy-to-prepare sauce livens up dishes from scrambled eggs to broiled fish to steak.

> *6–8 large dried red chiles*
> *2 large cloves garlic, peeled*
> *½ teaspoon oregano*
> *3 tablespoons cilantro or 2 teaspoons ground*
> *   coriander*
> *⅓ cup hot water*
> *salt to taste*

Place all the ingredients in a blender and puree.

Makes about 1 cup

$\mathcal{C}$HRISTMAS BISCUITS

The combination of red and green chiles gives these quick-to-prepare biscuits their name.

*1¼ cups all-purpose flour, measured after
  sifting*
1 cup coarse cornmeal
½ teaspoon salt
2 teaspoons baking powder
½ teaspoon baking soda
⅔ cup cheddar cheese, grated
⅓ cup vegetable shortening
*¼ cup chopped, canned jalapeño peppers, well
  drained*
¼ cup pimientos, chopped
⅔ cup buttermilk

Preheat the oven to 450 degrees with the rack in the center position. Line a heavy-duty baking sheet with foil. Sift the flour, cornmeal, salt, baking powder and baking soda together into a mixing bowl. Stir in the cheese. Use two knives to cut in the shortening until the mixture resembles coarse meal. Stir in the jalapeño peppers, the pimientos and the buttermilk. Lightly flour a work surface and turn the dough out onto it. Knead 10–15 times and then pat into a ½-inch thickness. Cut 2-inch circles and place them on the baking sheet, just touching. Bake for 12–15 minutes, reversing the sheet front to back once during the baking. Serve warm.

Makes about 26 biscuits

Chocolate

*My*y association with chocolate has afforded me some unforgettable experiences, and the friendships of some wonderful people. Sally and Tom Jordan, winemakers par excellence and creators of the extraordinary Jordan cabernet sauvignon, are world-class chocolate lovers. I had the pleasure of visiting their Alexander Valley vineyard to work with their very talented chef, Franco Dunn, to create a meal in which every course included chocolate in one form or another. Franco made prawns with a butter sauce thickened with a small amount of white chocolate and garnished with red peppercorns and toasted hazelnuts, and a duck with a sauce containing unsweetened chocolate. Dessert (my department) was a mélange of fruits in two sauces (white chocolate and Drambuie, and apricot and Amaretto). I personalized each plate by writing the guest's name in chocolate on the rim. The ethereal Jordan chardonnay and deep, luscious cabernet enhanced this special meal.

Another unforgettable chocolate experience took place half a world away from California — in Italy.

There is nothing in all the world quite like the grand Hotel Cipriani. The low, pale gold stucco building sits on its own private island across the harbor from the most magic city of all: Venice. The hotel's boat launch whisks its guests from the bustle of Piazza San Marco across the Grand Canal and the harbor right to the heavenly sanctuary of the island. In front of the hotel is a small garden shaded by trees bearing what look like golden pomegranates. On closer inspection they in fact appear to *be* golden pomegranates. "Let's look for the Rolex tree next," mutters David, my cynical husband.

I knew that if I spent my fortieth birthday at the Cipriani I would feel less depressed than if I spent it, say, in Harvard Square seeing *The Rocky Horror Picture Show* for the third time. This is what my seventeen-year-old son had suggested. Not even a Mud Pie from Steve's Ice Cream (my fifteen-year-old's idea) would be as good. Twenty-five giant kisses and a night with my four-year-old's soft blanket, no matter how generous the thought, would not take the place of a night in that famous hotel. Ever since I had read about the Cipriani in an ancient, dog-eared copy of a slick *Town and Country*–type magazine that was piled up along with the prerequisite *Cosmopolitan*s and *Redbook*s at my hairdresser's, I had wanted to go there. Anything described as the "ultimate in luxury hotels, over-looking the most breathtaking scenery in the world" sounded like a place I could be very happy. This was my husband's attitude: If you pay, I'll go, but don't come crying to me when they don't treat you like royalty. You'll be just another American tourist who will be ignored while the beautiful people (he meant the RICH beautiful people) get all the attention. I gave him the double positive (yeah, yeah) and called the travel agent. The good news, she reported back, was that they had space, the bad news was that according to the thinness of our American Express card we could only afford to stay one night. That was good enough for me.

Every other person in the motor launch was wearing white de-signer outfits, sunglasses and tans. I had never seen so much luggage with little *V*'s on it before. Their hair didn't blow into their mouths because they had seen it all before and were not staring open-mouthed at the splendor before us. They also didn't seem at all nervous about wearing their gold necklaces, bracelets and watches while cruising around the tourist hot spots of Italy. I thought longingly of my one good ring, safe at home, wishing that I had it so that it could, in some way, cancel out my grimy, travel-stained trench coat and our mismatched blue duffel bags. I winced as I glanced at all those travel tags I had left on my bags to show that I had "been around." Dog-eared and ripped, the tags looked as if they had gone through several spin cycles in the washing machine, which would also explain why the bags looked like lumpy blue Christmas trees someone had discarded in the gutter during a rainstorm.

A nattily uniformed bellman helped us off the boat and steered us toward the trees of golden fruit. Off to our right we were able to spot the Cipriani's famous swimming pool — the largest outdoor heated pool in the world. On chaise longues around the edge of the pool were couples with perfect bodies who looked as though they probably played polo when they weren't lying around swimming pools. On our left was a long, wide terrace facing out toward the water. The tables were being set for dinner. We entered the lobby, which mirrored the same understated elegance as the garden and the building's exterior. It was lined with polished wood-framed glass cases in which were displayed the baubles of the upper crust that were for sale in the hotel's shops: skirts and jackets made of the softest suede; mink-trimmed, black-sequined sweaters; handbags that cost as much as four years at Princeton; delicate, hand-painted enameled china pitchers; and jewelry — serious jewelry: watches dripping with diamonds, ruby and emerald bracelets that would require arms strengthened by months of Nautilus exercises to support.

As we stood in the Cipriani's polished stone and deep-stained wood lobby, brushed by on either side by handsome couples dressed in identical fluffy white terry-cloth robes with the Cipriani logo emblazoned on the lapel, looking like they had stepped out of the pages of *Town and Country*, striding purposefully toward the pool or sauna or tennis court, we felt most definitely out of place.

We made our way to the front desk and told the concierge our names. I truly expected him to give us the old up and down, sniff disdainfully and tell us that our reservation had been canceled because we weren't up to par. Instead he gave us a warm smile and said, "Ah yes, the Brodys. Signorina Paola Starace would like to greet you personally. She is the hotel's public relations person." He buzzed the phone on his desk.

David and I exchanged looks. Why on earth would the public relations person at the Cipriani want to meet us? Through the doorway with an energetic pace came a petite woman with shining eyes and an extended hand. "The chocolate lady! I have been waiting for you! Welcome to the Cipriani." She grasped our hands in a firm, welcoming handshake. This warm and enthusiastic greeting was not exactly what I had expected. I asked her how she knew about my chocolate persona (I knew that my chocolate book had not yet made it to the shops in Venice). She replied that my travel agent (Ste. Debby-Sent-from-God) had telexed a note with my deposit saying that I was a food writer, specializing in chocolate, and that we had chosen the Cipriani for a birthday celebration.

"You should know that chocolate is my obsession, my adored food. Everywhere I travel I buy it so that I can have a chocolate experience in each country. I even have a stash hidden in my room for the times when I get the craving in the middle of the night. When I heard you were coming I couldn't wait to meet you — at last, a person who takes this passion as seriously as I do." Now here was a person after my own heart.

She continued, "At the Cipriani we have our own very special chocolate dessert. With your permission I will ask the chef to prepare it for you this evening. Meanwhile please make yourselves at home. I hope you like your room; it has a very special view. Please try the pool — there is nothing like it in the world." I had died and gone to heaven — and this angel wanted to feed me chocolate too.

The room was perfection: walls of the softest, palest peach trimmed with cream. French doors opened up onto a spacious veranda on which large fruit trees in clay urns gave shade from the midday sun. Below lay the garden with its heavenly smell of orange blossoms and deep lavenders and pinks of begonias. Beyond, across the shimmering water, like a silvery mirage on the horizon, floated Venice. David was in the bathroom trying to figure out what all the knobs, buttons, buzzers and switches were for. I ran my hand across the luxuriously soft cream-colored sheets — so this is what royalty sleeps on.

"Hey, look. Here's our robes. Now we can look like everyone else." David came out of the bathroom with two of those fluffy white terry-cloth robes over his arm. Hit the pool. And what a pool it was. Endless turquoise water, warm as toast. It was like swimming in the Caribbean Sea, except that every time I raised my head and squinted I could see gondolas gliding by in the distance. I dove under the surface and floated effortlessly through the womblike water. There were only the sounds inside my head: "Don't get used to this, kid," they warned me. "Come on," I pleaded, "it's my birthday. Let me pretend that I'm rich and tan and on permanent vacation at the Cipriani."

Wet and wrinkled and blissfully at peace, we wrapped ourselves in our robes and sat by the pool and watched the muted red-orange autumn sun set in the mist over the harbor, then made our way back to our room to take a nap before dinner. David was fiddling with the bathroom controls again and I was testing those sheets when someone knocked at the door. It was a bellman bearing gifts. There was a bottle of champagne in an ice bucket and several small gift-wrapped packages. "Happy Birthday," said the card, "from Paola Starace." Inside the little packages were the most exquisite chocolate bars. These were from Paola's secret cache: two from Germany filled with crunchy nougat surrounded by dark chocolate, and two from Italy made with *gianduja* — milk chocolate infused with hazelnuts. It was clear that this was going to be an outstanding birthday. David, rosy-cheeked and relaxed from his hours of water play, opened the champagne. I opened the chocolate. Lying under the silky sheets, sipping champagne and nibbling the delicious chocolate and listening to the gently muted sounds of the evening, we redefined the concept of the cocktail hour.

From our table on the veranda we could see the twinkling lights of Venice. The night air was soft and warm. Gondoliers at full voice steered their sleek boats full of rapt tourists past our island while we made the same wish on every star that appeared in the black sky. "Next year at the Cipriani!" we said, clinking our glasses together. Paola joined us for a glass of champagne and we thanked our wonderful new friend profusely for her extravagant gifts and warm hospitality that made this birthday so special. She talked about her fascinating job, which entails her spending several months of every year traveling around the world to promote the hotel. She told us of eating chocolate in places as exotic as New Zealand and as familiar as upstate New York. She divulged the names of her beloved shops in Vienna and Salzburg, Rome and Paris. I promised to send her my favorite American chocolates as soon as I got home.

Our dinner was one of the most delicious and certainly the most romantic we'd ever enjoyed. But dessert — that was paradise. A parade of waiters surrounded our table. One carried plates, one carried serving utensils and the third carried the chocolate birthday soufflé, bedecked with glowing candles. The waiters sang "Happy Birthday" — fast, so the soufflé wouldn't deflate before we got to eat it — and all the other diners chimed in (fortunately the dessert was large enough for everyone to have a taste). I took a bite and closed my eyes. I was floating on a deep blue sea, champagne bubbles making my body weightless. The exquisite warmth of the deep, rich chocolate set off fireworks of delight in my head. David didn't look too unhappy either.

I got a postcard from Paola just the other day. She thanked me for the chocolate bars I had sent and reminded me that she was expecting us at the Cipriani for birthday number forty-one. I have just a few months to convince David that life won't be bearable unless I can eat that chocolate soufflé at least once a year.

☙ Chocolate ❧

THE fruit of the cacao tree (which grows within 20 degrees north or south of the equator in places like the Ivory Coast and Ghana) looks like an elongated melon sporting variegated hues of yellow and brown. Split open, it reveals an inner mucilage containing several handfuls of white beans. These beans, once dried and fermented under coconut mats in the tropical sun, turn brown and offer up the heavenly smell of chocolate. The beans are shipped to manufacturers and immediately sorted and roasted. The outer husks are removed and the beans are ground. The cocoa butter (a clear fat) is removed from the ground beans and the end product is cocoa. When cocoa butter is put back in and the mixture conched, or moved, over a series of rollers for up to seventy-two hours, the result is baking chocolate. When sugar is added during the conching process, the result is (depending on how much sugar has been added) either bittersweet, semisweet or sweet chocolate. The addition of milk solids creates milk chocolate. White chocolate is simply cocoa butter, sugar and milk solids.

All chocolate should be stored in a cool, dry place away from heat, humidity and sunlight. Since chocolate absorbs any odors, keep it well wrapped in heavy-duty plastic in sealed containers. Do not keep chocolate in the refrigerator because it will develop a coating of moisture that invites mold. This moisture will also cause the chocolate to seize, or harden, when it is melted. Since dark chocolate will keep for up to seven years under ideal conditions, it is not necessary to freeze it. You may want to freeze white and milk chocolates, which have only a six-month shelf life because of the milk solids.

When freezing, make sure to wrap the chocolate in several heavy-duty plastic bags and defrost it wrapped so that the moisture collects on the plastic. It is always more economical to buy chocolate in bulk, and the easiest way to do this is to contact a local bakery supply house. Make sure you buy *real* chocolate as opposed to summer or compound coating in which palm kernel or coconut oil is substituted for the cocoa butter that gives chocolate its magical melt-in-your-mouth quality.

As far as choosing which brand of chocolate to cook with, remember, if it's good enough to eat, it's good enough to cook with.

Serves 6

$\mathcal{S}$OUPE DE FRUIT

This visual masterpiece combines the finest of fresh summer fruit, two easy-to-make-ahead sauces and the unusual personalized garnish of your guests' names written in chocolate around the rim of the plates. It is best to use larger dinner plates with a shallow well and a wide rim.

FOR THE CHOCOLATE WRITING:

1 cup heavy cream
12 ounces semisweet or bittersweet chocolate,
*   finely chopped*

In a small saucepan scald the cream and add the chocolate, stirring over low heat until the chocolate melts. Place the pan in a larger pan full of ice water and stir gently until the mixture cools and begins to thicken slightly. Using either a pastry bag with a medium writing tip or a paper cone, practice writing until you feel confident to work on the plates. Write the guest's name around the rim of the plate. Remember, you can always wash and dry the plate and begin again. There is plenty of chocolate "ink" in this recipe. If the chocolate seems too stiff, return it to the pan and warm gently over very low heat. The plates can be decorated the night before and stored in a cool place but not refrigerated.

FOR THE FRUIT:

About 1 cup per person of some of the following fruits: peaches, apricots, nectarines (all blanched, skinned and sliced), kiwis (peeled and sliced), cherries (pitted and halved), purple grapes (halved and seeded), raspberries, blackberries and black raspberries

FOR THE WHITE CHOCOLATE DRAMBUIE SAUCE:

9 ounces white chocolate (I use Tobler Narcisse)
1 cup heavy cream
1 tablespoon finely grated lime peel
¼–⅓ cup Drambuie

Break the chocolate into pieces and place them in the bowl of a food processor. Scald the cream in a small saucepan and with the processor's motor running, add the cream to the chocolate. When the mixture is completely smooth, add the lime peel and the Drambuie to taste. Serve warm or at room temperature. This sauce can be frozen.

Makes 2½ cups

FOR THE ORANGE APRICOT SAUCE:

⅔ cup granulated sugar
2 cups water
12 ounces (2½ cups) dried apricots (try to find the soft ones)
finely grated rind of 1 large lemon
strained juice of 1 large lemon
2 cups orange juice
⅓–½ cup Grand Marnier or Amaretto

Combine the sugar and water in a medium-sized skillet over high heat, stirring until the mixture begins to simmer. Turn to low and add the apricots. Cook over low heat, stirring occasionally, until the apricots are very mushy. This will take between 15 and 25 minutes.

Use a slotted spoon to remove the apricots to the work bowl of a food processor. Add the rind and lemon juice to the cooking liquid and simmer over low heat for a few more minutes. Add this liquid to the processor. Process with the pusher in place until the apricots are pasty. Add the orange juice and the liqueur to taste. For a thinner sauce add a bit more orange juice. This sauce can be frozen.

Makes 3½ cups

TO ASSEMBLE:

Use a small ladle to spread each of the sauces on one half of the plate. Arrange the prepared fruit artfully on top of the sauces. Serve at once.

CHOCOLATE SOUFFLÉ NERONE
HOTEL CIPRIANI

6 tablespoons sweet (unsalted) butter
½ cup flour, unsifted
1¼ cups milk, heated
⅓ cup unsweetened cocoa
½ cup granulated sugar
4 ounces bittersweet chocolate, coarsely chopped
½ teaspoon vanilla extract
6 extra-large eggs, separated
⅛ teaspoon salt
boiling water

Preheat the oven to 425 degrees with the rack in the center position. Generously butter a 1½-quart (6-cup) soufflé dish and sprinkle it with granulated sugar. In a large, heavy-bottomed saucepan set over moderate heat, melt the butter. Lower the heat and whisk in the flour. Cook, whisking constantly, for 5 minutes. Do not let the mixture brown. Off the heat, dribble in the hot milk and whisk until it is incorporated. Return to the heat and cook 2–3 more minutes, whisking constantly. The mixture will be very thick. Remove from heat.

Sift together the cocoa and ¼ cup of the sugar. Add to the flour mixture along with the chopped chocolate. Stir until the chocolate melts and the mixture is smooth. Set aside to cool for 10 minutes. Stir in the vanilla extract. The base can be made this far up to 3 hours before completing the soufflé.

Beat the egg yolks into the chocolate mixture, two at a time, stirring well to incorporate. Beat the egg whites with the remaining ¼ cup of sugar and the salt until they are shiny and hold firm peaks. Stir a generous spoonful of the whites into the chocolate mixture to lighten it, then fold the rest of the whites in.

Pour the mixture into the prepared soufflé dish. Smooth the top with a rubber scraper, then run the scraper around the rim of the soufflé to form a shallow indentation. Set the dish into a roasting pan and place it into the oven. Pour boiling water to come halfway up the sides of the soufflé dish. Try not to leave the oven door open for any length of time while you do this.

Immediately lower the oven temperature to 400 degrees. Bake for 50 minutes or until lightly set. If the top is browning too fast, lower the oven temperature to 375.

Serve immediately.

Serves 6

CHOCOLATE ALMOND CAKE
HOTEL CIPRIANI

FOR THE CAKE:

*1½ cups (5¼ ounces) ground almonds (they
  don't have to be blanched for this recipe)*
½ cup boiling water
*7 ounces bittersweet chocolate, chopped into
  small pieces*
*½ cup plus 3 tablespoons sweet (unsalted)
  butter at room temperature*
¾ cup granulated sugar
4 extra-large eggs, separated
*1¼ cups all-purpose flour, sifted before
  measuring*

Preheat the oven to 325 degrees, with the rack in the center position. Butter a 9-inch springform pan, line the bottom with a circle of parchment or wax paper, butter the paper and dust the pan with 2 tablespoons of the ground almonds. Pour the boiling water over the chocolate and stir until it is melted and smooth. Cream the butter and sugar until light and fluffy, then beat in the egg yolks one at a time. Blend in the remaining almonds and then the chocolate and finally, with the mixer on low speed, the flour. Mix only until incorporated. Beat the egg whites until stiff but not dry and fold them into the chocolate/almond batter. Scrape the batter into the prepared pan and bake for 35–45 minutes or until the center of the cake tests moist but not wet. Let the cake remain in the pan for 15 minutes before unmolding. Turn the cake out onto a serving plate with 4 strips of wax paper under the edges and, while it is still warm, glaze with the following raspberry glaze.

FOR THE RASPBERRY GLAZE:

½ cup best-quality raspberry jam
2 tablespoons Framboise or other fruit liqueur

Heat the jam and the liqueur briefly and then strain through a sieve.

After the cake has cooled completely, cover it with the following chocolate glaze.

FOR THE CHOCOLATE GLAZE:

3 ounces semisweet chocolate, chopped
1 ounce unsweetened chocolate, chopped
4 tablespoons sweet (unsalted) butter at room temperature
1–2 tablespoons rum

Melt the chocolates in a small bowl set over a pan of gently simmering water. Stir until smooth. Stir in the butter and rum. Cool slightly, then pour the glaze over the top of the cake and use a long metal spatula to spread it smoothly over the top and sides. Remove the wax paper.

Serves 8–10

BITTER CHOCOLATE ICE CREAM HOTEL CIPRIANI

4 extra-large egg yolks
1 cup plus 2 tablespoons sugar
½ cup unsweetened cocoa
2 cups heavy cream
1 cup milk
4 ounces unsweetened chocolate, chopped

In the work bowl of a food processor or an electric mixer, beat the egg yolks and sugar until pale and thick. Add the cocoa and mix very well. Heat the cream and milk to a simmer and stir in the unsweetened chocolate, whisking until it melts. Pour the hot cream mixture over the egg mixture and mix well. Chill very well before freezing in an ice cream machine. Serve with the following chocolate sauce.

Makes 2 pints

CHOCOLATE SAUCE HOTEL CIPRIANI

6 ounces bittersweet chocolate
½ cup milk

Break the chocolate into small pieces and melt them in a metal bowl set over a pan of gently simmering water. Stir in the milk and cook the mixture in the water bath for 2 more minutes. Serve warm or at room temperature.

Makes 1⅓ cups

Coffee

I used to make a living making birthday cakes. I would spend hours laboring over each creation, making chocolate roses and elaborate patterns out of tiny gold *dragées*. The cakes would be tied with ribbons and would sit on fine embossed doilies that I ordered from Switzerland. I had only one problem with this line of work — I clutched when I was asked to personalize a cake. First of all, my handwriting is so bad that it makes any doctor's look like master calligraphy and second, there is the terror of knowing that you have only one chance to make good on the top of a cake — there is no such thing as a frosting eraser or Chocolate Out. "Happy Birthday, Marlene" or "Best Wishes on Your Golden Anniversary" would keep me up nights.

One Christmastime I got an order for a very large cake — actually it was a series of ten chocolate jelly rolls set end to end. The woman was ordering the cake for her husband's fiftieth birthday and she wanted me to write the names of the guests on the cakes — all one hundred and fifty of them. I thought for a moment about the sleepless nights this project would cost me, and then I thought about how much I like to swim in the Caribbean in February. So, I took the job.

I was very organized. I made the cakes the day before and frosted them so that I wouldn't have to worry about anything but the writing the day they were to be picked up. Early that morning, before anyone else was up, I started to get ready to tackle the project. First I needed to wake up. I brewed a pot of coffee and poured a big mugful. Just the smell made me feel great. I get my kicks from caffeine. Hold the decaf, please. I love coffee. I love it steamy, strong, clearing my head like an express train, making my mornings seem full of potential. I like it in big, thick mugs, topped off with cream and sweetened with a bit of sugar. I like it in France in wide cups as deep as bathtubs — half hot milk, half espresso — and I like it in Italy, thick and rich and topped with clouds of frothy steamed milk. I like it in New Orleans, fragrant with chickory, and I like it in the coffee shop down the street, where the cook adds two tablespoons of grounds for every cup of water.

The coffee tasted so great I had two cups. I filled my pastry bag with frosting, spread the guest list out on the counter and got to work. Later that morning my husband wandered downstairs and eyeballed my efforts.

"Gee, did you make this writing so squiggly on purpose? 'Haprth Brizdath, Kemmeshd,' " he read. "These people have some strange names. 'Marlkg and Chrushty'? 'Brb and Gerthtuf'? How many cups of coffee did you drink before you wrote this?"

I looked over his shoulder and had to admit that the letters did look as if they'd been written by someone holding the pastry bag in her mouth. I got out the hundred and fifty candle holders and placed them strategically in and around the names.

"No one would have been able to read this anyway," I assured him (and myself) as I lavished daisies and greens from the florist on top of the creation. The result didn't look so bad — and I don't write on cakes anymore unless I am drinking decaf.

❧ Coffee ❧

AMERICANS drink 300 million cups of coffee every day, which makes it this country's favorite beverage. If you consume one pound of roasted coffee per week, your annual consumption equals the yearly yield of about forty-five coffee trees.

The coffee bean is one of two seeds found in the fruit of the coffee tree, which grows in tropical countries such as Mexico, Brazil, Kenya and India. In the case of the best (and most expensive) coffee the beans are hand-harvested, and only those that are tree-ripened are picked. Once the coffee bean has been picked, it can be processed in several different ways, depending upon the country in which it was grown. The processed green beans are then exported and handed over to the roaster, who uses his expertise to heat the beans to the right temperature to produce the distinctive aroma and delicate taste that are extracted when the ground beans are treated with hot water. During roasting the bean gradually achieves shades that progress from light to very dark brown, almost black in color.

There are about one hundred different types of coffee available. The blending of beans, and the subsequent roasting process, creates the differences among coffees. In general, price can be a good indicator of coffee quality.

There are several important rules to follow in the making of a great cup of coffee:

. Use fresh beans. Keep both unground beans and ground coffee in the freezer in a sealed, heavy-duty Ziploc bag or in a covered tin. The shelf life of roasted coffee beans is one month if kept in the freezer. For ground coffee it's one week.

. It's important to use the right grind for your method of coffee preparation. Whether you use a filter system or a percolator, make sure you get the beans ground to the right consistency.

. Never make coffee with water that has been softened chemically.

. Always measure the water and the grounds. A good rule of thumb is two level tablespoons of coffee for every six ounces of *cold* water.

. If you use an electric percolator, never brew less than three-quarters capacity of the pot. Otherwise, you will end up with weak coffee.

- If you grind your own beans, make sure to keep the grinder clean. If old coffee collects inside, your coffee will have a rancid taste.

- Make sure your coffee maker and all its parts are spotlessly clean and free of sediment.

- Coffee tastes best immediately after brewing. Hold it only for forty-five minutes and at a temperature no higher than 180 degrees.

- Never reheat or boil coffee.

COFFEE CRÈME BRÛLÉE

5½ cups heavy cream
3 rounded tablespoons powdered instant
  espresso
8 extra-large egg yolks
⅔ cup granulated sugar

Preheat the oven to 350 degrees and place the rack in the lower third of the oven. Set eight 8-ounce custard cups or ramekins into a shallow roasting pan or jelly-roll pan with at least 1-inch sides. The cups should not touch.

Heat the cream in a medium-sized saucepan just until small bubbles form around the rim. Add the coffee and stir until it has dissolved. In a metal bowl combine the egg yolks and sugar and whisk for 1 minute. Whisk a little of the hot cream into the yolk mixture and then combine both mixtures. Divide among the custard cups. Place the pan with the cups into the oven and add about half an inch of boiling water. Bake 40 minutes or until the custards are set. Remove the custards from the water. Cool at room temperature for 20 minutes and then refrigerate them until cold.

FOR THE TOPPING:

2–3 tablespoons boiling water
1⅓ cups dark brown sugar, firmly packed

Set the broiler on high with the rack in the top position. Make a thick paste with the water and brown sugar, and using the back of a teaspoon, spread about 2 tablespoons of the mixture on top of each custard, all the way to the rim of the cup. Set the cups on a heavy-duty cookie sheet under the broiler (about 3 inches away from the element) until the sugar bubbles and just begins to get very brown. If you can smell the sugar burning, then it's time to take them out. You can also broil the custards two at a time in a toaster oven set on "Top Broil." Refrigerate until serving time.

Serves 8

COFFEE GRANITA

If you are an iced coffee fan, this is the dessert for you.

> *2 cups strong brewed espresso or ¼ cup instant*
> *espresso powder mixed into 2 cups boiling*
> *water*
> *¾ cup granulated sugar*
> *whipped cream and cinnamon for garnish*

Combine the coffee and sugar and stir over low heat until the sugar dissolves. Cool completely, then freeze in either an ice cream machine or in a shallow pan. If you choose the pan method, remove from the freezer when frozen, then chop into pieces and process in a food processor until smooth. Serve with softly whipped cream and a sprinkle of cinnamon.

Serves 4

IRISH COFFEE

> *2 tablespoons sugar*
> *4 cups strong, freshly brewed coffee*
> *½ cup Irish whiskey*
> *1 cup heavy cream whipped with 3 tablespoons*
> *confectioners' sugar and 2 tablespoons Irish*
> *whiskey*

Combine the sugar and coffee in a 1-quart pan and stir over low heat until the sugar dissolves. Off the heat add the whiskey and divide among 4 goblets. Top with the whipped cream.

Serves 4

COFFEE ICE CREAM SUNDAE WITH MILK CHOCOLATE COFFEE SAUCE

2 cups whole milk
2 cups heavy cream
½ cup instant coffee (regular or decaffeinated)
5 egg yolks
1 cup granulated sugar

Heat the milk and heavy cream together in a 2-quart heavy-bottomed saucepan. Stir in the coffee and stir until it has dissolved. Bring the mixture to a simmer. Combine the egg yolks and sugar in the large bowl of an electric mixer and beat until the mixture is thick and light in color. With the machine on a slow speed, dribble in the hot milk/cream mixture and mix until it is combined. Return this mixture to the saucepan and cook over low heat, stirring constantly, until the custard coats a spoon. Strain into a metal mixing bowl and chill. Freeze in an ice cream machine.

Makes 1 quart

FOR THE MILK CHOCOLATE COFFEE SAUCE:

12 ounces best-quality milk chocolate (not
  chocolate chips)
1 cup heavy cream
1 tablespoon instant coffee
2 tablespoons light corn syrup
2 tablespoons sweet (unsalted) butter
⅓ cup Kahlúa or Tia Maria

Break the chocolate into small pieces and place them in the work bowl of a food processor. Scald the heavy cream and add the coffee, stirring until it dissolves. Pour the hot cream over the chocolate and process in the food processor until smooth. Add the corn syrup and butter and process until smooth and finally, add the liqueur. Cool slightly.

Makes about 2½ cups

1 cup heavy cream, chilled
2 tablespoons confectioners' sugar
1 tablespoon instant powdered espresso

Beat the cream in a chilled bowl with chilled beaters until it holds soft peaks. Beat in the sugar and coffee.

TO ASSEMBLE:

Place a scoop of the coffee ice cream in each dish and pour about 1 tablespoon of Kahlúa or Tia Maria on it. Top with the sauce and a large dab of the whipped cream.

Serves 6–8

$\mathcal{M}$OCHA SOUFFLÉ ROLL

This dessert will head your list of easy-to-make favorites once you master the jelly-roll technique. You have a choice of fillings: mocha cream or ice cream.

FOR THE SOUFFLÉ ROLL:

10 ounces bittersweet chocolate, chopped into
small pieces
10 extra-large eggs, separated and at room
temperature
1 cup granulated sugar
2 tablespoons instant espresso
unsweetened cocoa

Preheat the oven to 350 degrees with the rack in the center position. Line a 17 x 11-inch heavy-duty jelly-roll pan with parchment, or butter the pan and line it with wax paper. Butter and flour the wax paper.

Place the chocolate in a metal bowl set over a pan of gently simmering water. Stir occasionally until the chocolate melts. Remove the chocolate from the heat.

Beat the egg yolks and half the sugar in an electric mixer at high speed until the mixture is thick and light yellow in color. Beat in the coffee. On low speed add the chocolate, mixing only until incorporated.

Beat the egg whites with the remaining sugar until they hold soft peaks. Fold the whites into the chocolate mixture and spread the batter on the prepared pan. Bake for 7 minutes and then reverse the pan back to front. Bake another 6 minutes. The cake will feel dry to the touch and slightly springy when it is done. Let the cake cool in the pan. To unmold, run a sharp knife around the edges to release the cake. Sift some unsweetened cocoa on top of the cake and cover with 2 long strips of plastic wrap that overlap in the center and extend at least 6 inches beyond the long sides of the pan. Place a large board or cookie sheet on top of the cake and flip it over. Peel off the parchment or wax paper.

FOR THE WHIPPED CREAM FILLING:

¼ cup confectioners' sugar
3 tablespoons unsweetened cocoa
1 tablespoon instant powdered espresso
1½ cups heavy cream, chilled

Sift the confectioners' sugar together with the cocoa and coffee. Whip the cream until it holds stiff peaks and fold in the coffee mixture. Reserve about half a cup for garnish. Spread the cream evenly over the cake to within 1 inch of the edges. Using the plastic wrap to guide you, roll the bottom (long) edge of the cake away from you. Continue rolling — *don't worry if the cake cracks* — until the cake is completely rolled, but still on the cookie sheet. Cover with the plastic wrap and freeze for about 1 hour; this makes the cake much easier to work with. At the end of the hour, gently lift the cake onto a long cake plate, or board covered with foil. Have someone help you do this. Remove the plastic wrap. Refrigerate until ready to serve. Use the reserved mocha cream and a pastry bag fitted with a star tube to garnish the cake with whipped cream rosettes.

FOR THE ICE CREAM FILLING:

1½ pints best-quality coffee ice cream

Soften the ice cream by beating it for 1 minute in the metal bowl of an electric mixer. Spread it over the cake to within 2 inches of the edges. Proceed to roll it as in the above recipe. Wrap it in plastic wrap and foil and freeze for several hours. Unwrap and serve with the following coffee chocolate sauce.

FOR THE BITTERSWEET CHOCOLATE COFFEE SAUCE:

1 cup heavy cream
¼ cup instant powdered espresso
10 ounces bittersweet chocolate, chopped
2 tablespoons sweet (unsalted) butter at room
   temperature

Scald the cream in a medium-sized, heavy-bottomed saucepan. Add the espresso powder and stir until it is dissolved. Off the heat, add the chocolate and stir until it has melted and the mixture is very smooth. Stir in the butter, bit by bit. Serve warm.

Makes 2½ cups

Soufflé roll serves 8–10

Crayfish

$\mathcal{D}$on't even ask how I found myself, one perfectly gorgeous spring day, riding in a baby-blue Rolls-Royce Corniche convertible down Fifth Avenue. Well, as long as you ask. . . . My escort, the owner of the Rolls, was a wildly successful orthodontist from Long Island who did some investing on the side. Some enterprising travel agents had introduced us in hopes of talking him into backing a plan that would have me teaching a group of swells all about chocolate while we cruised the Mediterranean in the *Sea Goddess* (a fancy yacht that transports the swells in the lap of luxury around the world from one watering hole to the other). After our meeting he invited me to lunch. Never one to turn down a meal in the restaurant mecca of this country, I said sure and hopped into the Rolls as if I kept one in the driveway behind my twelve-year-old orange Volvo. Please God, I begged silently as we glided down Fifth, just this once, let someone I know see me. Even in this city where everything goes, people turned their heads to stare as we went by. Would I like to make a call on his car phone? he asked after I remarked that I had never ridden in a car with a telephone before. "Uh, sure," I said and tried to think of someone who would be impressed. I called home. "Hey, guess where I am?" I asked the child who answered.

"Mom, I know you're in New York, but where are my gray gym shorts and the other tube sock with the green stripe on the top?"

"I'm riding down Fifth Avenue in a Rolls-Royce!"

"Yeah, and I've just been drafted by the Celtics."

"Really, I'm not kidding. It's baby blue and has this neat silver ornament on the hood. . . ."

"Mom, I really need those shorts." This is the kid who started saving for a Porsche with the income from his lemonade stand?

No garage would take the Rolls, so the orthodontist parked it at a meter outside the restaurant. If it had been my car, I would have ordered the food to go rather than leave it where all manner of humanity could place their fingerprints on its glossy exterior.

The restaurant, while not quite so fancy as the transportation, was pretty posh, and from the attitude of the staff, took itself pretty seriously as well. We drank some lovely champagne while we perused the menu.

"The special today is pasta with lobster," said the waiter, who went on to describe the dish. That sounded fine, I said, and ordered the special. A short while passed as we sipped the champagne and chatted about how we would entice the swells aboard the yacht with mountains of chocolate and promises of exotic ports of call.

The waiter returned with a shallow white dish full of delicious-smelling pasta that he placed before me with a flourish. I looked at my dish with surprise. That wasn't lobster nestled in between strands of pasta. I said to my host, "Look, crayfish!" Thinking I was displeased, he called the waiter over and demanded to know why the kitchen was trying to cheat me out of the lobster.

The waiter, duly offended at this accusation, said very huffily, "Madame, those are tiny lobster tails flown in from South America. We would never serve crayfish as a substitute." He assured me that I was mistaken. I didn't bother telling him that, as a native New Englander, I had been eating lobster since I could say "Pass the melted butter," and that my friends in New Orleans had acquainted me with crayfish in every form from boiled to deep fried. I knew what was what.

I tried to explain what neither the waiter nor my escort seemed to understand — that I was *delighted* to find crayfish in my pasta rather than lobster, that I ranked crayfish as one of my all-time favorite things in the world to eat. I tried to tell the waiter that he should stop apologizing, because he had made me very happy. While this conversation was taking place I was gobbling up the pasta as fast as good manners would allow. The crayfish were sublime. They were sweet and tender and tasted as good as the ones I had gorged myself on in New Orleans so many times. My host was looking dubious; he was, after all, a man who was used to getting exactly what he wanted. He was sure we were somehow being cheated.

While he and the waiter were arguing over the genus and species of the tender, tasty red morsels, I licked my plate clean. I told the waiter that, on second thought, perhaps he was right — they could have been baby lobster tails. Did he think he could bring out another plate of them just so I could be sure. Perhaps he could bring them out without the pasta. Did the kitchen have some sauce rémoulade they could serve on the side?

≽ Crayfish ≼

CRAYFISH, crawfish, crawdaddy or stone crab, perhaps it's that its flavor is similar to lobster that makes crayfish such a prized catch, but I think that it's because they are so much fun to eat. Whether you choose to boil, fry or sauté them, choose them with your nose. As is true with all fresh seafood, they should have no odor except perhaps the faint smell of the ocean. In the areas far removed from the sea you might have to settle for frozen crayfish tails. No matter. While they're not exactly as fresh as those right out of Louisiana's waters, you can make some tasty dishes out of them. As with other seafood, keep crayfish well chilled and use them as soon as possible.

$\mathcal{M}$R. B'S CRAYFISH AND FETTUCCINE

This delicious dish and the one following are the creation of Gerard Maras, who is the chef at Mr. B's Restaurant on Royal Street in the New Orleans French Quarter. Ralph Brennan, owner of Mr. B's, is the president of Gerard's fan club, which is made up of adoring and wildly appreciative devotees of his fine culinary talents.

If no fresh crayfish are to be found, use frozen crayfish tails, available at many fish markets and specialty stores.

> *4 ounces fettuccine, cooked al dente and*
> *drained*
> *1 tablespoon olive oil*
> *1 tablespoon sweet (unsalted) butter*
> *¼ cup diced green pepper*
> *¼ cup diced red pepper*
> *⅓ cup diced onion*
> *1 cup crayfish tails, cooked and peeled*
> *½ teaspoon Creole seasoning (see p. 95)*
> *pinch of crushed red pepper*
> *1 medium tomato, chopped*
> *2 tablespoons scallions (green part only), sliced*
> *6 tablespoons sweet (unsalted) butter, cut into*
> *pieces and very cold*
> *whole crayfish for garnish*

Toss the cooked fettuccine with the oil and set aside, covered to keep warm. Place the 1 tablespoon of butter in a large, heavy-duty sauté pan set over moderate heat. When the butter is melted and hot, raise the heat, add the green and red peppers and onion and cook for about 2 minutes, shaking the pan to keep the peppers from burning. Add the crayfish tails and the seasonings and cook an additional 2 minutes, then add the tomato and scallions. Sauté briefly and then start adding the cold butter, one piece at a time, stirring constantly and vigorously with a whisk or fork. When all the butter has been added, check the seasoning and remove from heat. Divide the pasta among 2 heated dishes and spoon the sauce over it. Garnish with fresh, boiled crayfish.

Serves 2

MR. B'S FRIED CRAYFISH SALAD WITH SEASONAL GREENS

FOR THE CREOLE MUSTARD DRESSING:

1 egg
2 tablespoons lemon juice
1 teaspoon Worcestershire sauce
2 tablespoons Creole seasoning (see recipe
  below)
½ cup vegetable oil

Whisk together all the ingredients in a small bowl until completely blended. Cover and chill for 2 hours or more before serving. Just before serving, whisk again to blend.

Makes ¾ cup

FOR THE GREENS:

Use some of the following greens: red leaf, green leaf, romaine and Bibb lettuce, and radicchio, escarole and chickory. Wash and dry the greens well, rip them into small pieces and chill until ready to assemble the salad.

FOR THE FRIED CRAYFISH:

1⅓ cups crayfish tails, cleaned and peeled
½ cup Louisiana hot sauce
3 cups all-purpose flour
⅔ cup cornstarch
2 tablespoons Creole seasoning (see recipe
  below)
vegetable oil for frying

Combine the crayfish and hot sauce in a small bowl and let the crayfish marinate while you prepare the greens. Combine the flour and cornstarch and seasoning in a medium-sized bowl. Heat about 1½ inches of oil in a deep skillet or electric frying pan to 350 degrees. Remove the crayfish from the marinade, dredge them in the flour, shake off the excess and fry until golden brown — about 2 minutes. Drain on paper towels.

TO ASSEMBLE:

Arrange the greens on 4 chilled plates and top with the fried crayfish. Drizzle on the Creole mustard dressing.

Serves 4

FOR THE CREOLE SEASONING:

2 tablespoons dried oregano
⅓ cup salt
¼ cup ground black pepper
2 tablespoons cayenne pepper
2 tablespoons dried thyme
⅓ cup paprika
3 tablespoons freeze-dried onion or onion flakes

Combine all the ingredients and mix thoroughly. Pour into a large glass jar and seal so it is airtight. This seasoning will keep indefinitely.

Makes 1½ cups

$\mathcal{C}$RAYFISH BISQUE

6 tablespoons butter
1 red pepper, chopped
1 green pepper, chopped
1 medium onion, chopped
6 tablespoons flour
¼ cup fresh parsley, chopped
2 cloves garlic, minced
2 cups chicken stock
1 cup medium cream
1½ pounds crayfish tails, cleaned and peeled
Tabasco sauce to taste
salt and pepper to taste

Melt the butter in a 2-quart pot and sauté the two peppers and the onion until soft and translucent. Stir in the flour, parsley and garlic and cook over low heat, whisking occasionally, for 10 minutes. Whisk in the stock and cream and cook for 20 minutes, stirring to prevent the bottom from burning. Add the crayfish tails, cook 10 more minutes, then correct the seasoning with the Tabasco and salt and pepper.

Serves 8

CREOLE QUICHE

This unusual layered quiche has two fillings — one crayfish, the other a delicious Creole mixture — and a unique custard topping. You can substitute shrimp, crabmeat or lobster meat for the crayfish.

FOR THE FILLING:

2 tablespoons butter
2 cups (about 1/2–3/4 pound) crayfish meat, cut
* into small pieces (reserve 8 whole crayfish*
* for garnish)*
2 tablespoons lemon juice
2 tablespoons dry sherry
1/4 teaspoon dried tarragon
1/4 teaspoon nutmeg
1/3 cup Swiss cheese, thinly sliced
1 cup Swiss cheese cut into 1/2-inch cubes

Melt the butter and stir in the crayfish along with the lemon juice, sherry, tarragon and nutmeg. Cook for 5 minutes over moderate heat, then set aside while making the pie shell.

FOR THE PIE SHELL:

1 1/2 cups sifted all-purpose flour
1/4 teaspoon salt
1/2 cup vegetable shortening, or 1/4 cup
* shortening and 1/4 cup cold butter cut into*
* small pieces*
1 egg, slightly beaten

Preheat the oven to 450 degrees with the rack in the center position. Combine the flour and salt in a large mixing bowl. Cut in the shortening (or combination of shortening and butter) until the mixture resembles coarse meal. Stir in the beaten egg until the mixture is crumbly. Press and pat into a 10-inch pie plate. Crimp the edges. Line the shell with a piece of foil and bake for 10 minutes, then remove the foil and bake for an additional 5 minutes.

FOR THE CREOLE MIXTURE:

3 tablespoons olive oil
1 cup onions, finely minced
1 garlic clove, mashed
1/3 cup diced green pepper
1/3 cup diced red pepper
1 16-ounce can tomatoes, well drained, peeled,
*   seeded and chopped*
1/2 teaspoon dried thyme
1 teaspoon dried tarragon
1 bay leaf
dash of Tabasco sauce
dash of cayenne pepper
salt and freshly ground pepper to taste

Heat the oil in a heavy skillet. Add the onion and garlic and cook over moderate heat until they are soft. Do not let the garlic brown. Add the green and red peppers and cook 5 more minutes. Add the tomatoes, thyme, tarragon and bay leaf and cook over low heat for about 15 minutes, stirring occasionally until the mixture is a thick puree. Add the seasonings. Remove the bay leaf. Let this mixture come to room temperature while you make the custard layer.

FOR THE CUSTARD TOPPING:

3 eggs, beaten
3/4 cup light cream
3/4 cup sour cream
1/4 teaspoon salt

Combine all the ingredients and whisk together until smooth.

TO ASSEMBLE:

Lower the oven temperature to 350 degrees. Scatter the cubed Swiss cheese on the bottom of the pie shell. Add the Creole mixture in an even layer, pressing down with the back of a spoon to fill the air pockets. Add the crayfish filling in an even layer, and cover this with the sliced Swiss cheese. Pour the custard topping over this. Sprinkle with additional nutmeg and a pinch of cayenne. Place the quiche on a sturdy cookie sheet or jelly-roll pan and bake for 30–40 minutes or until nicely browned. Cool 15 minutes before slicing.

Serves 8

Heavy Cream

So, you're going to Devon? You absolutely must stay at my mother's third husband's inn," said my ex-best friend Simon, whose family's marital hyperactivity seemed to keep justices of the peace quite busy in England. "He and his second wife own this charming guest house in a quiet village, off the beaten track. They'd be thrilled to meet you; they'll entertain you in grand style." How could we lose? We rerouted our trip so that we could spend two days in the village where one of Simon's stepfathers and his wife had their inn. Simon promised to write ahead to make the reservation.

The Red Dog Inn was a gray stucco affair located, to our surprise, across the road from an industrial park. It was composed of several segments stuck together in a rather haphazard fashion that faced out onto a semicircular asphalt drive. There was no thatched roof to soften the roofline that jigged and jagged over the length of the building. As we pulled in, my heart sank. This was not quite what we had been hoping for. There were a few scraggly flowers in the window boxes, but there was also a beer bottle in the birdbath.

"Want to make a run for it?" asked David.

Yeah, I wanted to go home and have a little talk with Simon.

Just then the front door opened and out walked a tall, thin man with terrible posture who grinned and waved wildly as he walked toward our car. He was still waving wildly when he was three feet from the car. Perhaps he thought we had bad eyesight, or was this the international sign for something? A washed-out blond in tweeds and sensible shoes followed him. She was not smiling. Welcome to Fawlty Towers. I was surprised to see that there wasn't a mangy red dog following at her heels.

"Well, well, here we have the Brodys!" the man said, still grinning. He had stopped flapping his hands around and was rubbing them together, sort of in the lugubrious way Count Dracula would when he welcomed his victims into his castle. His wife looked confused and not at all pleased to see us. We shook hands all around and Simon's mother's third husband ("Call me Ray") said, "How is Simon? We haven't seen him in years." Years? "Just yesterday we received his letter telling us you were coming." Yesterday? He had said he would make the reservation weeks ago. "All the rooms were booked, so we had to make special accommodations for you." No wonder the missus didn't look too pleased. I saw a way out.

"We wouldn't hear of putting you to any trouble," I quickly said. "We can easily find another place to stay," I offered hopefully. Of course they wouldn't hear of it. And, it seemed there was no other place to stay. Ray insisted that we stay.

I was fascinated by Ray's maniacal grin. He wore it constantly except for a split second now and then when his cheek muscles went into spasm and he would have to let it go. He would twitch his mouth back and forth a few times as if he were sending a message to the central control and then the smile would flash back in all its brilliance.

"We've put you in James's room. He's away at school and I'm sure he wouldn't mind at all." Well, if it's no problem for James. . . .

Looking at the room, one would guess that James was not away at college. Judging from the size of the bed, most likely he was away at kindergarten. Judging from the amount of dust in the room, James had been away at kindergarten at least a year. Ray dropped our bags on the Day-Glo-orange fake-fur throw rug by the bed and said, "Drinks at six sharp by the bar. See you there."

David and I couldn't unpack because all the drawers were filled with James's toys and comic books. I began to say that I didn't think it could get much worse, when David sat down on the bed. It swallowed him up. What I mean is, the springs in the center of this narrow piece of sleeping equipment simply gave way (if they existed at all) and the bottom half of David's body disappeared. I must admit he looked kind of funny — sort of like a hand puppet — stuck in the bed like that. I stopped laughing the minute I sat down on the bed. It tried to eat me too. "I'm going to kill Simon. I mean it. The guy doesn't have a prayer." The dust activated my hay fever and I began to sneeze. David said, "I need a drink."

At the bar Ray poured us a healthy belt of brandy and started to reminisce about Simon. The more he talked (and the more he drank) it appeared that Simon was not his all-time favorite stepchild. As a matter of fact, the person whom he was talking about sounded like an awful guy — like someone who would send his best friends to a ratty inn, in an ugly part of England, run by a marathon grinner who hated his stepson and wanted to get back at him by torturing the stepson's unsuspecting friends in a bed that ate tourists. I couldn't wait to have a word with Simon.

At 6:00 P.M. an electric buzzer sounded. "That's the dinner bell," said Ray. "Our guests are expected to come promptly and not keep Cook waiting." Maybe we had come to boarding school by mistake. Well, in our haste to get to this godforsaken place we had missed lunch, so if he wanted to serve dinner at this ridiculous hour, I was game. White-haired couples started silently filing into the wood-paneled dining room. Was this a charter group of Gray Panthers? No, not enough vitality. We walked in too. The room was filled with eight card tables without cloths, set with thin paper napkins and cutlery that looked as if it was army surplus. Four bridge chairs surrounded each table. Oh, great! We got to play canasta if we finished our dinner. On a metal folding table on one side of the room twenty jelly glasses stood waiting. Someone had written on the table near my setting in tiny letters "Kill the cook." If I had had a pen I would have written "Beware of James's bed." After dinner I would have written "The cook tried to kill me." The kitchen door swung open and Constance, Ray's wife, appeared with an enormous tray on which were piled twenty white heavy-duty plastic dishes. She distributed them around the silent dining room. In unison twenty forks were raised and twenty knives tore into the minute piece of mystery meat (could this be the missing red dog?). Twenty forks tried to spear rock-hard slices of beet. Ray, over at the side of the room, poured wine from a plastic pitcher into the jelly glasses. Everyone got exactly half a glass.

"How come he was so generous with the brandy?" David muttered.

"Because he's going to charge us for it," I answered, staring at my plate. I had been chewing the mystery meat for three minutes and couldn't get it into a form that would go down my throat without choking me. I could just see David doing the Heimlich maneuver in the middle of the silent dining room. At ten past six everyone was done. The diners laid their forks down and looked expectantly at the kitchen. Were they hoping that whatever Cook was whipping up for dessert wouldn't be worse than the main course? Out schlepps Constance, twenty Pyrex custard cups balanced on her tray. Cornstarch pudding. My stomach was screaming with hunger. I would eat anything. I tasted. I would not eat this. David was really desperate. He ate his (that should have been in the *Guinness Book of World Records*) and he ate mine too. Six fifteen. Twenty chairs scraped back across linoleum and twenty starving people filed silently out of the room.

"Let's drown our hunger with alcohol, go to bed early and get the hell out of here first thing in the morning." A smart man, my husband. We headed to the bar. The bar was closed. We located Ray, who informed us that most of his guests, being of retirement age, went to bed early, so he closed the bar before dinner. "I'll share a little secret with you folks. I mentioned our cook before. Well, the fact is that Constance does all the cooking. That's how we manage to keep the costs down. We don't let many people in on that because it's better for our image if people think we have a professional in the kitchen. For my money Constance is better than any professional." Better than any professional food poisoner, sure. I didn't mention that I thought they held the food costs down by not serving any.

It was now 6:40. In the summertime in this part of the world the sun sets at 9:00 and at 10:30 it's still light enough outside to read a newspaper. The idea of retreating to James's room and the bed that ate tourists (and the dust that made me sneeze) was not exactly appealing. We decided to take a long walk. "Watch out for the no-see-ums," called Ray as we headed for the door.

We made our way up the road, away from the inn. Tiny little bugs started swarming around our heads, flying into our noses and eyes.

I began to sneeze again. "David, let's go back. These bugs are awful and OW! they bite." I was waving my arms wildly, which reminded me of something. I realized that was the very gesture Simon's stepfather had used as he had approached our car earlier.

"They're full of protein. Keep walking." We turned up a path and when I faltered (blinded by bugs and faint with hunger) David grabbed my hand and dragged me along. The path led toward a meadow bordered by hedges. The countryside was looking a lot prettier, when you could manage a glimpse through the swarming insects. After a while we saw some cows, a few sheep and even a small patch of wild roses growing over a garden gate. Things were definitely looking better. The path rounded a bend and there ahead was a little valley that nestled a cottage, a barn and a wooden silo. A cow lifted her head from grazing as we walked by. Birds dove in and out of the trees around us, scooping up thousands of the bugs that had been feasting on us, making it easier to see. I was relieved to be able to stop waving my arms, both because they ached like crazy and because I had not the slightest desire to emulate Ray. The farther behind we left the inn, the better we felt. Except we were ravenous. We approached the farmhouse and saw a sign hanging outside on a vine-covered post. "Cream Teas," it read. "We are saved," said David.

"No way, babe. Tea is served in the afternoon, not at seven at night." Always the optimist, David was determined to ask anyway. He knocked at the door, which was immediately opened by a plump white-haired lady wearing a blue and white gingham apron. An amazing smell wafted out of the kitchen. Now I know how people can say they've fainted with desire. David asked if cream tea was available. The woman must have seen we were in desperate straits. She asked where we had come from. We told her the whole story, and she laughed until tears came to her eyes. It seems we weren't the first victims of the inn of Simon's relatives. Certainly cream tea was available. She sat us down in the kitchen and chatted while she bustled about preparing food. It was hard to believe we were only a short distance away from James's Torture Chamber — we might have been on a different planet.

Our hostess set out blue pottery plates, oversized tea cups, heavy silver spoons, ivory-handled knives and big blue linen napkins. There was a thick white china jug of blue delphiniums and wild roses sitting on a crocheted doily on the dark oak table. From the old-fashioned refrigerator she brought out a glass jar of strawberry jam and a crock of clotted cream. As she swished the tea pot with boiling water she explained to us how she made the clotted cream by setting the extra-heavy cream from her own cows in a shallow pan on the back of the warm stove overnight. By morning the sweet cream is ivory-colored and thick enough that it can be spread on scones and crumpets. While the tea steeped we wished out loud that we could get clotted cream back home. "More reason to visit Devon," she said as she reached into the oven and pulled out a pan of scones that just happened to be baking there. God works in strange ways.

She split open the scones and fragrant steam rose from them. Here's the order she instructed: first the cream, then the jam. She poured black tea into the waiting cups and added milk and sugar. We slathered on the clotted cream and then spooned on chunks of glistening strawberry jam. I watched David as he took a bite. The look on his face was almost as delicious as the taste of the buttery scone, the sinfully smooth, rich cream and the intense flavor of the jam. It was a delectable and supremely satisfying combination of flavors and textures. With our hostess's encouragement we managed to finish off all the scones. The taste of that clotted cream will stay with me forever.

Knowing what was lying ahead in the bug and bed department, our gracious hostess insisted on pouring each of us a glass of homemade ginger wine "so you could get to sleep" and having her husband drive us home in his truck. We accepted both offers with great pleasure.

The wine soothed our reentry into the land of the starving sleepless, and we resolved the bed problem by sleeping on the throw rug. Even my sneezing didn't seem so bad. We were up bright and early for a quick getaway, and I think our strange innkeepers weren't too sorry to see us go. After all, we didn't fit the docile mold of their regular guests.

As we sped away with great relief, David, instead of going up toward town, headed in the direction we had walked the night before. "Where are we going?" I asked, knowing the answer full well.

"You know Simon probably was able to blot out the horror of the Red Dog with daily doses of clotted cream. One more cream tea and I can too."

❧ Heavy Cream ❧

CREAM, the part of milk high in butterfat and rich in flavor, is divided into three categories: heavy cream or heavy whipping cream, pasteurized or ultrapasteurized, which contains not less than 36 percent butterfat; light whipping cream or whipping cream, pasteurized or ultrapasteurized, which contains not less than 30 percent butterfat; and light cream, pasteurized or ultrapasteurized, which contains not less than 18 percent butterfat. Half-and-half is a mixture of ultrapasteurized or pasteurized milk and cream that contains not less than 10.5 percent butterfat. Whole milk, by contrast, has only 4 percent butterfat.

One of the benefits of ultrapasteurization is that heavy cream will keep for weeks under refrigeration. If you are like those cooks who prefer to use cream that has not been ultrapasteurized (because of the slightly cooked flavor that some cooks feel masks the real taste of the cream), simply buy milk that has not been homogenized (it will have been pasteurized) and skim the cream off the top. Regular pasteurized cream, which has a shorter shelf life than ultrapasteurized, is usually also available in health food stores.

Occasionally, cream will smell as if it has turned sour, but if you pour the contents into a clean bowl you will find that only the cream dried on the edges of the carton has gone bad and the rest is fine. Heavy cream can be frozen, although it is not advisable to try whipping it after it has thawed. Save it for another use.

❧ WHIPPED CREAM ❧

The secret to successful whipped cream is a cold metal bowl and cold beaters. The fat in heavy cream is more stable and better able to hold the air bubbles you beat into it in this cold state. Adding sugar at the beginning of the whipping process will yield a less voluminous whipped cream than adding it at the end. The higher the butterfat content of your cream, the thicker and more stable your whipped cream will be. If you need your whipped cream to stay firm for more than an hour or so, you can stabilize it. You can double or triple the following recipe. The dry ingredients will keep for a month in a covered plastic container.

⅓ cup instant dry milk powder
⅓ cup confectioners' sugar
¾ teaspoon arrowroot
2 teaspoons unflavored gelatin powder
hot water

Sift all the dry ingredients together. To assure even mixing, process them in a food processor.

For every cup of heavy cream to be whipped, use 2 tablespoons plus 2 teaspoons of the dry mix and 2 tablespoons plus 2 teaspoons of hot water. Mix until the dry ingredients dissolve (you may have to stir them over a very low flame — do not let the mixture boil). Cool 1 minute and then add to the cream halfway through the beating process. Do not overbeat, since the whipped cream will turn grainy.

CRÈME FRAÎCHE

While this is not quite the lusciously thick, tangy, sweet version found in France, it's a pretty good substitute and a damn sight cheaper than buying the imported or domestic commercial kind. Use crème fraîche as you would sour cream, or sweeten it with a bit of sugar or honey and use it on fruits and desserts. You can use it to thicken sauces and it won't curdle if boiled, unlike commercial sour cream.

It is imperative to use a thermometer when heating the heavy cream/sour cream mixture below to avoid overheating, which will kill the culture in the sour cream.

> *2 cups (1 pint) heavy cream*
> *4 tablespoons commercial sour cream*

In a small saucepan set over moderate heat, whisk the cream and sour cream, stirring constantly. Heat to exactly 85 degrees. Pour the mixture into a glass jar that has been rinsed with boiling water, filling it three-quarters full. (I use recycled peanut butter jars for this.) Screw the top on loosely and place the jar in a warm place — the closer to 80 degrees the better. The inside of a gas oven with the pilot light on is ideal. The cream will thicken in 12–16 hours. Refrigerate until ready to use. It will keep about 2 weeks.

Makes 2 cups

ULTI-GRAIN CREAM BREAD

The cream in this recipe replaces the shortening. It is typical of down-on-the-farm recipes, where excess cream found its way into all forms of baking. The cream makes the bread lighter and moister with a fine grain.

1 cup hot water
¼ cup molasses
¼ cup maple syrup
1 cup heavy cream
2 envelopes active dry yeast
½ cup quick or regular rolled oats
½ cup rye flour
1½ cups whole wheat flour
3 extra-large eggs, slightly beaten
1½ teaspoons salt
2½–3 cups unbleached flour
melted butter (optional)

In a large bowl combine the hot water, molasses, maple syrup and cream. The mixture should be warm but not hot. Dissolve the yeast in this mixture and allow it to proof (the mixture will turn foamy after about 10 minutes). Stir in the oats, rye flour and 1 cup of the whole wheat flour and mix well. Stir in the eggs and salt. Gradually mix in the remaining whole wheat flour and all but 1 cup of the unbleached flour.

Knead the dough either with a dough hook or by hand on a floured board for 10–15 minutes, adding more of the unbleached flour until the dough is no longer sticky. The dough should be quite soft. Place the dough in a buttered bowl covered with a clean dish towel and let it rise in a warm place until it has doubled. Butter two 8 x 4-inch loaf pans. Punch the dough down and divide it in half. Form each half into a loaf and place it seam-side down in the pan. Preheat the oven to 375 degrees. Let the loaves rise, uncovered, in a warm place until they have doubled in size and the dough reaches the top edge of the pan.

Bake the loaves for 25–35 minutes, until the loaf sounds hollow when removed from the pan and tapped on the bottom.

For a soft crust, brush the hot loaves with melted butter. Remove the loaves from the pans and cool on racks. These loaves can be frozen when completely cooled.

Makes 2 loaves

RASPBERRY-BLACKBERRY FRUIT FOOL

2 cups fresh or frozen raspberries
½ cup superfine sugar
2 teaspoons lemon juice
1½ cups heavy cream
⅓ cup confectioners' sugar, sifted
1 cup fresh or frozen blackberries
sprigs of fresh mint

Toss the raspberries with the superfine sugar and lemon juice in a small pan. Cook over very low heat for about 10 minutes, stirring constantly, until the raspberries give up their juice. Puree the fruit in a food processor and strain out the seeds. Chill. Whip the cream with the confectioners' sugar until it holds soft peaks. Fold in the puree lightly so that streaks show through the cream. Spoon into 6 chilled wine glasses and garnish with the fresh or thawed blackberries and sprigs of mint.

Serves 6

EASY CREAM SAUCE FOR CHICKEN OR FISH

This quick-to-make sauce simply involves adding cream and a few other ingredients to the pan juices left over from sautéing chicken breasts or fish. It is done at the last minute.

> *3–4 tablespoons butter*
> *½ cup dry white wine*
> *1 tablespoon shallots, finely minced*
> *1 cup heavy cream*
> *2 teaspoons Dijon mustard*
> *2 teaspoons dried tarragon*
> *1 teaspoon dried chervil*
> *1 teaspoon dried thyme*
> *2 tablespoons green peppercorns, rinsed of their*
> * brine*
> *salt and freshly ground white pepper to taste*

Sauté the chicken breast or fish in a large, heavy-bottomed skillet using the butter. Remove to a serving platter. (Pour off any excess fat from the chicken, taking care to leave the flavorful bits in the pan.) Add the wine and turn the heat to high. Cook until the wine is almost completely reduced. Add the shallots, the cream, the mustard and the spices. Cook on high heat until the cream reduces by one third. Add the green peppercorns and salt and pepper to taste.

Makes ⅔ cup

THE BEST FRENCH TOAST

Sunday night in our house means French toast. Our family is addicted to it, especially this version, which is heavy with egg and cream and cooked in lots of butter. The kids slather it with maple syrup made in nearby New Hampshire, but the grown-ups favor homemade Quick Blueberry Sauce (see p. 111).

1 loaf egg bread such as challah or Portuguese
  sweet bread, unsliced
3 eggs
1½ cups heavy cream
2 rounded tablespoons light brown sugar
2 tablespoons cinnamon
4 tablespoons sweet (unsalted) butter

Cut the challah into 1¼-inch slices. Mix the eggs and heavy cream together in a large, flat-bottomed bowl and stir in the sugar and cinnamon. Melt the butter in a large, flat skillet set on moderate heat. Dip the slices of bread into the egg mixture, turning to coat both sides. When the butter has melted and is sizzling hot, sauté the French toast a few pieces at a time for about 4 minutes on each side or until they are golden brown. Serve immediately with maple syrup or the following sauce.

Serves 4

QUICK BLUEBERRY SAUCE

1 quart fresh blueberries, fresh or frozen
  (preferably wild Maine blueberries)
⅓–½ cup granulated sugar
1 tablespoon instant tapioca
juice of 1 lemon

Place the blueberries in a medium-sized saucepan and sprinkle the sugar over them — use as much sugar as you need to just sweeten them a bit. Sprinkle in the tapioca. Add the lemon juice. Toss the berries and let them sit for 15 minutes. Cook over low heat, stirring constantly, until the berries give up their juice and begin to thicken. Cool a little before serving. This freezes very well.

Makes 1 quart

Duck

Back in the prehistoric days before Cuisinarts and vegicide (that's the slaughter of baby eggplants, zucchini, et cetera, before their prime to garnish those one-hundred-dollar entrees in temples of nouvelle cuisine), duck used to appear on menus in one familiar form: à l'orange. Then one day a chef somewhere in France was in a big hurry to turn out dinner to his patrons and didn't cook the duck long enough. Instead of meeting the diners' complaints about the rare meat with apologies, he cavalierly stated that this was the way duck was supposed to be served. The newly educated diners assumed that the chef knew what he was talking about, so they shut up and ate the undercooked duck. At the end of the meal they praised both the dish and the genius responsible for it. The smart chef, seeing a golden opportunity, pronounced the dish "nouvelle cuisine," raised the price and made it a staple of the menu. Some may say this story is apocryphal, but I'll bet that is exactly how rare duck came to be.

The chef in the restaurant where I used to work made miracles with duck. With the flash of a sharp boning knife he would remove the breasts from the duck, reserving the carcass to make stock for the sauce. The breasts, with the skin still intact, would then be placed in a dry marinade made of coarse salt, crushed peppercorns and bay leaves. They would remain there for several hours, while the chef spent time on the duck sauce. The carcass, along with carrots, onions and celery, was placed in a huge stockpot, covered with water and simmered for several hours. The resulting stock was cooled, defatted, and then returned to the stove to simmer until it reduced and the flavor intensified. The chef would add red wine to give it a hearty flavor and then thicken it ever so slightly with a slurry — a mixture of cornstarch and water. When the sauce was done its deep brown mirrorlike surface was flawless. The entire kitchen radiated with the heady aroma; deep and rich, it made you want to place your face directly over the sauce and hyperventilate until you passed out into the pot.

To prepare the duck, the chef wiped off the seasonings and heated a heavy-duty skillet until it was almost red-hot. He placed the breasts in the skillet, fat side down, and cooked them for three to four minutes, then he drained off the fat, flipped the breasts over and cooked them for an additional three minutes, pressing them down with a metal spatula. Then he slid them out of the pan onto a cutting board where, with a long, thin, very sharp knife, he deftly sliced them into thin strips. He fanned the rosy pink meat onto heated plates and ladled on some of the sauce. For something that took minutes to cook and seconds to arrange, the plates looked like a still life done by Rembrandt.

This dish was the chef's pride and joy, but while it caught on fast in France, many Americans had a problem getting used to the idea of eating rare fowl. The waiters would carefully explain that the duck dish on the menu was breast of duck served rare. I'll never forget the gentleman who called the waiter back to complain that his wife had ordered duck and was served flank steak instead. The waiter assured him that, while the meat on her plate might indeed look like flank steak, it was, in fact, duck breast. The diner insisted that it was steak. The waiter reported this to the chef, who waltzed out into the dining room bearing a whole duck, a cooked breast, his cutting board and his long carving knife. One glance at the knife and the doubting diners were ready to believe anything the chef said. The chef showed them where the meat came from on the uncooked duck and then, clearing away the fragile Limoges china with the sweep of his hand, put down his cutting board on the table and proceeded to carve up the cooked breast. The chef then speared a piece of meat and held it out to the woman. She looked as if she was eating hemlock until she realized that the morsel she had in her mouth was delicious. Goodbye, flank steak, hello, duck breast.

❧ Duck ❧

UNTIL very recently most shoppers had only frozen ducks available to them unless they lived near a poultry farm. Since its increase in popularity, fresh duck is now available in meat markets and some supermarkets. One of the more delectable species of duck available is the Muscovy duck, prized for its high meat yield. This duck has a thinner skin and less body fat than other domestic ducks (such as the Long Island duck) and a much more pronounced flavor. When shopping for duck, look for white skin, creamy white (or slightly off-white) fat and firm (not spongy) meat. There should be no odor to the duck. Defrost frozen ducks in the refrigerator and use immediately after thawing.

ROAST DUCK WITH APPLES AND CALVADOS

In her fine book *The Seasonal Kitchen*, Perla Meyers gives us this updated version of a classic dish. It's a real cold-weather treat. Serve with homemade steak fries (or oven-roasted potatoes) and sweet-and-sour red cabbage.

> *2 fresh ducks (4½ to 5 pounds each)*
> *salt and freshly ground pepper*
> *2 whole onions, each stuck with a clove*
> *2 tablespoons sweet (unsalted) butter*
> *1 finely chopped carrot*
> *½ cup finely diced celery*
> *1 bay leaf*
> *pinch of dried thyme*
> *¼ cup fresh parsley, chopped*
> *3 cups chicken stock (fresh, canned or 1*
> *   bouillon cube dissolved in 2 cups boiling*
> *   water)*

Preheat the oven to 450 degrees. Rinse the ducks, then dry them well both inside and out. Season with salt and pepper. Put a whole onion inside each cavity. Tie the duck legs together. Prick the skin of the thighs and breasts with a sharp knife.

In a flameproof baking dish large enough to hold both ducks comfortably, melt 2 tablespoons of butter. Add the vegetables and herbs. Place each duck on its side on top of the vegetables and place the dish in the oven. Reduce the heat to 350 degrees and roast the ducks for 2 hours, turning them once halfway through the cooking time. Baste the ducks a few times with the stock, and occasionally drain the fat from the bottom of the pan with a bulb baster or large metal spoon.

FOR THE APPLES:

> *6 large, firm baking apples, such as Cortland*
> *6 tablespoons sweet (unsalted) butter*
> *½ cup granulated sugar*
> *1 cup white wine*
> *⅔ cup golden raisins*

While the ducks are roasting, peel the whole apples and carefully remove their cores with a thin, sharp knife or apple corer. In an ovenproof casserole large enough to hold the apples, melt the butter. Add the apples, then sprinkle with sugar and wine. Cover the casserole and place in the oven for 30 minutes, until the apples are tender but not falling apart. Keep them at room temperature.

FOR THE SAUCE:

⅓ cup calvados
½ cup heavy cream
1 tablespoon cornstarch mixed with 3
    tablespoons cold water
2–4 tablespoons sweet (unsalted) butter, well
    chilled

When the ducks are cooked, remove them to a baking sheet. Preheat the broiler to high, then broil the ducks, breast side up, for 3 to 4 minutes, until the skin is crisp and brown.

Remove any remaining fat from the baking dish, place the dish over high heat and pour in the stock and the calvados, scraping the bottom of the pan well. Strain the sauce into a smaller saucepan.

Place the saucepan over high heat, add the cream and reduce the sauce to approximately 2 cups. Beat in the cornstarch paste and finally the butter. Cook 2 minutes until sauce is thickened.

TO SERVE:

Carve each duck into fourths, garnish each plate with an apple and a few raisins. You can either sauce the duck in the kitchen or pass the sauce separately at the table.

Serves 6

SAUTÉED DUCK BREAST

Here, in true nouvelle style, is the recipe for rare duck breasts. The sweet-and-sour sauce is a perfect complement. Once you've gotten the knack of the quick sauté, try duck breasts on the grill! Serve this with fresh asparagus and California Pistachio Pilaf, p. 238.

2 fresh ducks (3–4 pounds each)

Use a very sharp knife to remove the breasts from the ducks. Do not remove the skin. Trim the fat and skin so that it does not extend beyond the meat. Reserve the carcass for the stock. Rub the breasts with the following dry marinade.

FOR THE DRY MARINADE:

¼ cup coarse (Kosher) salt
1 tablespoon whole black peppercorns
several generous pinches dried thyme or several
  sprigs fresh thyme
6–7 cloves garlic, peeled and coarsely chopped
3 bay leaves, crushed

Place all the ingredients in a mortar and grind well with a pestle. This can be made, although not as effectively, in a food processor. Rub both the skin and flesh side of each duck breast with the dry marinade, wrap well with plastic wrap and refrigerate at least 4 hours or overnight.

FOR THE STOCK:

2 duck carcasses, liver and other organs
  removed
6–8 cups water
2 cups dry red wine
3 carrots, peeled and coarsely chopped
3 stalks celery, cut into 1-inch slices
2 large onions, coarsely chopped
1 bay leaf
1 teaspoon dry thyme or 1 sprig of fresh thyme

Place the carcasses in a stockpot. Cover with the water and add the above ingredients. Bring to a simmer and continue to cook for 2 hours. Do not bring to a hard boil. Drain off the liquid, discarding the solids. Cool well and remove all the fat. Reduce to approximately 4 cups.

FOR THE SAUCE:

4 cups strained and defatted duck stock
¼ cup Madeira
¼ cup honey or maple syrup
1½ tablespoons coarse mustard, such as
  Pommery
2 tablespoons cornstarch mixed with ⅓ cup
  water to make a paste
salt and pepper

Bring the stock to a simmer and add the Madeira, honey or syrup and mustard. Reduce to approximately 3 cups and add the cornstarch. Continue to cook until the sauce has thickened slightly and then add the salt and pepper to taste.

TO COOK THE DUCK BREASTS:

Heat a heavy-duty skillet until it is very hot. With a damp paper towel, rub the dry marinade from the ducks. (If you have trouble getting it off, you can rinse the breasts, but be sure to dry them very well.) Place all the breasts, skin side down, in the pan and cook over highest heat for 3–4 minutes. Drain off the fat and cook them on the other side for another 2–3 minutes, pushing them down into the pan with a metal spatula. You can tell they are done if when you press the flesh side with your fingers, there is a firm but not hard resistance. You can also cut into them with a knife to check. The meat should be red but not raw. Remove the breasts to a cutting board and slice, on the diagonal, into 5 or 6 pieces. Sauce and serve at once, 1 breast per person.

Serves 4

DUCK LIVER MOUSSE

This creamy-smooth, fantastically rich spread can be made with either duck livers or chicken livers. It must be made in a food processor.

*1 pound duck or chicken livers, rinsed and
   trimmed of fat
1 cup water or chicken stock
2–3 sprigs parsley
½ cup dry sherry
1 medium onion, finely chopped
3 cloves garlic, diced
1 bay leaf
1 cup (16 tablespoons) sweet (unsalted) butter
   at room temperature
¼ cup brandy or cognac (optional)
pinch of allspice
1 teaspoon powdered mustard
½ teaspoon nutmeg
1 teaspoon lemon juice
salt and freshly ground black pepper to taste
¼ cup (4 tablespoons) sweet (unsalted) butter,
   melted*

Place the livers in a small saucepan and add the water or stock, parsley, sherry, onion, garlic and bay leaf. Simmer for 15 minutes and then discard the liquid and bay leaf. Place the livers along with the cooked onion and garlic in the work bowl of a food processor and process until smooth. With the processor on, add the 1 cup of butter a few tablespoons at a time, waiting until the butter is incorporated before adding more. The mixture should be creamy and smooth. Add the optional brandy or cognac and season with allspice, mustard, nutmeg, lemon juice, salt and pepper. Scrape the mousse into a serving dish (I use a small white soufflé dish) and pour the melted butter on top. The butter keeps the mousse from drying out. Serve on toast or crackers.

Makes 2½ cups

WARM SALAD WITH DUCK CRACKLINGS

Assemble all the ingredients before you start to cook.

1 fresh duck, 4–5 pounds
2 tablespoons butter
3 tablespoons sherry
2 tablespoons honey
1 tablespoon soy sauce
2 shallots, minced
1 clove garlic, minced
2 teaspoons powdered mustard
¼ cup chicken stock (homemade or canned)
⅓ cup plain yogurt
8 leaves each assorted greens such as spinach,
*   red leaf lettuce, Boston lettuce and chickory*
3 scallions (green part only), thinly sliced
freshly ground pepper

Use a sharp boning knife to remove the breasts from the duck. Cut off the skin and slice it into strips about 2 inches long and ½ inch wide. Cut off as much of the other skin from the carcass as possible and cut this into strips. Cut off the legs and reserve them for another use. Heat a sauté pan or wok and cook the skin over high heat (draining fat as necessary) until the skin is very crisp. Drain on a paper towel. Combine the butter, sherry, honey, soy sauce and shallots in a wok or deep sauté pan. Cut each duck breast into 6 slices (the short way), add to the pan or wok and cook over medium heat for about 5–7 minutes. Remove the meat with a slotted spoon and cover with foil to keep warm. Add the garlic and mustard to the pan. Whisk in the stock and the yogurt. Cook another 2–3 minutes over moderate heat. Arrange the greens on 4 plates and top with the duck breast. Pour on a few tablespoons of the sauce and top with the cracklings and the scallions. Pass the pepper grinder separately.

Serves 4

Figs

I missed being a member of the counterculture generation of the swinging sixties not by virtue of my age but as a result of early onset parenthood. While all our friends were experimenting with everything from Mary Jane to mushrooms, David and I spent our "leisure" time doing Pampers and pediatricians. The only controlled substance we ever used was paregoric to soothe teething gums. While I did march for McGovern and chant with John Lennon to "give peace a chance," a baby in a stroller somehow cut into my image of myself as really "with it." We almost got to Woodstock, but I couldn't fit my pregnant body into my patched bell-bottom jeans and embroidered peasant blouse.

By the time our children were one and three, Crosby, Stills and

Nash were riding the Marrakesh Express and David and I were tired of being so out of it.

"Let's go to Marrakesh," says he.

"You wouldn't drive one hour to go to Woodstock and now you want to fly halfway around the world to Morocco?"

"Well, you're not pregnant now."

I didn't quite get the logic, but what the hell, the only exotic country I had ever been to was Los Angeles. I was game.

We left for Morocco one week after the Six Day War. I had forgotten that Morocco was an Arab country. Not only was I in the most foreign place I had ever seen, I found myself surrounded (and I do mean surrounded) by thousands of people undoubtedly hostile to my religious and ethnic orientation. I became paranoid. David kept telling me they were Berbers, not Arabs. Every time I turned around there was a hand on my chest or backside. "Friendly Berbers," David assured me.

Before we left for Morocco we were instructed to get the vaccine for cholera since the country was in the midst of an epidemic. The administering physician warned us that the shots were only 80 percent effective. We didn't know if that meant that we had a 20 percent chance of contracting cholera, or that if we did get cholera there was a 20 percent chance that we'd be dead. We were justifiably nervous about eating and drinking. Our appetites were dampened both by fear of cholera and by the temperature, which hovered for days on end in the low hundreds.

It was hard to find food sold at the crowded marketplace that either looked familiar or came packaged so that we could eat it without having to wash it first. As we wandered about in the blinding sun and debilitating heat in search of sustenance, young boys followed us asking if we wanted to buy marijuana and hashish. Our suspicions that they were selling shredded camel dung were borne out by the young American we ran into who offered us his gold watch for our Lomotil. I'll bet it was easier (and safer) to be a hippie at home.

We had finished off the last cans of 90-degree Coke that we had stashed in the car and were faint with hunger. We came upon a crowd gathered around a stand where a man was selling little, round-ish, squat greenish purple things with pointy short stems that looked as if they could be some kind of fruit or vegetable. I watched as Berber women, their black-lined eyes the only thing showing above their veils, reached with henna-stained fingers and stuffed the little things into their bags. The vendor saw us watching the goings-on and asked if we would like to buy. I asked what they were. He answered in Arabic and I shrugged my shoulders and started to walk away. He grabbed my arm — what a salesman — and picked up one of the little things and told me to try. The threat of instant cholera was doing battle with the thought of death from starvation. I started to shake my head no and then figured what the hell. I took a bite. A delicate yet intense sweetness filled my mouth. Inside the drab exterior of that small fruit was an explosion of pink, a shade so beautiful that all other pinks were dowdy by comparison. Crunchy with tiny seeds, the pulp was soft and somehow familiar-tasting. I reached for another one. What a way to die. Suddenly Morocco didn't seem so bad. We gobbled up a sackful of fruit and were none the worse for wear, but still ignorant of the name of what we were enjoying.

Shortly after our return we went to see the movie *Women in Love.* There is a marvelous picnic scene in which Alan Bates reaches into a bowl and picks a piece of fruit and starts talking about how women and figs are physically akin. FIGS! That's what those things were. I watched with rapt attention while he took a bite and held up the fruit to show the pink inside. I had a gustatory déjà vu and a flashback of Morocco. (A college English professor of mine called this a Proustian orgasm.)

So, our mysterious fruit turned out to be figs, faintly familiar, tastewise, in Morocco because of my childhood love of Fig Newtons. I couldn't wait for fall to bring the season's first crop to the stores. I bought tiny green figs and larger plump purple figs. While we enjoyed them, both out of the hand and in recipes, I reflected on the fact that we would never make it as members of the counterculture; we had gone all the way to Marrakesh and discovered a substance that needs to be controlled only in that if you eat too many you get a stomachache.

⊱ Figs ⊰

NATIVE to Western Asia and the Mediterranean, figs are one of the most ancient of fruits. They were undoubtedly among the first to be dried and stored for food. The bulk of this country's fig production takes place in central California's San Joaquin Valley, where types such as the black mission, white Kadota, white adriatic and white calimyrna (the California version of the smyrna fig) are grown in abundance. Fresh figs reach the market in the fall and have a short season. These delicate fruits should be consumed soon after picking (or purchase). Choose soft, dry, unblemished fruit. Check the bottoms for mold or soft, wet spots. The taste should be intensely sweet and the pulp tender, but not mealy. Fresh figs seem to lose flavor once they are refrigerated, but the cold air will prolong their shelf life. Dried figs are extremely high in calcium and potassium. Their taste is even more intensely sweet than that of the fresh variety. Select plump, moist figs that are free of tough parts. Dried figs will keep for months in a tightly covered container.

FIGS AND MELON WITH PROSCIUTTO

This arrangement makes a stunning first-course presentation or a beautiful centerpiece for a cocktail party.

> *fresh figs*
> *assorted melons such as Persian, casaba,*
>   *Cranshaw, cantaloupe and honeydew*
> *prosciutto or Black Forest ham, very thinly*
>   *sliced*
> *kiwi for garnish*

Slice the figs in half the long way. Cut the melons into cubes measuring 2 inches long and about ¾ of an inch wide. Cut the slices of ham in half the short way and use them to wrap about half the melon cubes and half the fig halves. Arrange the wrapped and unwrapped fruit decoratively on a platter, placing a small glass full of toothpicks in the center. Peel and slice the kiwi and use as a garnish for the platter.

FRESH FIGS IN PORT

A tasty fall dessert.

> *12 slightly underripe figs*
> *6 ounces (⅔ cup) cream cheese, well chilled*
> *1½ cups port*
> *¾ cup granulated sugar*
> *juice of 1 lemon*
> *finely julienned rind of 1 lemon*
> *whipped cream or crème fraîche for garnish*

Set the oven to 450 degrees with the rack in the center position. Slip the tip of a sharp-edged teaspoon into the bottom of each fig and insert about 1 tablespoon of cream cheese. Place the figs, stem side up, in an ovenproof baking dish with high sides. The figs should touch and fit snugly into the dish. Combine the port and the sugar in a small saucepan and cook over moderate heat, stirring until the sugar dissolves. Continue to cook until the liquid reduces by half and starts to get syrupy — about 15–20 minutes. Add the lemon juice and rind and cook 1 more minute. Pour the syrup onto the figs and bake for 15 minutes. Serve hot with a dab of whipped cream or crème fraîche.

Serves 4

FIG AND GINGER COMPOTE

Use this flavorful condiment with cold meats or poultry or with cheddar cheese and turkey in a sandwich.

> *2 dozen dried figs*
> *1 cup sweet sherry or sweet Marsala*
> *1½ cups orange juice*
> *2 tablespoons fresh ginger, finely chopped*
> *2 teaspoons powdered cloves*
> *1 lemon, cut in half and seeded*
> *1 cinnamon stick*

Place the figs in a saucepan or in a microwave-safe bowl and add the sherry or Marsala and almost enough orange juice to cover. Add the rest of the ingredients and simmer, covered, for 20–30 minutes (or microwave on high for 10–12 minutes), until the figs are tender. This compote will keep for several weeks, refrigerated. I store mine in a large glass jar.

Makes approximately 4½ cups

QUAIL WITH FIGS
MOROCCAN-STYLE

If you wish, Cornish game hens can be substituted for the quail.

1 stick butter
6 quail
1 cup red wine
1 cup chicken stock (fresh or canned)
2 tablespoons honey
2 tablespoons red wine vinegar
½ teaspoon ground turmeric
½ teaspoon ground ginger
½ teaspoon ground cardamom
½ teaspoon allspice
12 fresh figs
salt and freshly ground pepper
toasted slivered almonds (see note)

Melt the butter in a large, heavy skillet with a close-fitting top. Add the quail and brown over high heat on all sides. Add all the ingredients except the figs, salt, pepper and almonds, and cook the quail, covered, for 10–15 more minutes over moderate heat. Test for doneness by moving one of the legs — it should move freely. Remove the quail to a warm platter. Quickly toss the figs in the sauce left in the pan — just to warm them — and place the figs around the quail on the platter. Cook the sauce, uncovered, on high heat until it reduces to about 1½ cups. Season the sauce with salt and pepper and serve with the quail. Garnish with the toasted almonds. Serve with couscous or rice.

Serves 6

NOTE: To toast almonds, spread the almonds on a baking sheet and roast in a 350-degree oven for about 8 minutes, checking carefully every few minutes to make sure they do not get too brown. This can also be done in a toaster oven.

Fraises des Bois

When I first saw Switzerland, everything looked the way I had imagined it, except that the sky, so blue and filled with puffy white clouds in both my travel guides and my cherished edition of *Heidi*, was overcast and gray. After a week's worth of low dark clouds and raw weather I was unhappily resigned to the fact that this was the way Switzerland always looked in April. As we drove from Geneva along the lake and over to Montreux, trying to take in what we could see of the magnificent scenery through the fog, I couldn't help feeling that there was something missing, but I couldn't quite put my finger on what it was. All the right props were there: red and yellow tulips poking their heads out of melting snowbanks, alpine-looking buildings with gingerbread and half-timbers decorating their facades, and in the distance, large mountains engulfed in a soft gray mist that never quite cleared so that you could see what was going on behind it. The food we ate on the way was all right, but not inspirational; it was served by reserved but certainly pleasant enough waiters or waitresses, who I felt (and I supposed justifiably) viewed us as just two more tourists passing through. So, I thought . . . this is Switzerland. While I wasn't crushed with disappointment, I wasn't bowled over, either.

In Montreux we went to see Chillon, the castle where Swiss patriot François de Bonnivard was imprisoned and then immortalized in Byron's poem. This was a particularly cold, damp and dreary day and the dungeon where poor Bonnivard did time was, if you'll pardon the pun, really the pits. You could see scratchings he had made on the stone walls of the cell that I translated "The weather is terrible, be glad you're not here." Byron countersigned right under that. I, personally, was glad I had the option of leaving; I couldn't wait to get into the car and drive to sunny (I hoped) France.

The narrow road we were traveling rises steeply above Montreux and is studded with switchbacks that must afford breathtaking views when there is no fog. As we climbed higher the snow got deeper and the road narrower and steeper. Our little economy-sized rental car (the one without the snow tires) was fishtailing back and forth across the road as I dug my nails into my palms and silently reminded myself that my husband was a wonderful driver. Just as I was thinking that this mountain we were climbing was taking us straight to the ionosphere, the road leveled off and immediately proceeded straight downhill.

"Let's stop for lunch," I suggested, spying a roadhouse perched on the edge of a switchback.

"But it's four o'clock in the afternoon and we just ate lunch two hours ago. Remember? You ate my spaetzle and said it tasted as heavy as yours."

"Well, you weren't going to eat it and I thought it was important to fill up so we could weight down the car for the trip up the mountain. And speaking of the trip up the mountain, I need a rest before we take the roller coaster ride down." He took one look at how green I had turned and, sensibly, agreed that dessert was what I needed to make me feel better. One with lots of *schlag*, I added.

We entered the roadhouse, which was disguised as a chalet, and found ourselves alone in a large, clean (that's how you knew you were really in Switzerland — everything was so clean) dining room full of neatly arranged tables. We took seats near the window that under better weather conditions should have afforded a spectacular view of the valley below, but now framed yet another gray, misty scene.

The waitress looked up from polishing glasses. She looked depressed. David, who never notices if anyone is depressed, said, "Gee, she looks depressed." I said that if I had to stare out into endless gray I would be bonkers, never mind depressed. She handed us menus and, when we said we had stopped in just for dessert, took the menus back and said the chef had some strawberries if we wanted them. Strawberries sounded fine to us.

I sat with my chin in my hand staring glumly out of the window into the fog thinking about the fact that Heidi never mentioned this kind of weather. David pointed to a spot of faint gold down the side of the mountain. "Isn't that strange. I wonder what it is," he said. We both watched the spot get bigger, then, to our amazement, shafts of light broke through the dark clouds and turned the center of Lake Geneva, miles below us, into a golden pool. I swear to you, it looked like something Michelangelo would have painted on the ceiling of the Sistine Chapel. It was truly awesome. I looked at the beams of light, so ethereal, yet so powerful that I expected to see angels sliding down from heaven to skate on the lake. I whispered to David, "You know, when I was little, I thought those shafts of light were God."

"I can understand why," he answered.

We sat, absolutely mesmerized by the miracle going on below us, as the light, streaming through the molten sky, played along the surface of the partially frozen lake. Our reverie was broken by the approach of the waitress. We pointed out the window to the spectacle below. She shrugged her shoulders. Thinking she didn't see what we were talking about I tried, with my terrible French, to tell her to look down below at the lake. She gave a little smile and a Gallic shrug, indicating that she had seen it all before and was waiting for the sun to come out for good, not just play hide-and-seek with the clouds.

When I tore my eyes away from the window to see the small bowl she had set before us, I was surprised, to say the least. Here were some of the strangest, puniest strawberries I had ever seen. They were certainly the most anemic things going. In fact they were white instead of hearty red. The waitress saw my look of incredulity and said, "*Ce sont les fraises des bois* — wild strawberries." It was our turn to shrug. I picked up one by its thin green stem and took a closer look. It was a miniature, elongated version of the plump round berries from California and Florida that I was used to. I figured it would take more than this little bowlful to fill us up. Then I popped one into my mouth. I was astonished by the taste that dazzled my mouth. While it looked anemic and tiny, its flavor was anything but. It was amazing to think that anything that little could yield such an incredibly and deliciously sweet taste, a taste that was like essence of strawberry or strawberry perfume. I could tell by the look on his face that David was having the same reaction. We were both knocked over by the intensely pure taste found in these little berries. Our small bowls were just the right size. We ate slowly, relishing each bite.

With the combination of the magical light show outside and the splendid, soul-awakening taste in our mouths, Switzerland was beginning to look better and better and tourism here began to take on a whole new range of possibilities. If this in fact was the season for golden beams of light and fraises des bois, perhaps, we thought, we should stay another few days.

I found, to my delight, that my local nursery sold flats of fraises des bois. That summer I planted twenty of those strawberry plants in my garden. I grew both the white kind and the red kind. By the middle of the summer I was rewarded with two or three tiny sweet morsels every few days. By the next summer my crop was big enough to present my family with a small bowlful. While there were never enough to cook with (who would want to anyway?), there were always enough to give my mouth a flavor flashback of that day in Switzerland. Too bad I couldn't manage to get someone in to arrange a light show too.

❧ Fraises des Bois ☙

THESE tiny alpine strawberries come in red or pure white and taste like heaven. Their fragility does not make them a popular commercially grown fruit, so the best way to get them is to grow your own. This is as simple as growing regular strawberries. The plants can be ordered from White Flower Farm in Litchfield, Connecticut (see resource list). Their season begins in late spring and the plants will bear fruit up until the first frost. Unless you have given your garden over to fraises des bois, it is hard to have enough ripe berries on hand at any given time to actually make something. The best way to enjoy them is to go out to the garden, hunch down, lift the plants' leaves, gently pick the ripe berries and deliver them directly to your mouth.

RUBIES IN THE SNOW

This recipe is for the once in a lifetime that you find yourself with a bumper crop of fraises des bois.

FOR THE WHITE CHOCOLATE CUSTARD CREAM:

> *2 cups heavy cream*
> *3 ounces white chocolate (I use Tobler*
> *Narcisse), grated or finely chopped*
> *4 extra-large egg whites*
> *1 teaspoon vanilla extract*

Scald 1 cup of the heavy cream in a small saucepan set over moderate heat. Whisk in the chocolate and stir until it is blended (if there are lumps run it through the food processor). Place the other cup of cream and the egg whites in a metal bowl set over hot but not boiling water (you can use a double boiler). Dribble in the hot chocolate/cream mixture a little at a time and continue to cook, stirring constantly, until the mixture thickens slightly and coats a spoon. Remove from the hot water and immediately cover with plastic wrap to prevent a skin from forming. Cool 20 minutes and then stir in the vanilla extract. Chill well.

TO ASSEMBLE:

> *1 10-ounce jar finest-quality strawberry*
> *preserves*
> *2 tablespoons Grand Marnier or Kirsch*
> *1 quart fraises des bois*
> *white chocolate custard cream*
> *candied violets for garnish*

Heat the strawberry preserves over low heat until softened. Stir in the liquor. Divide the custard among 6 wine glasses and spoon the berries over it. Ladle the strawberry sauce over all and garnish with the candied violets.

Serves 6

Texas Ruby Red Grapefruit

I am not a winter person. My depression sets in with the gray skies of November and doesn't let up until the Red Sox return from Winter Haven. My spirits sink lower with every falling leaf, and the first snow heralds the onset of claustrophobia. My friends and neighbors ice-skate and ski. I sulk and memorize Club Med brochures. My family goes tobogganing and I curl up with *Silas Marner*.

One of the things that makes winter a little more bearable is the arrival once a month of the big box from Texas. Inside, nestled in red tissue paper, are a dozen and a half giant ruby red grapefruit. Each one weighs close to a pound and is so big that I can hardly fit them all into my refrigerator. I have to clear out all kinds of other things, and the result is indignant voices crying, "What the hell happened to all the blueberry yogurt?" and "Why are there grapefruit where the bologna is supposed to be?"

The sacrifice of room is worth it. After you taste one of these grapefruits you will be spoiled for any other kind. Visually, they're a treat. The surprise is that inside the smooth, pale yellow skin lies a deep rosy pink interior. Even the juice that sprays out with the first cut is pink-hued. And the taste — so clear and sweet — makes winter seem not so bad.

While there are lots of ways one can eat these monster-sized fruits, my favorite is the unadulterated way: Take a very sharp paring knife and cut the peel off (in one continuous spiral, if you're good), leaving on a thin layer of white pulp. This pulp is not unpleasant-tasting and is a wonderful source of fiber. Cut the grapefruit in half and place each half cut side down. Use a long, thin, serrated knife to cut one of the halves into four or five slices, keeping the slices together. Rotate the half one quarter turn and cut the slices into pieces. Repeat with the other half. Place all the pieces in a large bowl and enjoy. Spring is just around the corner.

⚡ Texas Ruby Red Grapefruit ⚡

WHILE the origin of the grapefruit is obscure, the ruby red was discovered in 1929 growing on a pink grapefruit tree in the heart of the lower Rio Grande Valley. It is so unique that it was the first citrus variety to be patented in the United States. A fantastic source of vitamin C and only one hundred calories per half, Texas ruby reds are shipped throughout the country starting in October and continuing through May, with peak supplies available from January into April. The ruby red from Texas is best distinguished from other grapefruits by the blush of pink showing through portions of the yellow skin area. Ruby reds will be thin-skinned and heavy for their size. The inside is distinctively rose-colored and the flesh is sweet and juicy. Select firm, well-shaped fruit and don't worry about the occasional marks on the skin — they don't affect the inside. Because the grapefruits are ripened on the tree, they are ready to eat when purchased. They can be stored in the refrigerator for up to three weeks.

Ruby reds are available both by mail order (see resource list) and in many supermarkets during the winter months. While you can use other kinds of grapefruit for these recipes, the flavor and color are not quite the same.

GRAPEFRUIT SORBET

¾ cup granulated sugar
1 cup water
3 tablespoons lemon juice
*finely grated rind of 1 ruby red grapefruit (use
    just the outmost part, not the white pith,
    which is bitter)*
*juice from the grapefruit, with the pulp but
    not the membranes*
1 drop red food coloring (optional)

Bring the sugar, water and lemon juice to a boil in a saucepan and simmer, stirring, until the sugar dissolves. Cool completely. Combine 1¼ cups of this syrup with the grapefruit rind, the juice and the optional food coloring. Before you freeze it, taste it to make sure you like it this sweet — or this tart. You can add slightly more syrup or more grapefruit or lemon juice. Process the sorbet in an ice cream freezer.

Makes 1½ pints

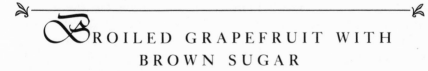

BROILED GRAPEFRUIT WITH BROWN SUGAR

This light first course is also a great way to start the day.

2 ruby red grapefruits
4–6 tablespoons dark brown sugar
cinnamon

Cut the grapefruits in half and use a grapefruit knife to loosen the sections. Spoon the brown sugar on top and sprinkle with cinnamon. Broil in the oven or toaster oven until the sugar begins to bubble. Serve immediately.

Serves 4

SAUTÉED SCALLOPS WITH GRAPEFRUIT

1 ruby red grapefruit
2 tablespoons sweet (unsalted) butter
2 shallots, finely minced
½ cup dry vermouth or white wine
1 pound sea scallops, quartered
½ cup heavy cream
¼ teaspoon nutmeg
salt and freshly ground white pepper
fresh chives, cut into ½-inch pieces, for garnish

Peel the grapefruit with a very sharp knife. Cut and peel away as much of the white pith remaining on the grapefruit as possible. Use a long, serrated knife to cut the grapefruit in half crosswise, remove any seeds and then slice each half into 8 sections. Cut away as much membrane as possible. Cut each slice in half. Reserve.

Melt the butter in a skillet and add the shallots. Cook for about 5 minutes over low heat. Raise the heat to high, add the wine and cook for 2 minutes. Add the scallops and sauté over high heat, shaking the pan briskly back and forth to move them around. Cook the scallops for 3–4 minutes, just until they turn opaque, then remove them to a heated platter. Add the grapefruit slices to the pan and cook only to heat them through. Arrange them around the scallops. Add the cream and nutmeg to the pan and cook for 2 minutes over very high heat. Stir with a wooden spatula to incorporate the bits on the bottom of the skillet. Add salt and pepper to taste. Spoon the sauce over the scallops and garnish with the chives.

Serves 4

CHOCOLATE-DIPPED CANDIED GRAPEFRUIT RIND

Now you can use the whole fruit — nothing is wasted. The combination of grapefruit and chocolate is unexpectedly delicious.

> *the intact rind of 4 ruby red grapefruit halves*
> *1½ cups granulated sugar*
> *1½ cups water*
> *6 tablespoons corn syrup*
> *½ cup superfine sugar*
> *8 ounces bittersweet chocolate*
> *2 ounces sweet (unsalted) butter*

Cut the grapefruit rind into strips approximately 1 inch wide and 2½ inches long. Use a small, sharp knife to remove as much of the white pith as possible. Place the strips into a saucepan, cover them with water and bring to a boil. Cook 1 minute, then drain the water. Repeat this step three more times. Drain and blot dry with paper towels.

Combine the sugar, water and corn syrup in a medium-sized pan and cook over moderate heat, stirring until the sugar dissolves. Boil for about 5 minutes, then add the rind. Lower the heat and cook until the syrup is reduced and thickened. With the heat on the lowest setting, continue cooking until there is barely any syrup left (watch the pot closely because it will burn once all the liquid is gone). Place the superfine sugar in a shallow tray and use tongs to dip the peels into it as you remove them from the pan. Let the rind dry completely on a cake rack.

Break the chocolate into small pieces and place it and the butter in a small metal bowl set over gently simmering water. Stir until melted and smooth. Dip one end of each strip of candied rind into the chocolate. Cool on wax paper. These can be stored for several weeks in a covered container.

Makes approximately 4 dozen pieces

GRAPEFRUIT UPSIDE-DOWN CAKE

This easy-to-make cake is made and baked right in a skillet. The first layer is a sugar syrup, the second, grapefruit sections and the third, the cake batter.

FOR THE GRAPEFRUIT:

2 whole grapefruits (preferably ruby reds)

Peel the grapefruits, cutting off as much of the white pulp as possible. Use a serrated knife to cut in between the sections to separate all of them into neat segments. Remove any seeds. Reserve while you prepare the syrup.

FOR THE SYRUP:

3 tablespoons sweet (unsalted) butter
1 rounded tablespoon dark brown sugar
2 tablespoons granulated sugar
⅓ cup light corn syrup
grated rind of 1 large orange
reserved grapefruit sections
8 maraschino cherries, halved

Preheat the oven to 350 degrees with the rack in the upper third, but not the very highest position. In a heavy, ovenproof skillet, 2½ inches deep, melt the butter. Stir in the sugars, the corn syrup and the rind, and stir over medium-low heat until the sugars are dissolved. Turn off the heat. Arrange the grapefruit sections around the outside edge of the pan and then spiral them inward to form a slightly overlapping layer in the center. Place the cherry halves, cut side up, randomly in the spaces among the sections. Prepare the batter.

FOR THE BATTER:

3 extra-large eggs
1½ cups granulated sugar
¾ cup whole milk
6 tablespoons sweet (unsalted) butter
1½ cups unsifted flour
1½ teaspoons baking powder
2 teaspoons vanilla extract
whipped cream

Beat the eggs for 5 minutes in an electric mixer set on high speed. Add the sugar and beat another 5 minutes. In a saucepan, bring the milk and butter to a boil over low heat. Sift the flour and baking powder together and stir into the egg mixture. Do not overmix. Pour in the hot milk and blend well. Add the vanilla extract. Pour the batter over the grapefruit, spreading it to smooth the top. Bake for 25–35 minutes, until a tester comes out clean and dry. Immediately cover the skillet with a serving platter several inches larger than the pan and invert the cake onto it. Serve warm with whipped cream.

Serves 8

Smithfield Ham

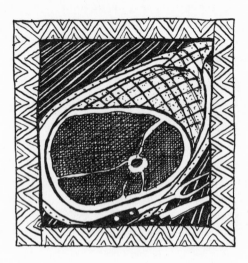

You can sing the Christmas carols, but when it comes to the part about Jesus Christ just move your lips. Then it's okay."

This was the ten-year-old wisdom of my best friend, Jenny Lindenthal, who was explaining to me how we could sing carols and not go to hell.

"Sort of like what we do with the Lord's Prayer, huh?" I asked. Jenny and I had got around this predicament by saying, "*Their* father, who art in heaven . . ."

The problem was that while I could live without the Lord's Prayer, I really loved Christmas carols. In fact, I loved everything about Christmas, except, of course, the fact that I couldn't celebrate it.

There were Jews (and still are) who have it both ways. Witness the proliferation of travesties called Chanukah bushes springing up in confused households where the motto is "Christmas is a secular holiday." While my parents were openminded about most things, there was no budging them on this point. They also made no attempt to make Chanukah a substitute for Christmas. Doubly deprived, I begged and pleaded, "Can't we just hang stockings?"

The reply was a patient, but firm, "No."

"Then how about midnight mass?"

"How about Chinese food and a movie," they countered. That's what we did every Christmas Eve — Chinese food and a movie. While millions of happy Christians got to sing "O Come, All Ye Faithful" and gorge themselves on Yorkshire pudding and candy canes, we got egg rolls and Walt Disney. It wasn't fair.

Everything about Christmas was wonderful and it was made a million times more so because I couldn't have it. What really made it terrible were the looks of pity I got from well-meaning strangers whose questions about what I wanted from Santa were answered by my stoic (martyred) reply, "I'm Jewish. I don't celebrate Christmas." I could have used the same facial expression if I was saying something like, "No thanks, my mother doesn't like me to eat chocolate layer cake with fudge frosting."

My active fantasy life made the latter part of the month of December a little easier to bear. I spent hours daydreaming about the perfect Christmas I would orchestrate if the opportunity ever presented itself. There were certain things I would have to have:

Snow. There would have to be a blizzard the week of Christmas that left everything covered with a pristine layer of deep, fluffy snow that sparkled under a clear blue sky. And no slush.

Grandmother. There had to be an apple-cheeked, white-haired grandma type — straight from central casting. One who wore gingham aprons, loved to play Chinese checkers, knew all the moves for cat's cradle, and taught you how to fashion hooked rugs from rags and how to knit. She always had a cookie jar full of homemade chocolate chip cookies and never yelled if you spilled cocoa on the carpet.

Sleigh and horses. To take you to Grandma's house over the perfect snow.

Boyfriend. To buy you tiny gold earrings or perfume (you made him a sweater with cables) and to take you to midnight mass.

Christmas carolers. Ringing your doorbell and singing all your favorites — "O Little Town of Bethlehem" and "We Three Kings."

Christmas cookies. Made by Grandma, covered with colored sprinkles, shaped into stars and snowmen, to give to the appreciative carolers.

Angel hair. To hang on the tree along with porcelain ornaments made for Czar Nicholas II and left to your grandmother, who smuggled them out of Russia in her girdle before the revolution.

Ribbon candy. To eat as much of as you wanted without anyone pointing out that you would make yourself sick eating all that ribbon candy.

Chocolate rum balls. Same as above.

Smithfield ham. Now, at the time I was conjuring up this fantasy of the perfect Christmas, I had never eaten Smithfield ham. However, my parents, good-thinking liberals that they were, subscribed, during my formative years, to *Saturday Review* magazine. Most of the articles were way above my head, but what I did love reading were advertisements and the classifieds. I always thought that one of the ways you could tell if you were really and truly grown-up was if you bought the things or went to the places advertised in the *Saturday Review*. I would spend hours browsing through the pages, picking out fine imported woolens, maple syrup and luxury yachts. Lying under our grand piano, where the light was so bad that my mother promised I'd lose my eyesight, I flipped slowly, dreamily through the pages, picking and choosing two weeks at an inn in Maine, a trip rafting down some obscure Peruvian river, a dude ranch in Wyoming. Every Christmastime there would be advertisements for Smithfield ham, which, according to the ad copy, was the only ham to consider for a traditional Christmas menu. Well, if that's what the *Saturday Review* said, it was good enough for me. I happily added it to my dream list.

It became easier to deal with Christmas as I got older and developed friendships with those lucky people who got to celebrate it. We had a deal: they would come to our Passover Seder and we would come to their Christmas dinner. Our kids, once they came to terms with the fact that they were stuck with being Jewish and that we weren't going to celebrate Christmas at our house, thought this was a great way of handling all those feelings about this holiday that they had obviously inherited from me. One of the things I liked best about this arrangement was that I was expected to contribute a dish to the dinner. For several years I made ultrafancy bûches de Noël, complete with meringue mushrooms, marzipan pinecones and candy rocks. Last year I decided that I wanted to do something different. I began to ponder what that something different would be, when, as if on cue, I opened one of those "gastro" magazines and saw an advertisement for Smithfield ham. Aha! Smithfield ham had been validated by *Saturday Review*. How could I lose? I ran to the bank, took out a small loan and sent off for a ham. It came packaged in a heavy-duty carton and wrapped in a burlap bag. It certainly looked interesting. Glazewise I let my imagination go wild. All my favorite flavors went into the saucepan: ginger, mustard, brown sugar, sherry and honey.

Everyone at Christmas dinner agreed that my fantasy all those years ago had become everyone's reality that night. The ham was tender, succulent and truly delicious. The glaze was perfection. I was getting ready to rest on my laurels when someone at the table mentioned that it was also customary for Smithfield ham to be served with beaten biscuits on Derby Day. All the guests, now enamored of this delectable and costly ham, looked at me expectantly. "Please," I demurred, "don't you know that Jews don't celebrate the Kentucky Derby?"

⅍ Smithfield Ham ⅃

To be a real Smithfield ham, it must, by federal and state law, be cured and smoked in the Town of Smithfield, Virginia. The hogs destined to become Smithfields must be peanut-fed (but not pen-fed on peanuts). Thus while they are young they are free-ranged, and roam the woods eating acorns, hickory nuts and beechnuts. Before slaughter they are allowed to forage in the peanut fields at harvest time, which results in their being juicier, more tender and less salty than hogs raised in other ways.

The Smithfield ham is dry-salted, a process that cures, dehydrates and preserves the meat. The salting takes about three months and then the hams are washed, coated with black pepper and smoked, very slowly, over apple and hickory wood. The smoking takes up to six months — sometimes even longer — and during this process, the hams lose about a third of their weight. The hams are then aged for an additional six months.

$\mathcal{T}$O PREPARE A FULLY COOKED
SMITHFIELD HAM

While it certainly is possible to buy an uncooked ham, the process of salting and baking it can be eliminated if you buy a fully cooked one. These hams come glazed with brown sugar and have a lightly salty, smoky flavor. The ham comes in a heavy, vacuum-sealed plastic film and will keep, under refrigeration, for up to four weeks. If, for some reason, the plastic has been punctured and some mold has formed on the surface of the ham, just wipe it off — it isn't harmful.

Even though the ham does come with a glaze, it is best, when heating it, to reglaze it with the following.

1/4 cup dark brown sugar, firmly packed
1/4 cup maple syrup
1/4 cup Dijon mustard
2 tablespoons soy sauce
1/4 cup dry sherry
2 tablespoons fresh ginger, peeled and finely chopped, or 1 teaspoon powdered ginger

Remove the ham from the refrigerator and allow it to come to room temperature before heating. Preheat the oven to 375 degrees. Place the ham in a foil-lined pan with low sides. Combine all the ingredients in a medium-sized saucepan and simmer for 5 minutes. Spoon or brush half the glaze onto the ham before it goes into the oven, and apply the rest every few minutes during the heating. Cook for about 20–30 minutes or until a knife inserted into the ham comes out warm.

TO SLICE:

Place the ham glazed side up. Using a long, thin and very sharp knife, cut paper-thin slices across the grain. Serve with assorted breads and the following layered mustard mousse ring.

LAYERED MUSTARD MOUSSE RING

This makes a spectacular and delicious accompaniment to Smithfield ham.

FOR THE BASE:

½ cup granulated sugar
1 envelope unflavored gelatin
¼ teaspoon salt
⅔ cup warm water
½ cup cider vinegar
4 extra-large eggs
1 cup heavy cream, whipped
½ cup sour cream

Mix together the sugar, gelatin and salt. Stir in the water and vinegar. Beat the eggs lightly in the top of a double boiler. Add the sugar mixture to the eggs and cook in the double boiler over gently simmering water, stirring constantly with a wire whisk until slightly thickened. Divide the mixture into three bowls. Prepare the mustard blends.

FOR THE MUSTARD BLENDS:

LAYER 1:

3 tablespoons Dijon mustard
1 teaspoon dried tarragon
2 tablespoons white horseradish, drained of
    liquid

LAYER 2:

3 tablespoons honey mustard (or 2 tablespoons
    Dijon mustard mixed with 1 tablespoon
    honey)
2 tablespoons Major Grey's chutney, finely
    chopped
½ teaspoon ground turmeric

2 tablespoons grainy mustard
1 tablespoon green peppercorns, drained of
liquid
3 tablespoons fresh parsley, minced
2 tablespoons fresh chives, minced

Combine the ingredients for each of the three mustard blends in small bowls or coffee cups and add one to each of the three bowls of base. Cover and refrigerate for 20 minutes. Meanwhile, whip the cream until it holds soft peaks. Chill while you prepare the mold.

Lightly oil a 1½-quart ring mold with vegetable oil. Mix 2 heaping tablespoons of sour cream and one third of the whipped cream into each of the mustard mixtures. Place the mustard/horseradish mixture in the bottom of the mold and freeze for 15 minutes. Layer the mustard/chutney mixture on top of the first layer. Freeze for 10 minutes. Finally, add the last mustard layer. Chill in the refrigerator very well, at least 4 hours.

To unmold, dip the mold very briefly in warm water, wipe the bottom with a towel and turn out onto a platter.

Serves 20

LACK BEAN SOUP

2½ cups dried black beans
3 quarts water
bone from Smithfield ham
2 large onions, chopped
1 cup celery, diced
3 large carrots, diced
2 bay leaves
½ cup fresh cilantro (coriander), chopped
½ teaspoon crushed red pepper
½ teaspoon ground cloves
2 tablespoons sherry or red wine vinegar
½–¾ cup Madeira
dash Tabasco sauce
salt and freshly ground pepper
2 chopped hard-boiled eggs for garnish
lime wedges

Rinse the beans well, then soak them overnight in a metal bowl in enough water to cover them (remember that they'll expand, so add several inches of extra water). Drain and place the beans in a large pot and add 3 quarts of fresh water. Add the ham bone, the chopped vegetables, herbs and spices. Simmer, partially covered, over low heat for about 2–2½ hours or until the beans are very tender. Add the sherry or vinegar, Madeira, Tabasco and salt and pepper to taste. Remove the bone and bay leaves. At this point you may wish to puree the soup in a food processor or blender. If so, puree the soup about a cup at a time. If you like a chunkier version, then serve it as is. Garnish with the chopped egg and pass the lime wedges separately for people to squeeze onto their soup if they wish.

Serves 8–10

WHAT TO DO WITH THE SMITHFIELD HAM LEFTOVERS

This succulent, flavorful meat makes wonderful sandwiches. Our favorite combinations involve spreading thin slices of dark pumpernickel bread with grainy mustard or sweet butter, laying on a slice of ham and covering it with a thin slice of red onion. If you want to add a cheese of some sort, it is best to stick to something nonsalty, like fontina or fresh mozzarella. You can make an elegant version of the English ploughman's lunch with slices of Smithfield ham, chutney, pickled onions and crusty bread. Lay out the fixings with a crock of mustard and let your guests help themselves.

How about a toasted cheese sandwich made with Smithfield ham and cheddar cheese? Try using the leftover slices of ham to make eggs Benedict. One member of our family swears that the combination of Smithfield ham and cream cheese is the only thing he'll have on his bagel. Spaghetti carbonara never had it so good: toss the hot pasta with an egg and a little heavy cream, lots of freshly ground black pepper and freshly grated Parmesan, then add the diced Smithfield ham.

SMITHFIELD HAM SPREAD

This recipe from the Williamsburg Inn can be served on cream biscuits (recipe follows) or spread on thin slices of pumpernickel bread.

> *1 pound (approximately 2 cups) Smithfield*
> *ham scraps*
> *2 cups mayonnaise (either commercially*
> *prepared or homemade)*
> *2 tablespoons grainy mustard*

Place the ham in the work bowl of a food processor and grind to a fine paste. Add the mayonnaise and mustard and process for another 15 seconds.

Makes about 3 cups

QUICK CREAM BISCUITS

2½ cups unbleached flour
6 teaspoons baking powder
1 teaspoon salt
1 tablespoon granulated sugar
½ cup frozen sweet (unsalted) butter, cut into
  pieces
2 cups heavy cream

Preheat the oven to 425 degrees with the rack in the center position. Line a baking sheet with parchment. Sift the dry ingredients into the work bowl of a food processor. Add the butter and pulse the machine on and off until the mixture resembles coarse meal. Whip the cream in a separate bowl. Distribute the cream in mounds around the top of the dry ingredients. Pulse the processor on and off until the dough just starts to form a ball. Do not overwork the dough. Scrape the dough onto a well-floured work surface and knead 10 times to make a homogeneous mass. Pat into a ¾-inch-thick circle and using a floured cutter cut into rounds measuring approximately 2–2¼ inches. Place 1½ inches apart on the baking sheet and bake for 18–20 minutes or until very lightly browned. If you find the bottoms are browning too fast, use a double baking sheet and increase the baking time by a minute or two.

Makes 15–18 biscuits

SMITHFIELD HAM AND CHICKEN CORDON BLEU

This is another specialty of the Williamsburg Inn that makes use of a native delight.

4 6-ounce boneless chicken breasts
2 tablespoons Dijon mustard
4 slices (6 ounces) Smithfield ham
4 slices (6 ounces) Gruyère cheese
1 cup all-purpose flour
2 eggs, slightly beaten
2 tablespoons peanut oil
2 tablespoons butter
1 cup dry, unflavored bread crumbs
1 cup chicken stock (commercially prepared or
homemade, or made with half a cube of
chicken bouillon to 1 cup of boiling water)
½ cup dry white wine
juice of 1 lemon
2 tablespoons butter

Preheat the oven to 350 degrees with the rack in the highest position. Pound the chicken breasts flat between 2 pieces of wax paper. Coat 1 side of each breast with Dijon mustard. Place 1 slice of ham on top of each breast. Top the ham with a slice of cheese. Fold the breast over the filling and secure with 2 toothpicks. Dip the breasts in the flour, then the egg, then back into the flour, shaking off the excess.

Heat the 2 tablespoons of oil together with 2 tablespoons of butter in a heavy skillet and sauté the chicken until it is golden brown. Add more oil if necessary. (Reserve the fat in the skillet.) Place the bread crumbs in a shallow dish and roll the chicken breasts in them to cover. Place the breasts on a foil-covered baking sheet, sprinkle with the rest of the crumbs and bake for 10–15 minutes or until a toothpick inserted in the center comes out hot. Pour out all but 2 tablespoons of fat from the skillet, set it over high heat and add the chicken stock, wine and lemon juice. Cook over high heat until the mixture reduces by half. Swirl in the butter and pour over the chicken just before it is served.

Serves 4

Hazelnuts

After *Growing Up on The Chocolate Diet* was published, I was besieged with requests to do all kinds of strange and wonderful things. And dangerous things. The danger came in the form of requests that I be a judge at various chocolate contests in which local bakers and restaurateurs submit their very best efforts: chocolate cakes, chocolate pies, chocolate cookies, chocolate candies, chocolate sculptures — the total chocolate experience, as it were. All these efforts are donated to raise money for some worthwhile charity. These chocolate items (usually fifty or so) are lined up along endless buffet tables so that the judges can move along tasting each one. This presents an awesome challenge to someone who gets pretty full after one bite of a brownie. I like chocolate very much, you could even say that I love it, but fifty desserts at one time? I know, I know, there are more painful ways of making a living.

When I know I have one of these affairs coming up, in the interest of my potentially expanding figure, I start the week with grapefruit and cottage cheese and try to stick to this sparse diet in hopes that the binges at the contest won't make me look like the Pillsbury Dough Boy. When I pass through the buffet line (did I mention that the creators of the desserts stand next to their desserts, expectant looks on their faces and large serving knives in their hands?), it's always easy to be enthusiastic for the first ten or so items; after that, chocolate overload sets in. Even though I take only a small taste, I am usually blotto by the fifth or sixth entry.

This winter I was one of a panel of judges at a chocolate dessert contest run by a local political organization. We got our scorecards and started down the line. The first few desserts were beautiful and quite delicious. Then I came to a chocolate layered gâteau with what looked like a thick layer of caramelized nuts in the center. One of the judges said: "Psst, try that one, it's unbelievable." Well, since I had to try it anyway, I was happy to hear that it was good. A young woman who was standing in for the chef cut me a small piece. I dug into the cake, and the flavor of toasted hazelnuts filled my mouth. I love toasted hazelnuts. Mmmm, bittersweet chocolate. Hmmm, crunchy chocolate meringue. What a combination! Ten seconds later, wiping my plate clean, I asked her for another piece. And then another. I had fallen behind the other judges, but I had found the ultimate in flavor and texture combinations. I would have been delighted to stay right where I was, eating this cake for the rest of the evening. It was made of two chocolate meringue layers, covered with buttercream, with a center of thick, chewy, chunky hazelnut nougat the texture of pecan pie, but with the amazing richness of toasted hazelnuts and honey. All this topped with a smooth-as-silk bittersweet chocolate cream. I was one happy, partial judge.

It took some arm-twisting on the part of the other judges to get me moving down the line. It was almost painful to force myself to taste all those other desserts (which, by the way, were delicious in their own right), I was craving those hazelnuts so. I am delighted to report that the hazelnut creation was the hands-down winner. I am embarrassed to admit that I had still one more piece after the cake was declared the winner. I tracked down the creator, a Paris-trained pastry chef named Barbara McPeak, who, happily for you and me, shared her recipe.

❧ Hazelnuts ❧

THE flavor of this versatile nut, also called the filbert, shines through after it is toasted. While hazelnuts are readily available in their shells, the time-consuming task of removing the dark brown outer skin is simplified by purchasing them shelled and husked. Health food stores are a good source for hazelnuts.

To toast and skin hazelnuts, preheat the oven to 400 degrees with the rack in the upper position. Place the hazelnuts on a heavy-duty baking sheet and bake for five to ten minutes. Shake the pan to rotate the nuts and bake another few minutes. Continue shaking the pan frequently after that to make sure the nuts don't burn. As soon as they are golden brown, remove the baking sheet from the oven and place a large terry-cloth towel over the nuts. Rub the towel vigorously over the nuts while they cool. As soon as you can handle them, rub the remaining skins off with your fingers. Don't worry if some of the nuts have dark spots — they will taste fine. These nuts freeze beautifully (in jars or Ziploc bags) and should always be frozen once shelled. Since it's such a pain to toast and peel them each time you need them for a recipe, it makes sense to toast several pounds at once.

ℬARBARA McPEAK'S FIRST PRIZE HAZELNUT CAKE

This is a three-layered creation with a fudgy chocolate bottom topped with two hazelnut meringue layers. Each layer has a thin coating of whipped chocolate cream and a thick hazelnut apricot coating. The whole cake is then frosted with the whipped chocolate cream.

FOR THE FUDGE LAYER:

10 ounces of bittersweet chocolate, chopped
6 tablespoons sweet (unsalted) butter at room temperature, cut into small pieces
3 tablespoons heavy cream
5 extra-large eggs at room temperature, separated
3 tablespoons granulated sugar

Preheat the oven to 300 degrees with the rack in the center position. Butter a 9- or 10-inch springform pan (you can also use a regular layer pan, but it's a bit trickier to get the cake out). Line the pan with a circle of parchment or wax paper, butter the paper and dust it lightly with flour.

Melt the chocolate in a small metal bowl set over a pan of gently simmering water. Off the heat, add the softened butter and stir until it is incorporated. Stir in the cream and egg yolks.

Whip the egg whites with the sugar only until they are very soft — just past the soupy stage. Fold the whites into the chocolate mixture. Place the mixture in the prepared pan and bake for exactly 15 minutes. The cake will not look done at the end of this time. *Do not attempt to remove it from the pan.* Refrigerate the cake until it is cold. To remove it from the layer pan, spin the bottom of the pan on a hot burner for 10 seconds, until the butter melts and the layer is released. Keep the layer cold until ready to assemble the cake.

5 ounces (1 rounded cup) whole hazelnuts,
  toasted (see p. 153)
2 tablespoons flour
3 tablespoons granulated sugar
4 extra-large egg whites at room temperature
1 cup granulated sugar
½ teaspoon lemon juice
1 teaspoon vanilla extract

Preheat the oven to 350 degrees. Trace two 9-inch circles on a piece of parchment. Butter and flour the circles. Place the parchment on a cookie sheet.

Place the toasted hazelnuts, the flour and the 3 tablespoons of sugar in the work bowl of a food processor fitted with the metal blade and process until the mixture is very fine. Set this mixture aside.

Whip the egg whites, gradually adding 1 cup of sugar, until the whites are shiny and hold soft peaks. Beat in the lemon juice and vanilla extract. Fold in the hazelnut/sugar mixture.

Spread the meringue onto the prepared circles and bake for 30 minutes. The meringues will brown, but they should not get too dark. Cool for 5 minutes before removing the meringues from the parchment. These layers can be made one day ahead and stored in an airtight container as soon as they are completely cool.

FOR THE WHIPPED CHOCOLATE CREAM:

3 cups heavy cream
10 ounces bittersweet chocolate, chopped
3 tablespoons bourbon

Place 1 cup of the heavy cream in a small saucepan and bring to a simmer, keeping the remaining 2 cups of cream chilled. Off the heat, add the chocolate and stir until it has melted and the mixture is smooth. Let cool to room temperature (do not let it get too cold). Place the cooled chocolate mixture in a metal mixing bowl and add the 2 reserved cups of cream. Beat with an electric hand mixer until the cream just begins to hold its shape — don't overbeat or it will curdle. Add the bourbon. Set aside half a cup of this mixture for decorating the cake.

FOR THE HAZELNUT APRICOT FILLING:

*1 12-ounce jar of good-quality apricot
preserves
3 cups toasted hazelnuts*

Place the preserves in a small saucepan and heat until they are softened. Place the hazelnuts in a heavy-duty plastic bag, seal the bag and then hit the nuts very gently to break them into halves or large pieces. Mix the hazelnut pieces together with the apricot preserves.

TO ASSEMBLE:

whole toasted hazelnuts

Place the chocolate cake layer on a flat cake plate. Spread a very thin layer of whipped chocolate cream on it. Place half the apricot/hazelnut filling on top of this. Use a little more of the chocolate cream to smooth out the filling. Place a meringue layer on top. Spread with a thin layer of chocolate cream and then the rest of the apricot/hazelnut filling. Add a thin layer of chocolate cream. Then add the last meringue layer. Use your hands to press the layers firmly together. Don't worry if the top layer cracks — it won't show.

Use the remaining chocolate cream to frost the cake. Use the reserved chocolate cream to pipe rosettes on top of the cake and then garnish with the whole hazelnuts. The cake should be refrigerated for several hours before it is served.

Makes one 9-inch three-layer cake to serve 12–14

SAVORY HAZELNUT SAUCE

This quick and easy-to-prepare sauce goes especially well with chicken or veal.

4 ounces sweet (unsalted) butter
2 cloves garlic, finely minced
¼ cup fresh flat-leaf parsley, finely chopped
1 teaspoon dried thyme
1 teaspoon dried rosemary
1 cup toasted, chopped hazelnuts (see p. 153)
2 cups heavy cream
1 teaspoon red wine vinegar
salt and freshly ground pepper to taste

In a large skillet set over low heat, melt the butter. Add the garlic and continue to cook for 1 minute. Add the parsley, thyme and rosemary. Continue cooking for another 2 minutes, stirring to prevent the garlic from browning. Add the hazelnuts and cream and simmer for 15 minutes or until the mixture has reduced by one third. Add the vinegar and salt and pepper to taste.

Makes 2½ cups

HAZELNUT BLUEBERRY MUFFINS

3 cups all-purpose flour, measured after sifting
4 teaspoons baking powder
¼ teaspoon baking soda
1 teaspoon salt
½ cup dark brown sugar, firmly packed
1 cup toasted, skinned hazelnuts, coarsely
* chopped*
⅔ cup orange juice
1 extra-large egg, slightly beaten
⅔ cup whole milk
½ cup butter, melted
finely grated rind of 1 large orange
1¼ cups fresh or frozen blueberries

Preheat the oven to 425 degrees with the rack in the center position. Generously butter enough muffin tins to make 2 dozen muffins. Sift the dry ingredients together. Stir in the sugar and hazelnuts and toss until they are lightly coated. Mix together all the remaining ingredients *except the blueberries* and stir into the dry ingredients just until they are incorporated. Gently stir in the blueberries. Bake for 20 minutes or until golden brown. If the muffins are browning too quickly before the centers are done, lower the oven temperature to 375 degrees.

Makes 24 muffins

HAZELNUT GELATO

1½ cups hazelnuts, toasted and skinned
1 cup whole milk
2 cups medium cream
6 extra-large egg yolks
¾ cup light brown sugar, firmly packed
2 tablespoons Frangelico (hazelnut liqueur)

Place the hazelnuts in a food processor and process until they form an oily paste. In a medium-sized, heavy-bottomed saucepan, scald the milk and cream. Beat the egg yolks with the sugar until the mixture is thick and light in color. Dribble in the hot cream/milk mixture and return to the saucepan. Cook over low heat, stirring constantly, until the mixture just coats a spoon. Strain into a metal bowl and chill. Stir 1 cup of the ice cream base into the hazelnut paste, and then stir in the rest. Process in an ice cream machine and serve semisoft with Frangelico-flavored Whipped Cream (see p. 159).

Makes 1½ quarts

FRANGELICO-FLAVORED WHIPPED CREAM

1 cup chilled heavy cream
3 tablespoons Frangelico
2 teaspoons vanilla extract
3 tablespoons confectioners' sugar, sifted

Whip the cream in a chilled bowl with chilled beaters. When it holds soft peaks, stir in the Frangelico, vanilla extract and sugar.

Makes 1⅓ cups

DORA APTER'S MANDELBREAD

Dora Apter was the wife of my father's first cousin Ben. She was a wonderful cook who left her family a legacy of exquisite culinary memories. These cookies are among my favorites from her vast repertoire.

4 extra-large eggs
1 cup granulated sugar
1 cup vegetable oil
4 cups all-purpose flour, sifted before
  measuring
1 teaspoon salt
4 teaspoons baking powder
1½ teaspoons almond extract
1 generous cup whole hazelnuts, skinned and
  lightly toasted (see p. 153)
⅔ cup sugar mixed with 3 tablespoons
  cinnamon
1 egg lightly beaten with 1 tablespoon water

Preheat the oven to 350 degrees with the rack in the center position. Line 2 heavy-duty baking sheets with foil.

Combine the eggs and sugar in the bowl of an electric mixer and beat for 5 minutes at high speed. Beat in the oil. Sift the dry ingredients together and on low speed add them to the egg mixture. Add the almond extract and nuts.

Knead the mixture by hand on a lightly floured board, adding a bit more flour if the dough is too sticky to handle. I find it helpful to use a pastry scraper when kneading this dough. Divide the dough into 5 portions and knead a tablespoon or so of the cinnamon sugar into each portion. Form each portion of dough into a log about 2 inches wide and 12 inches long. Place logs on the baking sheets, leaving at least 3 inches between each log. Brush each log with the egg/water mixture and sprinkle generously with the cinnamon sugar.

Bake for 30 minutes. Halfway through the baking, reverse the baking sheets shelf to shelf and back to front. Cut the cookies while they are still warm, on the diagonal, into 1½-inch slices. Place the slices on their sides and return to the oven to toast for 5 minutes.

Makes 4 dozen cookies

Lamb

iddle-class Jewish girls growing up in Hartford in the early sixties did not "come out." While white-gloved debutantes were all the rage at nearby Miss Porter's, our coming of age (old enough to drive, shave your legs, go out with boys that drove) was signaled by a ritual called the Sweet Sixteen Party. This event could take any number of forms: a family "do" (only girls in the most desperate social straits did that), a fancy party in a restaurant with dancing and boys (I didn't know any boys I'd want to be seen in public with), a party at home with dancing and boys (I still didn't know any boys), or a slumber party (now there's an oxymoron for you) with girlfriends. Since none of the other choices was feasible, I opted for the last one. My parents were so relieved that I hadn't made their lives miserable by whining for a car — like my friend Estelle (the mouth) Rudnick, who never gave up until she got one — that they decided to be graciously supportive of this affair. This meant my mother was willing to make whatever I wanted — food-wise — for the party.

"I want broiled lamb chops, mashed potatoes, canned peas and chocolate cream pie with whipped cream for dessert," I said reasonably.

"How about chili dogs or pizza?" my mother suggested rationally.

"I think we should have something I like since it's my birthday."

My mother said that she wasn't sure about how the other girls would feel about my favorite menu. I told her that everyone else had mundane things like chili dogs and pizza. I wanted something classy.

"And expensive," she muttered. I reminded her that lamb chops were a damn sight cheaper than a car, and besides, she only had herself to blame for my attachment to these particular foods.

The party was to be in our basement rec room, or "the boy pit," as my father called it. I thought that appellation was more wishful thinking than cynicism on his part. The eight lucky girls arrived at six sharp, in uniforms of Peter Pan–collared blouses with circle pin on the left (on the right meant something else), wrap corduroy skirts, knee socks and Weejuns (I believe tassels were in that year), carrying pillows, sleeping bags and overnight cases. The overnight cases were squat square pieces of Samsonite — usually aqua or pink, or if you were really "mature" white fake leather — with the handle located smack in the middle of the top, which made them hard to carry with your arm straight down by your side. On the inside lid was a rectangular mirror and below that a pleated pocket made from fake satin material with an elasticized top to hold assorted stuff. The overnight bags held the following gear: all the makeup you ever owned plus stuff you snuck out of your mother's vanity table; a bottle or two of perfume or toilet water, either Midnight in Paris, Canoe (a man's fragrance, but loved by all) or Elizabeth Taylor's favorite, Jungle Gardenia; frosted pink nail polish; two dozen hair rollers in various sizes with brushes inside to lacerate your scalp and split your ends; a jar of Jokar or Deb hair-setting lotion; a frilly pink hair bonnet with a ruffled edge so no one would suspect you had a head full of rollers; a can of hair spray and a teasing brush; a large jar of Noxema; eyebrow tweezers; eyelash curlers; a baby doll pajama set; dust mop slippers in iridescent pink or green; a couple of your favorite 45's; and a dog-eared copy of one of the following books (procured through the most devious means from under the mattress of your older brother's bed): *Peyton Place, The Bramble Bush,* or *A Stone for Danny Fisher,* with all the good parts marked. We staked out the basement with our sleeping bags before dinner. Since I was the birthday girl everyone wanted to sleep next to me, which made things a little crowded, but I was thrilled to think that a mere accident of birth could make girls who couldn't be bothered speaking to me the day before want to share my space so intimately.

Much to my mother's surprise, the dinner was a great success. I was in my glory at the head of the table watching my friends wolf down our very grown-up appetizers made from sour cream, cream cheese and a package of Lipton's Onion Soup whipped up in the brand-new kitchen marvel — the automatic blender. This was spread on Ritz crackers. As the smell of the broiled lamb chops began to filter from the kitchen into the dining room, I got that warm, happily expectant feeling you get when you know something really great is about to happen. The menu was a big hit. The girls loved those lamb chops as much as I did and they were not about to let me chew on their bones — no way. When my mom brought in the chocolate cream pie, my reputation as a birthday maven was sealed. These girls, used to the run-of-the-mill make-your-own sundae, were completely smitten by the ethereal magnificence of the ultimate birthday dessert. They were quiet, for the first time that evening, while they ate.

After dinner we adjourned to the basement, changed into our baby dolls, slicked down our hair with Deb, wound it around rollers, donned our curler hiders, made up each other's faces, put on the record player and waited. You know what we were waiting for — boys. Conversation quickly turned to what was the best way to get a boy to notice you. No one thought my suggestion about the art of making a perfect broiled lamb chop had much merit — until years later when that skill became so much more marketable than having a low score on a purity test or knowing the sequence of steps to the "Stroll."

❧ Lamb ❧

A LAMB is a sheep that is not yet a year old; the average age of one going to market is five to seven months old. Mutton is the meat of a mature sheep.

When selecting lamb, look for faint marbling (that's the pattern of fat) running through light red, moist meat. The fat should be creamy white in color.

It is best to use fresh lamb from the butcher or market within a day or two. While lamb can be aged (by the butcher), the resulting stronger flavor is a matter of personal preference. Store the meat in the coldest part of the refrigerator at a temperature of 32–40 degrees. If the meat is to be stored uncooked for more than two days, remove the original plastic wrapping and cover loosely with new plastic wrap. Fresh lamb can be frozen, with maximum storage time being three to four months.

Lamb is most delicious when cooked at a moderate temperature and served rare with an internal temperature of 130–140 degrees.

BROILED OR GRILLED LAMB CHOPS

8 double loin lamb chops
4 large garlic cloves, peeled
olive oil
A-1 or other steak sauce

TO BROIL:

Place the broiler on high with the rack in the position closest to the element (it may be necessary to lower the rack if the fat begins to burn). Smash the garlic with the flat side of a heavy knife and rub both sides of the lamb chops with it — including the bone. Drizzle a little olive oil (about 1 teaspoon) on each chop and rub it in with your fingers. Drizzle about 1 teaspoon steak sauce over each chop and smear it around with the back of a spoon. Broil the lamb chops about 5–6 minutes (for medium rare) on each side.

TO GRILL:

Follow the same directions and grill over charcoal or charcoal and mesquite for the same amount of time as with broiling.

Serves 4–6

GRILLED BUTTERFLIED LEG OF LAMB WITH MINT MAYONNAISE

This recipe is a favorite of my wonderful butcher, John Dewar.

FOR THE LAMB:

*1 leg of lamb (about 6 pounds in weight),
    boned and butterflied
12–15 cloves garlic, peeled and cut into slivers
4 or 5 sprigs fresh rosemary or 3 tablespoons
    dried rosemary
3–4 tablespoons fresh thyme or 2 tablespoons
    dried thyme
coarsely ground black pepper
1 cup olive oil*

Place the lamb in an enameled roasting pan, just big enough to hold it. Use a small, sharp knife to make little slits in the meat. Insert the slivers of garlic. Sprinkle the herbs over the meat. Grind pepper over the meat and press it in with your fingers. Rub the olive oil into the meat. Cover it with plastic wrap and refrigerate it for several hours or overnight. Grill over mesquite and charcoal, about 8 minutes on each side. Cut into the meat to see if it is done — it should be quite pink inside and charred on the outside. The meat can also be broiled. Set the rack about a third of the way down from the element and broil on high for the same amount of time. Slice the meat into thin slices and serve with rice pilaf, cold bean salad and the following mint mayonnaise.

Serves 10–12

1 extra-large egg
2 teaspoons garlic, minced
1 tablespoon Dijon mustard
3 tablespoons cider vinegar
1 cup olive oil
½ cup fresh mint leaves or 3 tablespoons dried
mint leaves
2 teaspoons granulated sugar
½ teaspoon salt
freshly ground pepper

Place the egg, garlic, mustard and vinegar in the work bowl of a food processor or blender. Process for 15 seconds, then begin to dribble in the oil, very slowly at first, until the mixture begins to emulsify. Add the rest of the oil, then the mint and sugar. Process until the mint leaves are incorporated. Add the salt and pepper to taste.

Makes 1⅔ cups

RACK OF LAMB WITH GRAINY MUSTARD

This recipe for an elegant presentation is the specialty of Stephen Elmont, president of Creative Gourmets, Ltd., of Boston.

1 lamb loin, at room temperature, fat very
well trimmed and chine bone removed (your
butcher will do this for you)
2 sticks (½ pound) sweet (unsalted) butter
3 cloves garlic, peeled and minced
3 tablespoons shallots, peeled and minced
2 cups fresh coarse bread crumbs
⅓ cup grainy mustard, preferably Pommery
2 tablespoons fresh rosemary or 1 tablespoon
dried rosemary
¼ cup fresh parsley, chopped

Preheat the oven to 400 degrees. Place the rack of lamb, meat side up, in a heavy-duty roasting pan and insert a meat thermometer into the meat. Melt the butter in a large sauté pan set over moderate heat. Lower the heat and add the garlic, shallots and bread crumbs. Cook, stirring occasionally, until the mixture is golden brown. In a small bowl combine the mustard, rosemary and parsley. Spread the mustard mixture on the lamb. Top with the bread crumb mixture, using your hands to pat it into place. Roast for approximately 35 minutes or 120 (for rare) degrees on the meat thermometer. Slice into chops with a heavy chef's knife and serve 2–3 per person. Serve with tiny red russet potatoes tossed in butter and fresh asparagus or snow peas.

Serves 2–3

$\mathcal{L}$AMB SIRLOIN CHOPS WITH AVOCADO RELISH

This special recipe comes from the American Lamb Council.

FOR THE RELISH:

1 fully ripe avocado, peeled and diced
1 large tomato, peeled and finely chopped
1 small red onion, finely chopped
1 small green pepper, finely chopped
2 tablespoons diced green chiles
2 tablespoons lemon juice
½ teaspoon salt
¼ teaspoon freshly ground pepper

To make the relish, combine the vegetables, lemon juice, salt and pepper in a mixing bowl.

4 lamb sirloin chops, ¾ inch thick

Broil the lamb chops 4 inches from the broiler for 6–7 minutes (for medium rare) on each side (if you are preparing the lamb on a grill, cook for the same length of time). Serve topped with the avocado relish.

Serves 4

Lobster

Shortly after we moved to Boston I found myself at a formal dining party at the home of a dear friend. Since this was one of those grown-up dinner parties where you are expected to be mature enough to make lively conversation with strangers, I was not seated next to my husband. I sat instead between a young and very straight doctor and a middle-aged and very gay artist. The occasion for this gala dinner was the birthday of my friend's husband. We started with mint juleps, and I thought they were so good I had two in quick succession. By the time I got to the table I could have conversed in any language with any person living or dead. The doctor was sweet but extremely limited in his outlook. He glanced across the table at his wife before he answered any question that I asked him. I wasn't giving him the third degree; why did he have to get his wife's nod to tell me in which of the upwardly mobile Boston suburbs they had overpaid for their house?

The artist, on my other side, was much more interesting, and he had had one more mint julep than I, so he was very easy to talk to. Since his lover, seated on the other side of the table, was engrossed in conversation with my husband, eye contact between the two was not only unnecessary, it was impossible.

The first course, much to my delight, was a lobster salad. It was made with three kinds of melons — cantaloupe, Persian and casaba — scooped into balls, and big chunks of lobster meat, coated lightly with an orange mayonnaise, sitting on a chiffonade of Boston and red leaf lettuce. This was served in a giant, wide-mouthed Burgundy glass. It was a stunning presentation and as delicious as it was beautiful. I dug right in and ate as quickly as good manners and conversation would allow. The combination of textures and flavors — four different kinds of sweetness and the citrus accent — was fantastic. As I relished the very last bit of lobster I noticed that the doctor had eaten all his melon and none of the lobster. How could someone not eat the food that I considered the cause of ultimate eating euphoria? He caught me staring in wonder at his dish. I asked him if he kept Kosher. He looked at his wife; she nodded. He said no, he was trying very hard to restrict his intake of cholesterol to cut down his chances of getting heart disease. I silently wondered (1) how he would handle the main course, which was standing rib roast, and (2) if it would be terribly tacky to offer to eat his lobster. I looked across the table at his wife, wondering if I could get her to nod no to the last question, when something completely unexpected happened. Someone (and it had to be one of the men sitting on either side of me) had put his hand in my lap. Not only put his hand in my lap but started to nuzzle it around. I froze and stared straight ahead, not knowing quite what to do. We were seated so close together that it was impossible to tell, without actually looking down, which man it was. While the hand became more intimately acquainted with my lap, I tried to collect my thoughts before I made a complete fool out of myself and embarrassed the wrong man. This whole thing just doesn't make sense, I thought. One of these guys doesn't like women, and the other is so repressed that he can't breathe without consulting his wife. Could it be that one of them is acting out? What did Emily Post say to do in a situation like this? I had to act fast because the maid was about to take away the doctor's dish and then she would get to eat all that lovely lobster in the kitchen. I didn't feel right about laying claim to the guy's food until I found out if he was the one pawing me. I figured I had to be straightforward about this, so with more conviction and courage than I felt, I reached down toward the offending (and offensive) hand. What I came up with was the tiny kitten that our hostess had given her husband for his birthday. As I held the kitten aloft the relief on my face was so evident that everyone at the table must have known what I had been thinking. The doctor turned scarlet and the artist laughed until he cried. With some leftover boldness I snatched the doctor's dish away from him just as the maid approached — and winked at the wife.

❧ Lobster ❦

ACCORDING to Roger Berkowitz, co-owner of the Legal Sea Foods restaurants in Boston and Cambridge, Massachusetts, real lobsters are found only in the frigid waters off the coast of New England and northeastern Canada. Hybrid types such as the rock lobster of Florida have smaller claws and are prized for their tail meat. Roger suggests driving your fishmonger crazy by asking for the female of the species because they tend to have wider tails, and therefore more meat. You also get the bonus of the eggs, a truly delicious delicacy. The larger the lobster, the better the meat-to-shell ratio. It is not true that larger lobsters are tougher — it is true, however, that people tend to overcook large lobsters, making them tough. To choose a live lobster for cooking, pull the tail section straight out. It should immediately curl back. If it doesn't, choose another lobster.

You can steam lobsters in two inches of water in a large pot. Bring the water to a rolling boil, drop the lobsters in and cover the pot. Or boil by filling the pot with water and proceeding as with steaming. It's important not to overcook them. Roger's rule of thumb is eight minutes per pound for lobsters under five pounds. For those over five pounds, five minutes per pound is ample. If you split the lobster open after cooking and the meat is still gelatinous and, if it's a female, the eggs are black and slick, it isn't done. Simply throw it back into the cooking water for several more minutes. Roger says that even though the lobster thrashes around after you put it in the pot, it is dead the instant it hits the hot water. That's why it's important to have the water at a rolling boil when you put the lobster in. He also says that the story about the digestive system being poisonous is an old wives' tale. That doesn't mean, however, that it is something that you would want to eat, primarily because of its texture (fibrous) and also because of its taste (unpleasant). The green part, called tomalley, is the liver, and not only is it edible, it's delicious.

DURGIN PARK'S LOBSTER STEW

Durgin Park is a Boston institution, where tourists and natives alike go to savor the essence of what this city is about. You'll find yourself sharing a table with total strangers and having the time of your life eating the freshest seafood available. The waitresses look tough — and they are! The lobster stew is a classic.

> *1½ pounds cooked lobster meat*
> *8 tablespoons (¼ pound) butter*
> *½ cup dry sherry*
> *4 cups light cream*
> *salt and pepper to taste*

Cut the lobster meat into 1½–2-inch chunks. Melt 4 tablespoons of the butter in a large skillet with high sides set over high heat. When the butter is hot, add the lobster and sauté over medium heat for 4 minutes. Add the sherry. Simmer gently for 5 more minutes. Add the remaining butter and the cream. Heat until steaming, but not boiling. Add the salt and pepper to taste. Serve in heated bowls and accompany with oyster crackers.

Makes 4 meal-sized servings

ℒOBSTER MILANESE LEGAL SEA FOODS

1 1¼-pound lobster per person
3–4 large or jumbo shrimp per lobster
virgin olive oil
1 clove garlic, peeled and finely chopped
cayenne pepper

Roger Berkowitz created this easy-to-fix recipe. It's a popular choice at Legal Sea Foods — once you make it you'll understand why.

Fill a large pot with water, cover and heat until the water comes to a rolling boil. Drop the lobsters in and cook them for only 30 seconds, to kill them. If you are not squeamish, you can simply plunge a knife into the space between the back of the lobster's head and the body to sever the nerve. Shell and devein the shrimp by running a sharp knife down the back of each shrimp and removing the dark vein found there. Cut each shrimp in half lengthwise. Place each lobster on its back and split open the body. Bend back the shell so that the tail meat is exposed. Sprinkle generously with olive oil and rub some of the garlic into the meat, and eggs if the lobster is a female. Butterfly the shrimp, lay them along the sides of the lobster and dribble more oil on them. Sprinkle with cayenne pepper.

Turn the broiler on to high with the rack in the upper, but not the highest, position. Broil for 10 minutes. If the top starts to get too dark, move the lobster a little farther away from the heating element.

𝒦AREN'S MELON AND LOBSTER SALAD

This mayonnaise is made with the egg white only.

2 large egg whites
¼ teaspoon granulated sugar
⅓ cup Dijon mustard
¼ teaspoon salt
¼ teaspoon white pepper
½ cup peanut oil
¼ cup almond oil (available at health food stores)
3 tablespoons raspberry vinegar
3 tablespoons frozen orange juice concentrate, thawed slightly
freshly grated rind of 1 large, brightly colored orange
2–3 tablespoons Grand Marnier

Place the egg whites in a blender or food processor with the sugar and 1 teaspoon of the mustard, the salt and the pepper. Process or blend for 15 seconds. Dribble in the oil very slowly until a thick emulsion is formed. Add the rest of the oil. Empty out about three quarters of the mixture and reserve. To the remaining mixture in the processor or blender, add the remaining mustard, the vinegar, the orange juice concentrate, the orange rind and the Grand Marnier (to taste). Blend until smooth. Whisk this mixture into the reserved mayonnaise. Chill until ready to use.

TO ASSEMBLE:

1 pound lobster meat
3 cups mixed melon balls (cantaloupe, honeydew, Persian, casaba)
fresh mint for garnish

Cut the lobster meat into 1-inch pieces and mix with the melon. Toss with enough dressing to make the mixture moist but not drippy. Spoon into very large wine goblets. Garnish each with a fresh mint leaf.

Serves 4

Macadamia Nuts

When the producer of an afternoon talk show on our local NBC affiliate called and asked me to be on her show to talk about what America eats for dessert, I accepted with great delight. "We have some ice cream experts to do a taste test and Mrs. Fields, the cookie lady, will be the other guest," she told me. At the mention of Mrs. Fields I conjured up a roly-poly grandmotherly type, complete with silver bun and wire-rimmed glasses. As nice as it would be to meet the figurehead, I thought, it would be far more interesting to get to know the power and brains behind all those neat shops, which seemed to be proliferating on every street corner like so many chocolate bunnies.

I arrived at the studio and was ushered into a room to await the arrival of the other guests. The ice cream people arrived, lugging dozens of pints of wonderful-looking frozen delights. The show's host, Buzz Luttrell, came in to get acquainted, and as we chatted, technical people came in and out carrying props and boxes of chocolate. In the midst of all this, the door suddenly flew open. In swept a gorgeously chic and effervescent young blond woman. She had a smile that looked like Miss America's and a figure to match. Her huge blue eyes sparkled with good humor and intelligence as she was introduced around the room. Unlike me, Debbi Fields remembered all our names after she heard them once. So much for the granny image. It took about two minutes of conversation to figure out that the figurehead was the brains and power behind the phenomenally successful business. It was clear that this was one smart, beautiful, successful and, on top of it all, perfectly lovely woman. Before I allowed myself to get depressed I got down to business:

"I want you to know that I once had a screaming tantrum because my husband came home from your store without the macadamia nut coconut cookies."

"I know just how you feel," she answered — this woman who looked like she never allowed a morsel of anything more fattening than a breath of air past her lips. "I adore macadamia nuts. I like them better than any other kind of nut, in fact, and I get to eat them all the time now that we have our own processing plant in Hawaii."

Knowing full well that macadamia nuts could not exactly be classified as diet food, I asked her how she was able to eat those tender, tasty tidbits and still get into her clothes.

"Well," she answered, straight-faced, "I knew that if I was going to eat all those macadamia nuts, something just had to go. So I gave up celery."

⊰ Macadamia Nuts ⊱

MACADAMIA nuts are the only native Australian plant developed as a food crop. Although plantations have been started in California, Hawaii continues to be the prime location for high-yield trees. The shells of macadamia nuts are extremely tough and hard to crack. Sophisticated technology has resulted in the development of equipment that will shell the nut and leave it whole. After the outer husk is removed, the in-shell nuts are dehydrated and then the shell is cracked. The kernels are cleaned and sorted and roasted in refined coconut oil. Salt is added at this point and the top-grade nuts are sealed in either glass jars or tins. First-grade vacuum-packed macadamia nuts may be stored for up to two years in a cool, dry place without any serious loss of quality.

MACADAMIA NUT CHICKEN SALAD

This unusual chicken salad (it is also delicious with duck meat) is perfect for summer luncheons or light suppers.

3 cups cooked chicken or duck, cut into chunks
3 tablespoons frozen orange juice concentrate, thawed
1 cup finely diced celery
1 medium red onion, finely diced
1 small can water chestnuts, drained, rinsed and cut into coarse pieces
rind of 1 large orange, finely julienned
2 large oranges, peeled, seeded and sectioned (cut sections in half if they are large)
1 7-ounce jar whole macadamia nuts, shaken in a strainer to remove excess salt
1 cup mayonnaise or ½ cup mayonnaise mixed with ½ cup plain yogurt
½ teaspoon dried tarragon
salt and freshly ground pepper to taste

Place the chicken in a medium-sized metal bowl, add the orange juice and toss. Cover and refrigerate for 30 minutes. In a large bowl combine the celery, onion, water chestnuts, orange rind, orange sections, and macadamia nuts. Add the mayonnaise and toss. Add the chicken (with the juice) and season with the tarragon and salt and pepper to taste. This is elegant served in a hollowed-out pineapple half with the pineapple used as garnish.

Serves 6

MACADAMIA NUT CREAM PIE

This recipe comes from Honolulu's Kahala Hilton and was created by Executive Chef Martin Wyss. It has a graham cracker crust made with macadamia nuts and a subtle coffee custard filling chockful of chopped macadamia nuts.

FOR THE CRUST:

1 cup graham cracker crumbs
½ cup chopped macadamia nuts
⅛ teaspoon mace
¼ cup granulated sugar
6 tablespoons melted butter

Preheat the oven to 375 degrees with the rack in the center position. Combine the above ingredients and then press into a buttered 9-inch pie plate. Bake for 8 minutes and then chill completely before filling.

FOR THE FILLING:

½ cup granulated sugar
⅓ cup cornstarch
pinch of salt
2 cups milk
3 extra-large egg yolks, lightly beaten
1 tablespoon sweet (unsalted) butter
2 tablespoons coffee liqueur
½ cup heavy cream
⅓ cup superfine sugar
½ cup chopped macadamia nuts

Combine the sugar, cornstarch and salt in a medium-sized, heavy-bottomed saucepan. Gradually stir in the milk. Stir in the egg yolks and whisk until blended. Bring to a boil over medium-low heat, and boil for 1 minute, stirring constantly. Remove from heat and add the butter and coffee liqueur. Stir until the butter has melted. Strain into a shallow bowl, cover with plastic wrap and refrigerate until very cold. Whip the cream with the sugar until it holds stiff peaks, and fold it along with the macadamia nuts into the cold custard. Pour the filling into the prepared pie shell, cover with plastic wrap and chill until firm.

TO SERVE:

> *1 cup heavy cream, whipped with 3*
> *tablespoons granulated sugar*
> *whole macadamia nuts*

Fit a pastry bag with a star tube and pipe rosettes around the rim of the pie. Garnish with the whole macadamia nuts.

Makes one 9-inch pie

PINEAPPLE AND MACADAMIA NUT BREAD

This makes a tasty, moist loaf.

> *2 tablespoons butter*
> *6 tablespoons sweet (unsalted) butter, softened*
> *1 cup light brown sugar, firmly packed*
> *2 teaspoons vanilla extract*
> *1 extra-large egg*
> *2 cups all-purpose flour, measured after sifting*
> *1 teaspoon baking soda*
> *½ teaspoon salt*
> *½ teaspoon baking powder*
> *1 7-ounce jar macadamia nut pieces*
> *1¼ cups flaked, unsweetened coconut*
> *1 20-ounce can crushed sweetened pineapple,*
> *drained (reserve 1–2 tablespoons of the juice*
> *for the glaze)*

Preheat the oven to 300 degrees with the rack in the center position. Generously coat either one 12 x 4 x 2½-inch pan or two 7½ x 3½ x 2¼-inch pans with the 2 tablespoons of butter and dust them with flour, knocking out the excess. Cream the 6 tablespoons of butter with the brown sugar and vanilla extract until light and fluffy. Beat in the egg and continue beating for 3 minutes. Sift together the dry ingredients and stir into the batter. Fold in the macadamia nut pieces, coconut and pineapple. Pour into the prepared pan or pans and bake about 1 hour or until a toothpick inserted in the center comes out clean. Cool in the pan(s) for 20 minutes, then unmold onto a rack and coat with the following glaze.

FOR THE GLAZE:

1 tablespoon butter, softened
1 cup sifted confectioners' sugar
1–2 tablespoons reserved pineapple juice
rind of 1 lemon, finely grated

Cream all the ingredients together until smooth and spread on the loaves.

Makes 1 large or 2 small loaves

MACADAMIA NUT ORANGE DESSERT SAUCE

This is delicious over pound cake topped with a scoop of vanilla ice cream. It makes a lovely gift, packed in a half-pint container and tied with a bow.

> *3 large, brightly colored navel oranges*
> *½ cup water*
> *¾ cup granulated sugar*
> *½ cup light corn syrup*
> *1 tablespoon lemon juice*
> *⅔ cup macadamia nuts, broken into large*
> *   pieces*
> *3–4 tablespoons Grand Marnier*

Use a sharp knife to remove the peel from the oranges. Cut away as much of the white pith as possible. Cut the remaining zest into 1½ x ¹⁄₁₆-inch strips. Squeeze and strain the orange juice. In a small saucepan combine the juice, water and rind. Simmer for 5 minutes. Add the sugar, corn syrup and lemon juice. Stir over low heat until the sugar dissolves. Boil without stirring for 15 minutes. Cool completely and stir in the macadamia nuts and the Grand Marnier.

Makes approximately 1⅔ cups

Mangos

You must go to Canyon Ranch," said my good friend Dottie Sternburg. "It's the perfect place for you. It's just like summer camp for grown-ups." After a seemingly endless Boston winter I was ready for a week in the sun. My body was ready for some serious exercise and the thought of a week away from stove, typewriter and telephone seemed like heaven. I made my reservation.

Summer camp never looked so good! Situated in a Santa Catalina Mountain valley just outside of Tucson, Canyon Ranch is the ultimate in luxury spas. This is not a fat farm; it is a luscious oasis in the hot, dry Arizona desert where the body and mind are fine-tuned to a state called "wellness." The desert was a riot of blossoms when I arrived in May. Roses and jasmine climbed over the low apricot stucco buildings that housed the 150 or so guests of the ranch. My room faced out onto a carefully tended garden of exotic-looking cacti that sported strange and wonderfully fragrant blossoms. The sky was a brilliant blue and completely cloudless. I had never smelled air so clean and sweet. My ears, accustomed to a constant barrage of city noises, drank in the silence, which was punctuated only by the gentle cooing of doves.

Days at Canyon Ranch were a curious mixture of pushing my body as hard as I thought I could and then pampering it with delicious (low calorie) meals and endless massages, herbal wraps, facials and the like. Every morning at 6:30 I joined a small group of walkers who set off at a breakneck pace to cover five miles in one hour. After a sumptuous breakfast of fresh fruits, homemade whole-grain cereals and herbal tea, I spent the next three hours in intensive aerobic exercise classes whipping my body back into respectable shape. Lunch included perhaps consommé and a salad of smoked pheasant, goat cheese and radicchio. I spent the afternoons much like the mornings, ending with a five-mile run, and then a whirlpool and massage before dinner. I was in bed by nine every night.

While I was fairly sore and stiff the first few days, toward the middle of my stay I began to feel renewed. I became reacquainted with muscles I hadn't used in ages. I had lost weight and inches without ever being hungry. I had pushed myself, physically, beyond my own self-imposed limits. I was having a wonderful time. One challenge remained. Canyon Ranch has a serious hiking program founded and run by a dynamo named Phyllis Hochman. If I really wanted to challenge my strong new body, an eight-mile hike with Phyllis would (I had heard) do the trick. At seven the next morning six of us were driven by van halfway to the top of one of the mountain ridges surrounding the valley. While it was fairly warm in the valley, the temperature dipped into the chilly fifties on the mountain. My skimpy running shorts did little to cover my legs and I was grateful that I had been smart enough to bring a sweatshirt. Silver, Phyllis's tiny dog, streaked ahead of us as we took to the trail. As we climbed, the temperature fell. My lungs, which do most of their work at sea level, were still not used to the altitude. I felt as if I had a watermelon in my pack. We hiked for about an hour before resting. Phyllis cheerily informed us that we were about to start the uphill part of the trail. With effort I raised my head to take in the trail, which seemed to climb straight upward. Only two more hours to go. Everyone else looked thrilled at the idea. I looked at my blue knees and tried to catch my breath. I was having trouble on the flat trail. Surely I would humiliate myself once we started upward. As we slowly climbed (walk three steps, rest, walk three steps, rest) I was overcome with self-pity. Why the hell was I here? Dying of hypothermia and having my lungs ripped out at the same time wasn't fun. I could be home, hunched over my typewriter in an overheated room listening to the phone ring and the kids squabble. "You're a wimp," I told myself with disgust. I said it again and again, matching the refrain to my footsteps. That's how I made it through the next hour. We stopped for another rest, while the clouds swirled around us obscuring the sun. The winds had picked up and the temperature was still dropping. Phyllis decided that it was too cold to stop; breakfast would have to wait until we got off the mountain. I couldn't do it. My body was running on empty. I needed sugar and fast. Phyllis noticed that she was about to lose me and began to rummage around in her pack. "Make it be chocolate," I silently prayed. With a flourish she pulled out, of all things, a mango. Its dull green and blush peach mottled skin did nothing to make me hopeful that this would give me the wherewithal to move my exhausted body off the mountain. She got out her Swiss Army knife and deftly peeled off the skin, exposing the lush deep-orange interior. She handed me a dripping slice. I gulped it down. The sweet pulp filled my mouth and put a dent in my mighty thirst. I ate another slice (this one I took the time to chew). By the third slice I was beginning to feel human. My blood sugar was rising and so was my energy level. Phyllis handed me the rest of the mango. I felt as if I could have run up the rest of the mountain — well, not quite. I tried not to wolf the whole thing down, taking little bites every fifty steps (sort of as a reward). The last hour of the hike, my feet no longer dragging, I daydreamed about all the delicious things I would make with mangos once I got home. Propelled by hunger and cold, we finished the hike in record time. The sun gave us a warm welcome as we drove back down into the valley.

I returned home from Canyon Ranch lighter by five pounds, thinner by six inches and imbued with the knowledge that I had discovered strengths and endurance that I didn't know my body had. In my suitcase I had, besides souvenirs for the kids, two nice fat mangos, just to remind me — I am not a wimp!

❧ Mangos ❧

SHAPED like fat teardrops and tasting like the very essence of summertime, the mango, cool and fragrant, accounts for more than one half of the fruit grown in India. During its peak season, May and June, more than 1,400 different varieties are harvested there. Of those, the most expensive and sought-after is the alphono variety, which will sell in India for up to ten dollars a dozen as opposed to other types which sell for a few cents each.

The mango is believed to have many magical qualities, including being an aphrodisiac. Select fruit that is firm, but yields slightly to pressure, with no soft or mushy spots. Look for mangos that are free of black spots as well. Mangos will ripen off the tree, so you can buy hard fruit and ripen it at room temperature. When the skin yields to pressure from your fingers, then it is ready to eat. Ripe mangos can be stored for several days in the refrigerator.

Mango lovers worldwide know that the best way (actually the only way) to get to the flesh remaining near the pit (after you have sliced off the other part) is to lean over the sink and use your teeth.

MANGO AND WATERCRESS SALAD

1 head Bibb lettuce
1 bunch watercress
1 large mango, peeled and cubed
6 strips well-cooked bacon, crumbled
1 red onion or vidalia onion, very thinly sliced

Place a few leaves of the Bibb lettuce on each of 6 small plates (or 4 larger ones). Arrange the rest of the ingredients on the lettuce.

FOR THE DRESSING:

¾ cup olive oil
⅓ cup red wine vinegar
3 teaspoons Dijon mustard
½ teaspoon dried tarragon
2 teaspoons light brown sugar
salt and pepper to taste

Whisk the oil into the vinegar and then whisk in the other ingredients.

Serves 4–6

COLD CREAM OF MANGO SOUP

This thick, rich soup should be served very cold in little bowls before a light meal on a hot summer night.

>*2 large, ripe mangos, peeled and sliced*
>*1 cup heavy cream*
>*2 cups plain yogurt*
>*2 cups fruity white wine*
>*½ teaspoon curry powder*
>*1 cup unsweetened, shredded coconut, toasted*
>   *(see note) for garnish*

Place the mango slices, heavy cream and yogurt in the work bowl of a food processor or blender. Puree well. Add the wine and curry powder and blend. Chill very well and serve garnished with the coconut in chilled bowls. Pass the remaining coconut in a separate bowl.

Serves 8

NOTE: To toast the shredded coconut, spread it in a thin layer on a heavy-duty cookie sheet and place it under the broiler for a few minutes. Or you can place the coconut in a large, heavy skillet and shake it back and forth over high heat until toasted.

CHICKEN BREASTS WITH MANGOS

This is a simple and elegant presentation with an exotic garnish.

>*6 boneless chicken breasts, with skin left on*
>*salt and pepper*
>*1 12-ounce bottle Major Grey's chutney*
>*1 6-ounce can frozen orange juice concentrate*
>*½ cup water*
>*1 large onion, peeled and sliced*
>*½ cup golden raisins*
>*1 cup dry white wine*
>*salt and pepper to taste*
>*1 large mango, peeled and sliced, for garnish*

Preheat the oven to 400 degrees. Salt and pepper each breast and spread both sides with a tablespoon of the chutney. Lay them skin side up in a shallow roasting pan and spread the remaining chutney over the breasts. Mix the orange juice concentrate with the water and pour it over the chicken. Scatter the onion slices and the raisins around the chicken. Cover the pan with foil and bake for 20 minutes. Remove the foil and bake an additional 20 minutes. Remove the chicken from the pan and scrape the remaining juices into a saucepan. Add the wine and cook over moderate heat for 10 minutes. Add the salt and pepper to taste. Place the mango slices in the pan and cook for 1 minute, just to heat. Place 1 chicken breast on each plate, garnish with the sliced mango and spoon a little sauce on top.

Serves 6

JOHANNA GILL'S MANGO LIME SHERBET

My friend Johanna, an art historian, has raised sherbet to an art form with this recipe.

> *2 ripe mangos (or enough to yield 2 cups*
> *pulp), peeled and sliced, pits reserved*
> *1½ cups water*
> *1 cup granulated sugar*
> *4 tablespoons lime juice*
> *finely grated rind of 2 limes*

Puree the mango pulp in a food processor or blender. Combine the water and sugar in a saucepan and stir over moderate heat until the sugar dissolves. Add the mango pits, cover and simmer for 5 minutes (this adds flavor to the syrup). Remove the pits from the syrup, and combine the puree, syrup, lime juice and lime peel. Cool completely before freezing in an ice cream machine.

Makes 1½ pints

Mascarpone

We are driving along the hairpin curves of Italy's Amalfi Drive in a Fiat Panda, a car that is really two motorized lawn chairs. It emits a noise that makes you think you forgot to empty the grass catcher. There are no seat belts — they wouldn't do any good. I am trying to train my husband to say "look to the right" or "look to the left" instead of removing his hand from the steering wheel to point out each vista adjacent to a horrifyingly steep drop-off plunging straight down to the Tyrrhenian Sea.

We are traveling in search of *tirami su. Tirami su*, which means "wake me up" or "wake up my mouth" in Italian (although it sounds like Japanese to me) is an Italian dessert made with mascarpone, a fresh, soft, sweet cream cheese; a special kind of biscuit called

Savoiardi; coffee; eggs and a little bit of chocolate. I had never tasted *tirami su*, but the week before we left for Italy the *New York Times* had run a big article in the food section about it. The gist of the article was that each restaurant makes its own version and each formula is more delicious than the next. This dish sounded like it was the holy grail of desserts and I was in the mood for a quest.

That's how we found ourselves on the way to Ravello and the Villa Maria, where, rumor had it, we could get *tirami su*. Italy in autumn is hot, hazy and simply wonderful. The grapes are ready for harvest, the olives are ripening and the sea and sky are as blue as the bottom of a swimming pool. I was faintly aware of all this as we careened around buses full of tourists who, unlike me, had the good sense to let somebody who didn't think he was A. J. Foyt drive.

To get to Ravello we followed the narrow road straight upward for five kilometers. Arriving in a small piazza we parked our car (a.k.a. the dubious vehicle of choice). The gardens in Ravello are magnificent, and even though a particularly dry summer had done in many of the flowers, we spent several hours wandering amid majestic cedars, giant cacti and the last fragrant roses of summer. We rested on a marble bench set into a wall at the edge of a garden that overlooked a drop straight down hundreds of feet to the sea.

Our reverie was interrupted by the sound of church bells signaling one o'clock. We made our way toward the white stucco wall surrounding the Villa Maria and peered into the courtyard. A dozen tables, set with sparkling white cloths and light blue napkins, were scattered under the gnarled oak trees. A group of Italian students was seated at one table laughing and eating pasta. Four men sat at another table playing cards and drinking wine.

Our lunch was simple and delicious: salad of mozzarella, garden-ripened tomatoes and fresh basil followed by *crispini*, thin savory crepes filled with cheese and slivers of ham topped with a creamy, herb-scented sauce. Now, for dessert. We put in our order. The waiter shook his head. Finished. All out. No more today. Come back tomorrow and we could have all the *tirami su* we wanted. I was devastated. We explained about the quest for the *tirami su* and the waiter listened sympathetically. He told us to wait and then disappeared into the kitchen. Upon his return he told us that if we came back at five that afternoon we could have some *tirami su*. We were terribly impressed by a chef who could be so accommodating.

When we returned to Villa Maria it was totally deserted. The cloths were off the tables and the card players had left. We tentatively knocked on the door of the kitchen. "*Avanti.*" In we went.

There was our waiter, devoid of waiter's jacket, sitting with his feet up relaxing over the newspaper. He jumped up when he saw who it was and quickly ushered us out into the courtyard. Back into the kitchen he went and then raced out with an armful of linen, china, silverware. We protested that he was going to too much trouble. No, no. It was important to eat the dessert in the proper setting. He quickly but carefully set the table and seated us. He disappeared into the kitchen again and this time when he returned he was carrying a large oval dish with low sides. He set the dish down on the table and let us gaze on it for a minute. Then with tremendous reverence he scooped out two very healthy portions. He waited expectantly as David and I picked up our forks and took a taste. The combination of the creamy-smooth mascarpone, already so rich and now made even richer with egg yolks, along with the coffee, chocolate and liqueur-soaked cookies, resulted in a taste that should have been called "heaven in your mouth." We told the waiter that it was truly sublime and asked if the chef was around so we could thank him for making us this divine treat. The chef hadn't made the *tirami su*. Our waiter had! He said that this particular dessert was his favorite dish and he thought that anyone who shared his passion for it should not be disappointed. We couldn't believe it — this man had spent his afternoon off making dessert for two strangers. We insisted that he join us for a glass of wine, and of course a dish of *tirami su*. The afternoon wore on and the shadows got long. We sat under the oak trees, licking our plates clean, and talked in our bad Italian and his better English. He talked about his mother's cooking and how she taught him just a few dishes. The one we were eating was his proudest effort. As we left, I told him that I was going to include him and *tirami su* in a book I was about to write. As he waved good-bye he shouted, "Hey, don't call it *tirami su* in that book. Name it after me — Camillo de Ravello!"

⤐ Mascarpone ⤗

MASCARPONE, with its wondrously delicate flavor, is Italy's answer to England's Devonshire cream. Originating in the Lombardy region, it is a fresh (as opposed to cooked) high butterfat (80 percent) cow's milk cheese. It is notoriously fragile with a very short shelf life. Its consistency ranges from custardy to firm to pourable (the latter indicating that it has turned). It has a fresh sweet taste that will remind you of eating solid heavy cream. Cheese expert John Greeley states that mascarpone never tastes the same once it leaves Italy. Be that as it may, I am grateful every time I see it in a shop. It can be found in the cheese or dairy department of Italian groceries and in many cheese shops as well as in large general grocery stores. It comes in little tubs like yogurt. Take care to buy *plain* mascarpone for these recipes, not the kind layered with savory herbs. Be sure to taste the mascarpone before putting it in a recipe. If it tastes anything but sweet and fresh, return it.

I usually buy mascarpone whenever I find it available. I use it on top of hot soups instead of a dollop of sour cream, I use it to make the most elegant macaroni and cheese casserole in the world, by mixing about half a cup into the cheddar cheese sauce. I use it on pasta with lots of fresh grated Parmesan cheese. Best of all, I use it on top of fresh strawberries, sprinkled with dark brown sugar. The following recipes involve a few more steps than the simple ideas I just mentioned, but the results are worth the effort.

PESTO TART

This makes a smashing presentation: a wreath of green surrounds a creamy white topping and underneath there is the surprise of a pesto layer.

FOR THE PESTO:

2 cups fresh basil, leaves only, loosely packed
5 cloves garlic, peeled
⅓ cup plus 2 tablespoons olive oil
⅓ cup walnuts
⅓ cup (1⅓ ounces) Parmesan cheese, grated
½ teaspoon salt
freshly grated pepper
1 egg yolk

Place the basil and garlic in the work bowl of a food processor. Process for 20–30 seconds or until well chopped. Dribble in the ⅓ cup oil (place the other 2 tablespoons in a small bowl) and process to make a smooth paste. Add the walnuts, cheese, salt and pepper. Process 15 seconds. Measure out 3 tablespoons of the mixture and stir into the reserved oil. Set aside to garnish baked tart. Add the egg yolk to the remaining mixture in the food processor and process to blend, 15 seconds.

FOR THE TART SHELL:

1¼ cups all-purpose flour, unsifted
¼ teaspoon salt
½ teaspoon dried basil
½ cup dried parsley
6 tablespoons cold butter, cut into pieces
2 tablespoons vegetable shortening
3 tablespoons cold water

Mix the dry ingredients and herbs in a bowl. Use two butter knives to cut in butter and shortening until the mixture resembles coarse crumbs. (This can be done in the food processor; pulse machine on and off to cut in the shortenings.) Sprinkle the cold water evenly over the mixture and stir briefly to moisten. Form dough into a ball, kneading once or twice until the dough holds together. Wrap in plastic and refrigerate for 30 minutes.

Preheat the oven to 375 degrees with the rack in the upper third of the oven, but not the highest position. Lightly grease either a 10-inch fluted tart pan with removable bottom, a 10-inch fluted porcelain tart pan or a 10-inch pie plate. On a lightly floured board, roll out the dough so that it is 3 inches larger in diameter than the pan. Place the dough in the pan, and crimp the edges. Pierce the bottom and sides with a fork and line the shell with aluminum foil. Bake 12 minutes. Remove the foil and bake an additional 5 minutes. Cool on rack.

TO ASSEMBLE:

pesto mixture
3 extra-large eggs
1 cup mascarpone
½ teaspoon salt
¾ cup heavy cream
⅓ cup Parmesan cheese, grated

Lower the oven temperature to 350 degrees with the rack in the center position. Spread the pesto carefully over the bottom of the baked tart shell. In the clean work bowl of the food processor combine the eggs and mascarpone. Blend 20 seconds. Add the salt and heavy cream. Process 10 seconds. Carefully ladle the filling over the pesto layer, taking care not to disturb it. Place the tart on a baking sheet in the center of the rack and bake for 25–30 minutes or until puffed and golden. Remove tart but don't turn off the oven. Sprinkle the center with Parmesan cheese. Spoon the reserved pesto mixture around the edge of the tart and smooth it with the back of a spoon into a band about 1 inch wide. Return tart to the oven for 5 minutes. Serve hot or at room temperature.

Serves 10 as an appetizer or 6 as a main course

CIRAMI SU

To be really authentic, you should use Savoiardi biscuits, which are available in Italian food stores (there is a mail-order source listed in the back of the book). They are the fat, dry ladyfingers that are traditionally used in this recipe. However, you may substitute your own homemade ladyfingers or even soft macaroons, or use the recipe for Italian Sponge Biscuits, p. 196. You may make this dessert in any shape dish — round, square, rectangular, oval. The number of lady fingers you will need will depend on which size and shape dish you choose.

1½ cups very strong coffee or espresso
1½ cups granulated sugar
½ cup coffee liqueur or brandy
enough Savoiardi biscuits (or a substitute) to
  fill a medium-sized serving dish or platter
  approximately 12 x 14 inches or 14 inches in
  diameter in 4 layers
2 cups heavy cream
4 extra-large egg yolks
6 ounces bittersweet chocolate, finely chopped
4 extra-large egg whites
2 cups mascarpone
cocoa

In a small saucepan heat the coffee and ½ cup of the sugar, stirring until the sugar dissolves. Add the liqueur or brandy. Dunk enough biscuits briefly in this mixture to line the bottom of the dish. Take care not to leave them in the liquid so long that they fall apart. Reserve remaining liquid.

Scald the heavy cream in a 1½-quart saucepan. While it is heating, beat the egg yolks with ½ cup of the sugar. Dribble in the hot cream and blend. Return to the saucepan and stir constantly over low heat with a rubber spatula until the mixture just begins to thicken. Off the heat, add the chocolate and stir until it has melted. Strain if necessary. Place this mixture in a metal bowl over a larger bowl filled with ice water or in the freezer to get *cold* and *firm* before you start the next step.

Beat the egg whites with the remaining ½ cup of sugar and fold into the mascarpone.

The chocolate mixture must be cold and firm when you put the *tirami su* together or it will leak out from between the layers of biscuits. On top of the layer of soaked biscuits spread a layer of half the egg white/mascarpone mixture. Dip more biscuits into the coffee mixture and place these on top. Spread with the chocolate and more soaked biscuits. Finish with the egg white/mascarpone mixture. Sift the cocoa on top.

This dessert should be refrigerated for several hours to allow the flavors to blend before serving.

Serves 10

ITALIAN SPONGE BISCUITS

These need to be started the day before you plan to use them and baked the next day. Once baked, they will keep indefinitely.

> *3 extra-large eggs*
> *1 cup superfine sugar*
> *1¾ cups flour, measured before sifting*
> *1 teaspoon baking powder*
> *½ teaspoon vanilla extract*
> *additional superfine sugar*

Butter 2 large cookie sheets and line them with wax paper or parchment. Butter the paper and dust it with flour, knocking off the excess.

In the large bowl of an electric mixer beat the eggs at high speed, gradually adding the sugar. Beat for 10 minutes. The mixture will be thick and light yellow in color.

Sift the flour together with the baking powder. With the mixer on low speed, add the flour to the egg mixture, mixing only until no flour is seen. Mix in the vanilla extract.

Fill a large pastry bag fitted with a plain ½-inch tip with half the batter. Pipe the batter, using one downstroke and one reverse stroke right on top of the first, to form "fingers" 3 inches long and ¾ inch wide, 2 inches apart on the baking sheet.

This recipe makes 35 biscuits. Do not attempt to make any more, since this will result in biscuits that are too thin. Pipe any additional batter on top of those biscuits already formed. Sprinkle with the additional superfine sugar.

Let the biscuits stand, uncovered, at room temperature, overnight.

The next day, preheat the oven to 350 degrees with the rack in the center position. Bake 1 baking sheet at a time for 8–10 minutes or until the biscuits are pale beige. When completely cool, store in a tightly covered container.

Makes 35 biscuits

BAKED APPLES STUFFED WITH MASCARPONE AND CURRANTS

4 large baking apples, such as Cortlands
4 tablespoons currants
⅓ cup brandy
6 ounces mascarpone
½ cup walnuts, chopped
½ cup dark brown sugar, firmly packed
water

Preheat the oven to 350 degrees with the rack in the center position. Core the apples, leaving the bottoms intact, and peel off the skin around the top, leaving two thirds of the apple unpeeled. Use a grapefruit spoon to hollow out about a 1½-inch-wide by 2½-inch-wide deep pocket in the center (core) part of the apple. Place the currants and brandy in a small pan and heat them until the currants are somewhat softened. Combine the currants, remaining brandy, the mascarpone, walnuts and brown sugar. Fill the apples with this mixture and place them in a shallow ovenproof dish. Add about 1 inch of water. Bake for 30 minutes or until the apples are tender. Serve warm or cold.

Serves 4

MASCARPONE TORTONI

This is an updated version of a delicious classic.

2 tablespoons dark rum
1½ cups heavy cream
⅔ cup Amaretti cookies, coarsely crushed, plus
*   additional crumbs for garnish*
4 egg yolks
½ cup confectioners' sugar, sifted
8 ounces mascarpone
1 teaspoon almond extract

In a small bowl combine the rum, ½ cup of the heavy cream and the crushed Amaretti crumbs. Beat the egg yolks with the confectioners' sugar until thick and lemon-colored. Stir in the mascarpone and almond extract. Beat the remaining cup of heavy cream until it holds soft peaks. Fold in the beaten yolks and the Amaretti/cream mixture. Divide the mixture among 8 small fluted ramekins or small cups. Sprinkle the reserved crumbs on top. Freeze until firm, about 3–4 hours, then remove to the refrigerator 30 minutes before serving.

Serves 8

Dried Mushrooms

About fifteen years ago my family went through a phase when (inspired, I guess, by Alex Haley) they put a lot of energy into finding their roots. For Tante Anna, this meant the lifelong fulfillment of a dream — a trip to Russia and Poland. On her way over she carried a suitcase full of *siddurim* (Hebrew prayer books) and *tallithim* (prayer shawls) to distribute to Russian Jews who had no access to such things. Finding herself with an empty suitcase and a love for dried Polish mushrooms, she returned with a suitcase full. She very generously shared the mushrooms with us, and I found myself the owner of two long strings of hard, brown, irregularly shaped, strong-smelling dried mushrooms. Tante said they would keep forever and since I wasn't into cooking yet, I put them in a sealed mason jar, where they remained on display on a shelf in my kitchen.

Several years ago during a trip to Europe, my husband and I came down with bad colds that sent us to bed for a few days. The hotel cook sent us up his idea of comfort food: thick slices of crusty bread slathered with sweet butter and huge bowls of mushroom and barley soup. The smell of the soup alone was an instant cure; the rich and savory steam opened up our clogged noses so that we could taste the full flavor of the pungent mushrooms and the crunchy barley. We ate it with enormous soup spoons, scooping up chunks of carrots and pieces of stewed *flanken* (pot roast). After our excellent and rapid recovery we went to thank the chef for the delicious medicine. He told us that he had made the soup with dried mushrooms and generously shared the recipe. I told him about Tante's mushrooms. The chef said he saw no reason why they shouldn't still be fine to use. Just rinse them well, he cautioned me.

My plans for making the soup were waylaid, for when we arrived home my mother entered the hospital for eye surgery. The operation had several stages and the healing process was dependent upon my mother's lying completely still for two endless weeks after the surgery. For someone as active and athletic as my mother this was extremely difficult. As much as she was determined to do everything she could to save her vision in that eye, her naturally energetic disposition made it hard. Forced to lie on her back with both eyes bandaged, she spent hours listening to the Red Sox lose to almost everybody in the American League. When her hospital roommate complained about the noise, we bought Mom a tiny radio with earphones. She went through dozens of batteries. Then, at last, the doctors said she could go home if she promised to rest and come in to have her eyes checked every other day. I brought her home to my house. It was only when she left her bed that I realized just how weak and uncoordinated she was. In order to insure that she would stay still, the doctors had given her massive doses of tranquilizers. The effect was appalling. She could hardly walk by herself and had neither the energy to stand nor the confidence to move about by herself. I quickly negotiated a deal with the doctors: if I made sure she stayed still, they would take her off the drugs. After looking at the doses she had been given, my neighbor, a doctor, cautioned me that she had to be taken off the tranquilizers slowly, because otherwise there was a danger of convulsions.

That first afternoon, I got my mother into bed and made her promise not to make a move without asking me first. Then I went into the kitchen to make her some comfort food, to help her get her energy and appetite back after her prolonged diet of hospital fare. I immediately thought of Tante's dried Polish mushrooms sitting in their mason jar. When I opened the jar they smelled just as they had when I put them in there (yes, ten years is a long time, but that smell is unforgettable). I pulled them off their string and put them into a pan of water to soak. I rinsed off the barley and put it into a pot with some beef bouillon cubes. I added lots of thick carrot slices, chopped onions and celery.

I rinsed the mushrooms several more times. From my uneducated vantage point they looked all right. I decided to make the soup and try it myself first, the queen's tester as it were, and if I didn't drop dead then I'd feed it to her. Several times Mom called down to ask what that wonderful smell was and when she could taste the soup. "Not so fast, Mom. First it has to pass the test," I kidded. Little did she know which test.

Several hours later the house was perfumed with the tantalizingly delicious flavor of the soup. David, the kids and even the dog had expressed a hungry interest in what was bubbling away on top of the stove. Finally, the soup was done. I ladled out a small bowlful. It smelled heavenly. With the addition of a small amount of salt and lots of freshly ground pepper, it tasted absolutely wonderful. I finished off my bowl and smacked my lips. The only bad side effect was that my bowl was empty. I pronounced the mushrooms just fine and ladled out soup for everybody else. Mom really loved that soup. She gobbled it up and asked for more. I was delighted to see that along with her appetite some color was returning to her face. When I came to get her empty bowl I suggested that she hurry up and get well so we could both thank Tante in person for the treat.

Later that evening I went in to check on Mom. She was lying on her side, facing the wall, with a quilt pulled up over her body and head. I thought this was sort of a strange position, but if she was comfortable, what the heck. I had to wake her to give her eye drops and as I reached out my hand toward her sleeping form she started to shake. I drew my hand back, alarmed. "Mom," I said softly, "are you all right?" The movement suddenly increased, so not only was she shaking but so was the bed. I froze. My mother was either having a convulsion from the withdrawal of the tranquilizers or she was dying from mushroom poisoning. I screamed for David. He arrived instantly and looked with a horrified expression at the quilt jerking on the bed. "Mom!" I shouted as I pulled back the blanket.

She hadn't heard me because she had her earphones plugged in.

She had tears streaming down her face. Was she laughing or crying? I pulled off her earphones and the tremors stopped immediately but not the laughter. She sat up in bed, effecting a remarkable recovery. "Hey, why did you unplug me?" she demanded. "I was listening to that hilarious Doctor Ruth tell all about good sex."

⊱ Dried Mushrooms ⊰

COOKS use dried mushrooms because all of the varieties of fresh mushrooms are not available all of the time. While they are not nearly so attractive as their fresh relatives, they have their strong points: they keep for several months when stored in tightly sealed containers, are easy to reconstitute and can be ordered by mail (see resource list).

In his excellent volume, *Joe's Book of Mushroom Cookery*, mushroom authority Jack Czarnecki tells all there is to know about every kind of edible mushroom. He advises that the concentrated flavor that comes from dried mushrooms and makes them better than those that are canned is a result of the absence of a heating stage (which kills flavor) in the drying process. Mr. Czarnecki says to look for mushrooms that are free of wormholes, and if possible, buy caps instead of stems and pieces — so you can be sure of what you are getting. If you wish to store the mushrooms for longer than several months, keep them in a plastic bag that you have pushed the air out of before sealing and freeze. If the mushrooms come in contact with moisture, they will turn moldy.

NOTE: There is always an abundance of grit to be found in dried mushrooms. It is imperative to soak the mushrooms thoroughly in boiling water (strain and save this liquid for the recipe), then to rinse them very well under cold running water for several minutes.

MUSHROOM AND BARLEY SOUP

You can use any sort of dried mushroom in this recipe. The stronger the mushroom flavor, the better your soup will be.

1½ ounces (about 2 cups) dried mushrooms
1 pound fresh mushrooms
3 tablespoons butter or oil
2 large onions, diced
2¼ cups (1 pound) pearl barley
3 stalks of celery, chopped
4 large carrots, peeled and sliced into ½-inch
  pieces
½ cup chopped fresh parsley
10 cups chicken or beef stock, homemade or
  canned
2 teaspoons dried thyme
1 teaspoon dried tarragon
salt and freshly ground pepper to taste

Place the dried mushrooms in a small metal bowl and pour boiling water to cover them. Swish them around to remove any grit. Soak them while you prepare the other ingredients. Clean and slice the fresh mushrooms into ¼-inch slices. Melt the butter in a large pot and sauté the onions in the butter. When the onions are wilted, add the barley, celery, carrots, parsley, stock and herbs. Remove the dried mushrooms from their soaking water and rinse them under the tap for a minute to remove any remaining grit. Strain the soaking liquid through a very fine strainer or a coffee filter. Add the fresh mushrooms and the dried mushrooms along with the strained soaking water to the large pot. Cover the pot and bring the soup to a simmer. Set the cover slightly off center and cook the soup over low heat for about 2½ hours or until the barley is soft and plump and the dried mushrooms are very tender. Add water if you like a thinner soup and salt and pepper to taste. This soup needs time to mellow under refrigeration and always tastes better the second or third day.

Serves 8–10

$\mathcal{M}$USHROOM ROULADE

When I had my catering business, this was one of the most popular dishes. It's really a mushroom soufflé baked flat in a jelly-roll pan and then filled and topped with a cream reduction sauce made with dried mushrooms. It's a time-consuming job but the results are certainly worth the effort. It freezes beautifully.

FOR THE ROULADE:

2 pounds fresh mushrooms
1 medium onion, finely diced
1 tablespoon butter
8 extra-large eggs, separated, at room
  temperature
6 ounces (12 tablespoons) butter, melted
⅓ cup flour
½ teaspoon salt

Preheat the oven to 350 degrees and set the rack in the center position. Grease an 11 x 17-inch heavy-duty jelly-roll pan and line the pan with parchment or wax paper. Grease and flour the paper and knock out the excess flour.

Chop the mushrooms in a food processor until they are in very fine pieces (you can also do this on a cutting board with a chef's knife). Place about 1 cup of mushrooms in a large clean dish towel and wring out as much moisture as you can by squeezing the towel. Repeat until you have removed the moisture from all the mushrooms.

In a small skillet, sauté the diced onion in the 1 tablespoon of butter. In the large bowl of an electric mixer, beat the egg yolks at high speed until they are very thick and pale yellow. On low speed add the mushrooms, onions, melted butter, flour and salt. In a clean bowl with clean beaters, whip the egg whites until they are shiny and hold firm peaks. Fold the mushroom mixture into the egg whites and smooth the mixture into the prepared pan. Bake 15 minutes or until the top is lightly browned and the roulade is well set. Cool in the pan (the roulade will be quite flat at this point) and then remove in the following way: release the edges of the roulade with a sharp knife. Cover the top with 2 overlapping strips of plastic wrap. The wrap should extend well beyond the sides of the pan. Place a large cookie sheet or board on top of the plastic wrap and flip both the cookie sheet and jelly-roll pan over so that the jelly-roll pan is on top. Remove the pan and carefully peel off the parchment. Cover the roulade with another piece of plastic wrap while you prepare the filling and sauce, or freeze it for completion at another time.

FOR THE FILLING AND SAUCE:

> *2 ounces (about 2⅔ cups) dried mushrooms*
>   *(porcini mushrooms are wonderful in this*
>   *dish)*
> *boiling water*
> *6 cups heavy cream*
> *2 shallots, peeled and finely chopped*
> *¼ cup fresh parsley, chopped*
> *1 teaspoon soy sauce*
> *½ teaspoon dried thyme*
> *salt and freshly ground pepper to taste*

Place the dried mushrooms in a small metal bowl and pour in enough boiling water just to cover them. Swish them around in the water to remove the grit. Continue to let them soak while you reduce the cream. Place the cream in a large saucepan — at least a 3-quart size — and bring the cream to a simmer. Watch it closely, because it can boil over very easily and make a terrible mess. Simmer the cream until it has reduced by half (this will take about 30–40 minutes). Add the shallots, parsley, soy sauce and thyme. Drain the mushrooms and rinse them under the tap to remove any remaining grit. Strain the reserved soaking liquid through a fine-mesh strainer or coffee filter. Cut the mushrooms into medium-sized pieces, then add them and their strained soaking liquid to the cream. Continue to cook at a low simmer for about 20 more minutes or until the mushrooms are tender. Add the salt and pepper to taste.

TO ASSEMBLE AND SERVE:

Spread about 1 cup of the sauce in a thin layer over the roulade. Roll it up the long way (that is, the long side will be facing you and you will roll the roulade away from you), using the plastic wrap to help roll it. You can freeze the roulade and the sauce at this point. Or you can make it a day ahead of time and refrigerate it. To heat, place the roulade (seam side down) on a well-greased jelly-roll pan. Loosely cover it with foil to keep it from drying out. Heat in a 350-degree oven for about 15 minutes if it has been at room temperature, or for up to 25 minutes if it has been refrigerated. Use a cake tester to see if the middle is hot. Heat the sauce separately. Slice the roulade and spoon some sauce over the top, or sauce each plate and place the slices, flat side down, on top of the sauce.

Serves 8 as a first course

℘ORCINI MUSHROOMS WITH POLENTA

In Northern Italy during the fall you can eat this dish in almost every good restaurant. I could eat it three times a day. Polenta is made from cornmeal and requires patience more than skill. I use dried porcini mushrooms, which are available in specialty food shops.

FOR THE MUSHROOMS:

*2 ounces (about 2⅔ cups) dried porcini
  mushrooms
2 cups heavy cream
2 cups boiling water
salt and freshly ground pepper to taste*

The mushrooms must be completed before you start the polenta. Place the mushrooms in a bowl and pour the boiling water over them. Let them sit for about 1 hour, swishing them occasionally to remove the grit. Strain the mushrooms, reserving the liquid, and rinse them under tap water to remove any remaining grit. Strain the soaking water through a fine-mesh strainer or coffee filter and reserve for the polenta. Simmer the cream in a large skillet and add the mushrooms and the boiling water. Simmer over low heat for about

30 minutes or until the mushrooms are very tender. Season with salt and pepper.

FOR THE POLENTA:

7 cups water (including water reserved from
soaking the mushrooms)
1½ teaspoons salt
1¼ cups coarse cornmeal
freshly grated Parmesan cheese
freshly grated black pepper

Bring the water and salt to a rapid boil in a large, heavy-bottomed pot. Sprinkle in the cornmeal slowly, stirring constantly. Lower the heat and continue stirring — don't stop — for about 20 minutes or until the liquid is absorbed. Immediately spoon about three quarters of a cup onto each of 8 plates. Spoon some of the mushrooms and sauce over each. Pass the grated cheese and pepper separately.

Serves 8 as a first course

$\mathcal{S}$AUTÉED MUSHROOMS AND PANCETTA

2 ounces (about 2⅔ cups) dried mushrooms
boiling water
2 strips pancetta (Italian bacon), diced
white and green part of 2 scallions, thinly
sliced
2 tablespoons cognac (optional)
freshly ground pepper

Cover the mushrooms with the boiling water and soak until they are tender, about 10 minutes, swishing them around to remove all the grit. Rinse them under tap water. Cook the pancetta in a large, heavy-bottomed skillet until it is crisp. Remove all but 3 tablespoons of the fat and add the mushrooms and scallions. Cook for several minutes over moderate heat, stirring frequently or shaking the pan briskly back and forth. Add the optional cognac and cook 2 more minutes. Season to taste with the pepper.

If you serve this as a first course, accompany it with thinly sliced, toasted bread.

Serves 6 as a vegetable and 4 as a first course

Oysters

*D*avid's sister, Abby Jane, is a wonderful cook. She loves oysters. Cooked or raw, fancy or plain, she eats them every chance she gets. She traveled to Mexico several years ago and upon her return she called me up and with great excitement told me of a delicious oyster preparation she had enjoyed there. She had never had this dish before and was hoping that I could give her some help in finding the recipe. As a matter of fact, the dish was so delectable, so memorably divine, that she and her friend had returned to this particular restaurant in Mexico City several times during their vacation just to enjoy this oyster treat.

I asked her to describe the dish. She said that it had looked like veal, but the waiter had insisted that it was oysters she was eating.

"It was so tender and delicate. It had the texture of oysters even though it didn't look at all like oysters."

"Did you get the name of the dish?" I asked.

Yes, she had carefully written it down. She said, "In Spanish it's called *ostra de pampa*, and in English, prairie oyster. I guess the prairie is the Western influence. Why are you laughing?" she asked.

It was a while before I could manage to stop laughing long enough to answer. I was just about able to catch my breath and managed to yell out, "Balls!" then was overcome again.

"Abby Jane," I had to dig my nails into my palm to keep myself from laughing again, "you know those oysters that you thought were so delicious?"

"Of course I know those oysters. That's why I called you. To find out how the hell to make them here in my kitchen so I don't have to go back to Mexico to eat them."

"Well, to make them, first you have to go to your local butcher."

"That's crazy. Why would I go to the butcher to buy seafood?"

"Because prairie oysters are beef testicles."

For a moment she was very quiet. Then she switched to denial. But to her great credit, Abby Jane is a good sport. After she looked up "prairie oyster" in the dictionary, she joined me, tentatively at first, but then with open throttle, in laughter. We all agreed that her trip to Mexico was most enjoyable — she really had a ball!

⪢ Oysters ⪡

OYSTERS are gathered twelve months of the year in cold waters off the Atlantic coast in places such as Maine, the Chesapeake Bay area, off the coast of Rhode Island and parts of New Jersey. The rule about not eating oysters in months whose names do not have the letter *R* in them is based on the fact that these months (May, June, July and August) are the warmest, which can result in a higher bacteria count in the oyster. State health departments carefully monitor bacteria levels, so if you get your oysters in a reputable place, you should have no problem. However, since oysters spawn during the summer, they are not as plump then, their texture tends to be mushy and the flavor is not at its peak.

Choose oysters that have no smell and whose shells clamp shut when gently squeezed. They will keep for several days under refrigeration, covered loosely with a moist towel. Do not submerge them or keep them in an airtight container because they will die from lack of oxygen. If you plan to serve them raw make absolutely sure they pass the squeeze test, and don't let them sit around at room temperature for any length of time. Serving them on the half shell on cracked ice that has been liberally sprinkled with coarse salt keeps them cool after they have been taken out of the refrigerator (see the following instructions for serving oysters on the half shell).

Some fish stores sell shucked oysters. These can be used in most recipes calling for cooked oysters. Again there should be no smell and they should be used within a day after purchase. These oysters can be frozen (in their liquid) and used quite successfully in soups and stews.

⊘YSTERS ON THE HALF SHELL

It's a little tricky getting the hang of opening an oyster. As soon as the critter suspects something's up, he flexes his muscles and squeezes his shell tightly closed. Since tiptoeing around as you prepare to attack won't fool him for a second, you have to arm yourself with a clam or oyster knife and a thick rubber glove. You can use a thick cloth glove, but getting it cleaned afterward is hard. A clam or oyster knife has a sturdy wooden handle and heavy metal (nonrust-type) blade with a rounded end. There is a flat metal shield at the end of the handle that will prevent you from ramming the knife all the way through the shell. This metal shield does not prevent you from ramming the knife through your other hand (the one holding the oyster), hence the rubber glove. Pick an unopened oyster. Hold it in the hand you don't write with. (This is the hand with the rubber glove on it.) Lay the oyster on a flat surface. Place your gloved hand firmly upon it. Grasp the knife in the other hand and hold it up against the oyster, near the hinge. Wiggle the knife around until you find a niche and then jam it in and twist. It will take a few times before you get the hang of it. Don't open the oysters too far ahead of the time you plan to serve them — they taste best right when they're opened. Layer them on ice sprinkled with rock salt to keep them cold for up to half an hour or refrigerate.

In our house we like our raw oysters with a squeeze of lemon juice; that's really the only way to savor the flavor. If you're of the cocktail sauce persuasion, enjoy. But give me my oysters plain.

Allow 6–8 oysters per person

BARBECUED OYSTERS

Don't let the cook who likes his meat well done make these. They call for a minimum amount of cooking over a very hot fire.

> *4 dozen shucked oysters*
> *2 sticks butter, melted*

Thread the oysters onto 4 skewers and baste them well with butter. Cook very briefly over hot coals, turning frequently. Serve as a first course on rounds of French bread spread with mayonnaise.

Serves 4

OYSTERS WITH ROASTED GARLIC

You will be amazed at the deliciously subtle taste of the baked garlic in this dish.

> *2 large, whole heads of garlic, the larger the*
> *cloves, the better*
> *1 cup (2 sticks) sweet (unsalted) butter*
> *½ cup vegetable oil*
> *32 shucked oysters with their juice*
> *2 cups heavy cream*
> *salt and white pepper to taste*

Separate the cloves of garlic and place them, unpeeled, in a small ovenproof dish. Cut the butter into pieces and place it over the garlic. Add the vegetable oil. Cover the dish with foil and bake at 250 degrees for 2–3 hours or until the garlic is very soft. Cool the garlic in the butter/oil mixture. When it is cool, carefully peel off the skins and set aside the peeled cloves, which will be very soft. Reserve the garlic butter in the refrigerator.

Drain the liquid off the oysters and reserve both. Combine the oyster liquid and the heavy cream and simmer until it reduces to 1½ cups. Season with salt and pepper.

TO ASSEMBLE:

Preheat the oven to 425 degrees. Place 4 oysters and 2 cloves of garlic in each of 8 small ovenproof ramekins. Pour in enough of the hot cream to cover. Bake for 15 minutes, top with a small piece of the garlic butter and serve immediately.

Serves 8 as a first course

OYSTERS WITH BEURRE BLANC AND CAVIAR

This particularly simple yet elegant recipe can be made quickly and served as a first course, especially if your fishmonger sells shucked oysters. If you have never made a butter sauce, it is a good idea to have a dress rehearsal (without the caviar and oysters) before the command performance. The sauce does not hold and must be served immediately.

FOR THE OYSTERS:

2 cups water
½ teaspoon salt
16–18 shucked oysters

Bring the water and salt to a gentle simmer in a shallow pan. Poach the oysters, 4 at a time, for 2–3 minutes. Remove with a slotted spoon and drain on paper towels.

FOR THE SAUCE:

3 tablespoons white wine vinegar
2 tablespoons clam juice
¼ cup dry white wine
2 shallots, very finely minced
1 cup sweet (unsalted) butter, cut into pieces
    and very cold
2 tablespoons black or red caviar
salt and freshly ground white pepper

In a heavy-bottomed skillet boil the vinegar, clam juice, wine and shallots until the mixture reduces to 1 tablespoon and just glazes the bottom of the pan. Lower the heat and whisk in the butter, piece by piece, to make a smooth, creamy sauce. You might have to remove the pan from the heat if the sauce looks as if it might be separating. You want the pan just warm enough so that the butter melts and an emulsion is formed. Gently stir in the caviar and then season with salt and white pepper.

TO ASSEMBLE:

Place 4 oysters on each plate and spoon some sauce over them.

Serves 4

BEER-FRIED OYSTERS

In the Louisiana po'boy tradition, we eat these on Italian rolls with Creole mayonnaise, hot sauce and pickles.

2 dozen shucked oysters, the larger the better
1 cup oyster-cracker crumbs
¼ cup beer
1 egg
½ teaspoon salt
freshly ground pepper
¾–1 cup solid vegetable shortening

Drain the oysters of their liquid and dry them well with paper towels. Place the cracker crumbs in a shallow bowl. Mix the beer, egg, salt and pepper in another bowl. Melt the shortening in a deep skillet or in an electric frying pan until it is very hot but not smoking. Dip the oysters into the crackers, then into the egg mixture and then back into the crackers, taking care to coat them well. Drop them into the hot shortening, 3 or 4 at a time, and cook for about 1 minute or until golden brown. Drain on paper towels and serve with tartar sauce or as the filling for a fried oyster po'boy.

Makes 24 fried oysters

FOR THE CREOLE MAYONNAISE:

1 cup mayonnaise (either homemade or
  commercially prepared)
2 tablespoons Creole mustard (available in
  gourmet shops) or grainy mustard
3 tablespoons sweet pickles, chopped
2–3 dashes of Tabasco sauce or Louisiana hot
  sauce

Place all the ingredients in a bowl and stir to combine.

Makes 1½ cups

Peaches

My neighbor Betsy Brown is a garden designer. She does all my flower arranging and I bake her chocolate cakes. She says it irks her when she sees flower arrangements containing things that are out of season. For instance, a fall bouquet with daffodils and tulips imported from South America intermingled with locally grown carnations and dahlias. She says it shows a lack of respect for the bounty and the order of the seasons. I feel exactly the same way when I walk into a grocery store in the dead of winter and see bright green stalks of asparagus (imported from Mexico) stacked next to knobby globes of celery root or shallow baskets of raspberries set like shining jewels (and costing just as much) among the navel oranges and Bosc pears.

I know on one level I should be grateful that Israel grows straw-berries to grace America's fruit tarts twelve months of the year and Australia produces blueberries that anyone (as long as they can jus-tify the price) can enjoy at Christmastime. It used to be that when the first figs appeared at the local Italian market, you could tell that fall was on its way; crisp red-green stalks of rhubarb meant spring. It was the peak of summer when you bit into that first luscious tomato. Now rock-hard, tasteless tomatoes vie with turnips and car-rots for space on winter shelves, along with avocados that will ripen some time in the next century.

There is something screwy about sitting around a cozy fireplace in long underwear, turtlenecked jersey, ski pants, high socks and boots drinking hot chocolate and enjoying a nice, fresh, juicy peach. Un-less you are in the Southern Hemisphere you don't eat peaches in February. This is the scenario for eating peaches: July afternoon, temperature in the mid-eighties, sky as blue as the bottom of a swimming pool, cicadas making a hell of a racket. You put on your bathing suit, drag the chaise longue into the sunniest part of the yard, turn the radio on (preferably to a station that plays a lot of Billy Joel and Stevie Wonder), open up any book by Danielle Steel, say a silent but fervent thank-you to God for taking away winter and then, and only then, close your eyes and bite into the first peach of the season. Let me tell you what this peach should look like. First of all, it should be big (the size of a baseball) and heavy in your hand. The word *lush* should instantly come to mind when you look at its rich, warm golden-pink hues blending into rosy pink and the softest gold. It should feel like velvet, smooth and soft, and its flesh should give very lightly to the merest pressure from your fingers. It should smell like a peach (something those imported winter varieties never do), and finally, when you take a bite, it should be so ripe that while an explosion of summertime is happening inside your mouth, peach juice runs down your chin inviting sugar-happy bumblebees to try to kiss your neck. This is a peach.

I can remember only once in my life when I passed up an opportu-nity to enjoy summertime peaches. We had been invited to our friends Sue and Phil Strause's house for dinner. It was the very beginning of August and I was in the very last weeks of my very last pregnancy. Phil, who happens to be our family pediatrician, had made a special cocktail for the guests to enjoy before dinner. Called Peach Fuzz, it was a kind of frozen peach daiquiri made with rum, frozen lemonade and the biggest, most luscious Georgia peaches I had ever laid eyes on. As much as I wanted one, I agreed with Phil that imbibing during pregnancy wasn't such a great idea, so, with great reluctance and frustrated longing, I passed. Phil, catching the look on my face as I watched David and the other guests enjoying their drinks, promised that after the baby was born we would be invited back again and he would make a batch of Peach Fuzz just for me.

Just one week later I went into labor. David and I had hopes that this would be your basic speedy delivery. So much for what we wanted. When close to midnight I was finally brought into the delivery room I was exhausted; I had by this time screamed at almost every person in sight. Just as the baby was about to be born and I felt myself going around the bend, the delivery room door opened. In walked Phil, dressed in a green scrub suit, carrying a silver thermos full of frozen peach daiquiris.

"You hurry up and have that kid so you can drink some Peach Fuzz," said he.

I was delighted to oblige.

❧ Peaches ❧

FRESH peaches are available during the summer months with the peak of their season in late July and early August. Peaches are divided into two types, clingstones, which have flesh firmly attached to the pit and are most often early-maturing varieties, and freestones, which have flesh that easily separates from the pit and mature later. While peaches can be home-ripened, it is best to buy almost-ripe peaches and enjoy them without having to refrigerate them for any length of time, as this speeds the deterioration of flavor. A bright, fresh appearance is a good clue to a high-quality peach. Background color should be either pinkish/yellowish or creamy. A light green background suggests that the peach was immature when picked and will not ripen well. Such a peach will become shriveled and have tough, poorly flavored flesh. The best peaches are fairly firm and free of bruises and soft spots.

The skin of cooked peaches is tough and tasteless and I suggest you remove it when using fresh peaches for any recipe, the exception being the Peach Fuzz. This is done simply by pouring boiling water over the ripe peaches, letting them sit for a minute or two, then slipping the skins off. If the skin does not come off easily, it means the peach is not quite ripe. Use a knife to remove the rest of the skin.

HOT PEACHES WITH BROWN SUGAR

Short of eating them out of your hand, this has to be the most delicious way of enjoying peaches. Next to a tuna fish sandwich, this is my all-time favorite comfort dish.

> 1 large Alberta peach, at room temperature,
>   perfectly ripe and blemish-free
> 2 rounded tablespoons dark brown sugar
> heavy cream (optional)

Place the peach in a small metal bowl. Pour boiling water over the peach and after 3 minutes, remove the peach with a slotted spoon and slip off the skin. Slice the peach into thick wedges and put them into a small bowl. Sprinkle the brown sugar over the slices and dribble on the optional heavy cream. The more comfort you need, the more cream you should use.

Serves 1 soon-to-be-happy person

PEACH FUZZ

Sue and Phil Strause use rum in their preparation but say it's fine to substitute gin if you wish. Stay away from peach brandy, though, because it's far too sweet and strongly flavored.

> 1 large or 2 medium very ripe peach(es)
>   (preferably Alberta freestone) with skin
> 1 6-ounce can frozen pink lemonade, softened,
>   but not defrosted
> 6 ounces rum
> crushed ice
> sprigs of mint for garnish

Slice the peach in half and remove the pit. Cut the peach into medium-sized pieces. Place the lemonade, liquor and peach into a blender (you can use the empty lemonade can to measure the 6 ounces of liquor). Add about a cup of crushed ice. Blend for 30–45 seconds. Pour into glass tumblers or wine glasses and garnish each with a sprig of mint.

Serves 4

MILLIE'S PEACH KUCHEN

One of my mother's finest desserts.

>*2 pounds (3–4, depending upon their size) very
>   ripe peaches, blanched, with skins removed*
>*2 tablespoons lemon juice*
>*1½ cups all-purpose flour, measured after
>   sifting*
>*2 teaspoons baking powder*
>*½ teaspoon salt*
>*½ cup granulated sugar*
>*2 extra-large eggs*
>*2 tablespoons whole milk*
>*grated rind of 1 lemon*
>*1 stick (4 ounces) sweet (unsalted) butter,
>   melted*
>*whipped cream for garnish*

TOPPING 1:

>*⅓ cup dark brown sugar, firmly packed*
>*½ teaspoon cinnamon*
>*½ teaspoon ground ginger*

TOPPING 2:

>*1 extra-large egg yolk*
>*¼ cup heavy cream*
>*1 rounded tablespoon light brown sugar*

Preheat the oven to 375 degrees with the rack in the center position. Butter a 9-inch springform pan and dust the inside with flour. Knock out the excess flour. Cut the peaches into slices and sprinkle with the lemon juice and set aside. Resift the flour with the baking powder, salt and sugar into a mixing bowl. In a small bowl beat the eggs and milk together. Stir in the lemon peel. Dribble this mixture over the flour, then stir in the butter with a fork. Mix only until the ingredients are incorporated. Spread the batter in the bottom of the prepared pan. Drain the liquid off the peaches and arrange them on top of the batter. Combine the ingredients for the first topping, sprinkle on the batter and bake for 25 minutes. Place the ingredients for the second topping in a small bowl and mix well. Pour this over the kuchen and bake 10 more minutes or until the top has set. Cool the kuchen in the pan for 15 minutes and release the springform. Serve with a dollop of whipped cream.

Serves 8

BEVERLY JONES'S COCONUT LAYER CAKE WITH FRESH PEACH FILLING

My recipe tester, Beverly Jones, created this heavenly combination of flavors and textures. This cake takes some time to make but the result is worth it. Just because a recipe is long doesn't mean it's difficult. This one has a lot of steps; read them all before you start.

FOR THE LAYERS:

1 teaspoon baking soda
1 cup buttermilk
4 ounces sweet (unsalted) butter at room
   temperature
1⅓ cups granulated sugar
2 extra-large eggs, separated
2 cups all-purpose flour, measured after sifting
½ teaspoon salt
2 teaspoons baking powder
grated rind of 1 lemon (reserve the juice for
   the filling)

Preheat the oven to 350 degrees with the rack in the center position. Grease two 9-inch cake pans, line the bottoms with a circle of parchment or wax paper, grease the paper and then flour the pans, knocking out the excess flour. Combine the baking soda and the buttermilk in a 1-quart bowl or pitcher and set it aside. (You'll need a larger bowl than you think because the mixture will foam up.)

Cream the butter and sugar in the bowl of an electric mixer until light and fluffy. The mixture should resemble whipped cream. Do not underbeat it. Add the egg yolks one at a time, beating well after each addition.

Sift the flour with the salt and baking powder onto a large piece of wax paper. With the mixer on low speed add the flour to the butter/egg mixture, alternating with the buttermilk mixture. Blend well after each addition, but don't overbeat. Stir in the rind. In a separate bowl beat the egg whites until they hold firm peaks and fold them into the batter. Divide between the 2 prepared pans, smooth the tops and bake for 30 minutes or until a cake tester comes out clean. Meanwhile prepare the peach filling.

FOR THE FILLING:

2 large, very ripe peaches, blanched, with
  skins removed
juice of 1 lemon
⅓ cup granulated sugar
¼ cup peach brandy (optional)

Slice the peaches into thin wedges. Toss the wedges with the lemon juice, the sugar and the optional peach brandy. Cover with plastic wrap and let sit at room temperature.

Remove the layers from the oven and turn them out onto a rack to cool completely. Drain the liquid from the peaches and brush it onto the tops of the layers while they are cooling.

TO ASSEMBLE:

2 cups heavy cream, whipped with 1
  tablespoon of vanilla extract and ⅓ cup
  superfine sugar
1 cup unsweetened, grated or flaked coconut,
  toasted (see note)

Place 1 cake layer on a flat cake plate with 4 strips of wax paper underneath to keep the plate clean. Arrange the sliced peaches on top of the layer and spread the peaches with one third of the whipped cream. Place the second layer on top (use two metal spatulas to do this) and use the remaining whipped cream to frost the top and sides of the cake. Take some coconut in the palm of your hand and press it onto the sides of the cake (some will fall onto the wax paper — just sweep it into your hand and use it for the other side of the cake). Sprinkle the rest on the top. Remove the strips of wax paper from under the cake.

Makes one 2-layer 9-inch cake

NOTE: To toast coconut, spread the coconut in a single layer on a baking sheet and bake in a 350-degree oven for about 10 minutes or until light brown. Or cook it in a large heavy skillet over high heat, shaking the pan briskly back and forth until the coconut is browned.

$\mathcal{P}$EACH ICE CREAM

This is wonderful served with the simple raspberry sauce found on p. 228.

> *4 very ripe peaches, blanched, with skins*
> *removed*
> *4 extra-large egg yolks*
> *⅔ cup light brown sugar, firmly packed*
> *3 cups heavy cream*

Cut the peaches into 1-inch chunks. In the bowl of an electric mixer, beat the egg yolks with the sugar until the mixture is light and fluffy. Scald the cream in a 1-quart pan and dribble it into the egg mixture. Mix well. Return the custard to the pan and cook over low heat, stirring constantly, until the mixture just coats the back of a spoon. Stir in the peaches and any accumulated juice. Cool the mixture before freezing it in an ice cream machine.

Makes 1 quart

Royal Riviera Pears

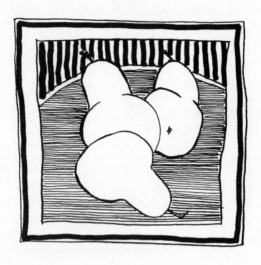

Art and gym were my areas of strength in high school. By the time I became a senior I had taken every art class in the curriculum. It wasn't that I was so good at art; it was that in this class I could spend my time daydreaming, which was what I was really great at. I was great at gym too, but that wasn't why I liked it. I liked it because the more time I spent hanging around in the athletic department, the better the chances were that I would get a glimpse of Mr. Mariani, the young and gorgeous boys' gym teacher. This feeling was shared by all the other girls in the school, who just about swooned whenever he walked by.

It was clear that no one would give me a job daydreaming after graduation. My parents (rightfully dubious about my artistic talents) suggested I start off with a studio class before I signed on at art school. The class was held in downtown Hartford at the studio of a painter who supplemented his income by giving classes to woefully untalented, aspiring Degases and Jackson Pollacks. The class I took was called "Drawing from Life." Every Wednesday night twelve students would sit around and try desperately to capture "the Essence, the Life" (as our teacher put it) of a very rotund, middle-aged nude woman lying next to an arrangement of plastic fruit. Every week it was the same model and the same bowl of fruit. Every week I drew a totally uninspired picture, yawned a lot and listened to my stomach rumbling with hunger. Every week I got to listen to the woman behind me complain about having to draw fake fruit. "If this is 'Drawing from Life,' why are we given that artificial fruit?" I was hoping she'd bring in some real fruit so I could have something to eat at the end of class.

One evening halfway through the term I ran into the plastic-fruit-hating lady in the parking lot on her way to class. Besides her box of charcoal she had a brown shopping bag with a big box in it. "I couldn't stand that awful fake fruit one more week, so I brought some really nice fruit from home." She showed me the box, which was from a place called Harry and David. Inside the box, carefully packed in shredded paper, were the most beautiful pears I had ever seen. They were full and round and pale green in color with lovely tiny golden flecks. She told me that her husband's business received a gift box of fruit every month, and these were left over from this month's shipment. "Every month we get something different," she explained. "Oregon peaches one month, fancy oranges another and then there's always a box of kiwi." I didn't know what kiwi were but thought that the pears were magnificent.

We walked into the studio together to find that the fruit situation wasn't the only thing that had changed. Our fat, naked lady was nowhere to be seen. The teacher announced that she was ill. He had placed a call to the agency and they were sending a replacement who was, unfortunately, late. We could get to work drawing the fruit. The pear lady volunteered that she had brought some real fruit, and the teacher was delighted to have her replace the plastic with the real. Since the pear lady was a minimalist (you could tell by the sketchy, faint lines she used to draw her figures), she placed only two of the pears on the model's stage.

I was pretty involved in my drawing of the pears and wasn't paying any attention to the arrival of the model. Then I heard the person next to me say something about a male model. I froze. Did he mean that in the next few minutes there was going to be a live, naked man on the stage? Where I could see him? Except for Joshua Katz, the eight-month-old baby I took care of on Saturday nights, I had never seen a naked male body. Growing up in a house where everyone was always fully clothed had dampened rather than ignited my childhood curiosity. When my friends and I played hospital in second grade, I kept my eyes closed.

My hands were shaking so that I could hardly hold the chalk, and my heart was pounding. My eyes were glued to my easel. I heard the dressing room door open and listened to the sound of bare feet pad onto the stage. I heard the pear lady gasp — was it delight or shock? Surely she had been viewing Mr. Pear in the altogether for years. The rest of the class was sketching madly. I had a little talk with myself about nature and beauty and the human form and how fear of the unknown is always worse. . . . As I lifted my eyes I prayed that he would at least be lying with his back toward me. No such luck. Posed full frontal, not four feet from the other side of my easel, was Mr. Mariani, the boys' gym teacher. I don't think I gasped out loud, but the magnitude of my shock at seeing the private parts of Mr. Mariani hanging almost within reach would have electrocuted a large dog.

The art teacher was making rounds, checking progress. I got to work on the pears, which, mercifully, were lying on the floor next to Mr. Mariani's beautifully proportioned feet. I drew them with slow, meticulous care — I had two hours to use up. I stared at those pears, analyzing every nuance, while I pondered Mr. Mariani's double life. The art teacher came by to say that my pears looked perfect and why didn't I start on the torso. I took a deep breath and allowed my gaze to travel from foot to hairy calf. How long can you draw a calf? I managed an hour. The knees took a long time too. Toward the end of the class, I had worked my way up to his muscular thighs and had even managed to sneak in a few discreet glimpses at the rest of his anatomy. As you can imagine, the whole experience was quite a revelation. In the last few minutes of the class, I realized that chances were I wouldn't have another opportunity like this handed to me. I put down my charcoal, forgot about the pears, sat back in my chair, inhaled a deep breath and took in the whole show. Here was material that would keep me in daydreams for years.

The drawing that I made that evening was the only one that I kept from the course. I entitled it "Nude with a Great Pear."

❧ Royal Riviera Pears ❧

ROYAL riviera pears, also known as Comice pears, are prized for their large size, pure white flesh and their remarkable sweet, juicy flavor. The pears should be clean, uninjured by cuts or bruises, and fairly firm. Overripe condition is indicated by obvious softness and discoloration. Since pears develop their best flavor when ripened off the tree, allow the pears to ripen in temperatures between 60 and 70 degrees Fahrenheit for a few days before eating. When ripe, the gold-flecked, light green skin is easily marred, so the pears should be stored with tissue paper between them. While other pears can be used in these recipes, the unique flavor of the Comice tends to hold up better in cooked dishes. They are available by mail order and in some food stores during the winter months.

$\mathcal{P}$OACHED PEARS WITH RASPBERRY SAUCE

FOR THE PEARS:

8 ripe, unblemished royal riviera pears
juice of 1 lime
grated rind of 1 lime
1⅓ cups granulated sugar
2 cups fruity white wine
1 cup water

Peel the pears using a small, sharp knife (a peeler makes too many bruises) and leave the stems intact. Sprinkle each pear with lime juice to keep it white. Place the pears in a heavy kettle and add the lime rind, the sugar, the wine and the water. Cover, bring to a simmer and cook over low heat for about 20–25 minutes or until the pears are tender. Use a slotted spoon to remove the pears to a rimmed serving platter and pass the raspberry sauce separately.

FOR THE RASPBERRY SAUCE:

3 pints fresh raspberries or 2 10-ounce packages
frozen raspberries, defrosted (reserve the
liquid and use with berries)
⅓–½ cup granulated sugar
1 cup raspberry preserves
juice of 1 lemon

Cook the berries with the sugar (the amount of which depends upon the sweetness of the berries) over low heat until the juices are released. Add the preserves and the lemon juice. Pass through a strainer to remove the seeds.

Serves 8

PEAR AND HONEY CLAFOUTIS

A *clafoutis* is sort of a dessert quiche without the crust. It should be served warm, either plain or with vanilla ice cream.

> *3 royal riviera pears (about 1 pound total*
>   *weight)*
> *juice of 1 lime*
> *4 extra-large eggs*
> *⅓ cup granulated sugar*
> *2 tablespoons sweet (unsalted) butter, melted*
> *1 cup medium cream*
> *1 teaspoon powdered ginger or 1 tablespoon*
>   *chopped candied ginger (optional)*
> *finely julienned rind of 1 lime*
> *⅓ cup honey*

Preheat the oven to 350 degrees with the rack in the center position. Generously butter a 9-inch glass or pottery quiche pan. Place the quiche pan on a heavy-duty baking sheet lined with foil (this is to protect your oven in case of spills). Peel and core the pears and cut them into thin slices. Toss the slices in the lime juice. Whisk together the eggs, sugar, butter and cream. Stir in the ginger, if desired, and the lime rind. Pour a thin layer of the mixture into the quiche pan and then layer the slices of pear over it. Pour in the remaining mixture. Dribble the honey over the top. Bake for 25–30 minutes, until the top is puffed and browned and the filling is set.

Serves 6–8

HOT PEAR SOUFFLÉ

This low-cholesterol dessert soufflé rises dramatically and makes a spectacular presentation. You can either make individual soufflés or one large one. The base can be made ahead of time and kept refrigerated for up to a week or frozen for several months. You can also make this soufflé with ripe peaches and substitute peach brandy for the Pear William.

FOR THE SOUFFLÉ BASE:

1½ pounds very ripe royal riviera pears (this
*   equals about 3 large pears), peeled, cored*
*   and cut into quarters*
1 tablespoon lemon juice
½ cup granulated sugar
½ cup water
2 tablespoons cornstarch
¼ cup cold water
⅓ cup Pear William or other pear brandy

Puree the pears with the lemon juice in a food processor or blender. Combine the sugar and ½ cup water in a skillet set over medium heat. Stir until the sugar dissolves, raise the heat and boil for 3 minutes. Combine the pear puree and sugar syrup in the skillet and cook over medium heat; simmer for 5 minutes, stirring frequently. Combine the cornstarch and ¼ cup cold water in a small bowl. Whisk to a smooth paste, stir into the pear puree, return to a boil and simmer 4–5 minutes, stirring occasionally, until the mixture reduces somewhat and is very thick. The base should be the consistency of pudding. Stir in the brandy and cook 1 minute.

Makes 2 cups

FOR THE SOUFFLÉ:

2 tablespoons sweet (unsalted) butter, softened
granulated sugar
1 cup egg whites (about 8 large) at room
*   temperature*
pinch of cream of tartar
3 tablespoons confectioners' sugar, sifted
2 cups soufflé base at room temperature
¾ cup fresh or previously frozen raspberries,
*   blackberries or blueberries, drained of their*
*   liquid if previously frozen*
confectioners' sugar for garnish

Preheat the oven to 450 degrees with the rack in the upper third, but not the highest position. Use the butter to generously coat six 1-cup soufflé dishes or one 6-cup soufflé dish. Sprinkle generously with the granulated sugar.

Beat the egg whites with the cream of tartar until soft peaks form, adding the confectioners' sugar gradually during the beating process. Continue beating until they are firm but not dry. Add a generous spoonful of the whites to the base and stir to lighten, then fold all the whites into the base.

FOR THE INDIVIDUAL SOUFFLÉ:

Fill each dish about one-third full and sprinkle on a tablespoon of the berries. Divide the remaining mixture among the dishes, filling them to just below the rim. Smooth the tops gently with a rubber scraper.

FOR THE LARGE SOUFFLÉ:

Fill the bottom one-third full, add the entire cup of berries and fill with the rest of the mixture, smoothing the top.

Place the dish (or dishes) on a heavy-duty baking sheet. Bake the individual soufflés for 15–20 minutes. For the large soufflé bake 15 minutes at 450 degrees, then reduce the oven to 350 degrees and bake another 15 minutes. The soufflés are done when they have risen up out of the dishes (1 inch for the little ones and 2 inches for the big one) and the tops are well browned. The soufflé(s) should be fairly firm and not wiggle very much when moved.

Hold a strainer filled with a little confectioners' sugar over the hot soufflé and dust lightly. Serve immediately.

Serves 6

PEAR AND GOAT CHEESE SALAD

1 ripe, large, unblemished royal riviera pear
juice of 1 lime
4 large leaves ruby red lettuce
4 ounces goat cheese, such as Montrachet
(without the ash)
½ cup dykon radish, peeled and thinly sliced
1 red onion, thinly sliced

Peel the pear, slice it into ½-inch pieces and sprinkle with the lime juice. Arrange the lettuce leaves on 2 salad plates and arrange the pears on top of the lettuce. Crumble the cheese over the pears and arrange the rest of the ingredients on top. Serve with the following dressing.

Serves 2

FOR THE DRESSING:

1 clove garlic, crushed
½ cup olive oil
2–3 tablespoons red wine vinegar or balsamic
vinegar
1 teaspoon dried mustard
dash Tabasco
salt and pepper to taste

Place the garlic in the olive oil about half an hour before you plan to make the dressing. Combine the vinegar and mustard in a small bowl. Discard the garlic and whisk in the oil and then the Tabasco. Add the salt and pepper to taste. Add more vinegar if necessary.

Makes ⅔ cup dressing

ROYAL RIVIERA PEAR AND GINGER CONSERVE

My dear friend Michael Frishman's real specialty is chili, but when he heard I was writing a book that included a chapter on royal riviera pears, another one of his talents came to light — he makes exquisite preserves. He made up this recipe when he found that he had a plethora of ripe riviera pears on hand. It made me wonder why I never seem to have too many.

Please note that the large amount (one pound) of fresh ginger is not a mistake.

> *1 tangerine (Michael suggests mercot, or honey*
> *tangerines if they are in season)*
> *2 limes*
> *3 medium-sized Granny Smith apples*
> *3 very ripe royal riviera pears*
> *1 pound fresh gingerroot, weighed before*
> *peeling*
> *1 cup water*
> *2 cups granulated sugar*
> *1 cup honey*

Peel and seed the tangerine and chop finely. Cut the limes into thin slices and remove the seeds, then chop them finely. Core the unpeeled apples and pears and chop finely. Peel the ginger (the easiest way is to scrape off the skin with a small, sharp knife) and chop it in the bowl of a food processor until the pieces are very small, but the texture is not mushy.

Combine the fruit, ginger and water in a medium-sized saucepan, bring to a boil, cover and simmer over low heat for 30 minutes. Stir in the sugar and honey and continue stirring over low heat until the sugar has dissolved. Bring to a boil, lower the heat and then simmer, uncovered, stirring regularly to prevent scorching (especially as the jam thickens), for about 1 hour or until the jam is very thick. Spoon into canning jars that have been rinsed (along with their lids) with boiling water and refrigerate.

Makes about 2 quarts

Pistachios

There used to be a Planters peanut shop in downtown Hartford. On weekends a man dressed up in a peanut costume (I distinctly remember he wore black cotton gloves that fastened at the wrist with a tiny black button) would parade up and down in front of the shop, enticing people to come in and buy. My aunts took me there so we could load up on movie food before we went to the Saturday matinee at the Strand Theater, next door.

Inside was a case that contained neatly divided compartments full of nuts: there were roasted peanuts, Spanish peanuts, pecans, giant Brazil nuts, almonds, and cashews looking like tiny boomerangs. There were mixed nuts, spiced nuts and chocolate-covered nuts.

The array was dazzling, and choosing among the variety was difficult for most. But not for me. I took my nickel straight over to the glass vending machine on the black wrought-iron pedestal in the corner of the store. Standing on tiptoes, I carefully put my money into the little slot, used both hands to turn the dial (simultaneously bumping the glass top as hard as I could with my shoulder just as my cousin showed me — so more would come out) and then carefully cupped one hand under the little slot as I slowly raised the lid. Into my hand would rush a mound of red shells, smiling open at one end to reveal the bright green meat of the pistachio. With my hand still cupped in place I would give the machine another jolt and one more nut, accompanied by a shower of salt and flecks of nut debris, would be added to the pile in my hand. I would quickly deposit the handful in my jacket pocket and lick the salt off my hand.

Once inside the theater I checked out my goods. One or two unopened nuts was barely acceptable — any more and I was outraged, since these were impossible to open with fingers and teeth. My favorites were, of course, the fat ones, with crisp skin and lots of salt caked on them. The ones I favored the least, next to the closed ones, were the nuts with shells that, instead of opening on their hinges, broke in half, necessitating much more work to get the meat out. At the end of the show I sported red fingers and a pocket full of salt.

The first time I saw shelled pistachios I was thrilled. Imagine having the reward without all the work. But to tell you the truth, upon eating them I was disappointed. It just wasn't the same. I missed the challenge of the shell, the salt and even the red fingers.

⊱ Pistachios ⊰

THE pistachio is a relative of the mango and the cashew. While pistachios have grown in Europe, Asia and the Middle East for centuries, they have been a commercial crop in the United States only since 1976, when California harvested its first crop. When pistachios are ripe, they are covered with a beautiful rose-colored skin. This skin encases the ivory-shelled nut. This skin and the inner hard shell split when the nut ripens and is ready to be harvested. The rose-colored outermost skin must be removed very soon after harvest or it will stain the inner hard shell. Pistachios with natural-colored shells have had their outer skins removed soon after harvest. The commercially dyed red shells so commonly found encasing pistachios traditionally hid the natural staining that occurred before harvesting and processing methods were improved. The shells have also been dyed to distinguish pistachios from other nuts in vending machines.

In baking it is best, as a rule, to use natural, unsalted nuts unless otherwise indicated. Pistachios should be stored in an airtight container to keep them from becoming soggy and stale. While unopened tins of pistachios will keep for up to three years, it is advisable to keep untinned or shelled nuts in a heavy-duty plastic bag in the freezer. Health food stores and shops specializing in Middle Eastern supplies often sell high-quality pistachios.

If a recipe calls for blanched pistachios, pour boiling water over shelled pistachios and let stand for five to ten minutes. Drain off the liquid and slip off the skin. After blanching, pistachios should be dried in a warm (250-degree) oven. Place the nuts in a single layer on a cookie sheet and dry for forty minutes to one hour. Check often to make sure they do not burn.

FLOUNDER WITH STEAMED SPINACH AND PISTACHIOS

You can substitute any white fish fillets for the flounder in this recipe.

1 cup water
1 chicken bouillon cube
1 pound clean, fresh spinach with stems
  removed
1 medium onion, minced
4 tablespoons butter
1½ pounds flounder fillets
1 cup white wine
2 shallots, minced
salt and pepper to taste
¾ cup pistachios, coarsely chopped

Bring the water to a boil in a large pot. Add the bouillon cube. When it dissolves, add the spinach and onion and cook, covered, until the spinach is wilted but not mushy. Drain and keep warm.

Melt the butter in a skillet and cook the fish over moderate-high heat for about 2–3 minutes on each side. Divide the spinach among 4 plates and place the fish on top. Add the wine and shallots to the skillet and cook for a minute or so, until the liquid reduces slightly. Add salt and pepper to taste. Add the pistachios and cook for 1 minute. Pour the glaze over the fish and serve immediately.

Serves 4

CALIFORNIA PISTACHIO PILAF

1 cup sliced mushrooms
½ cup brown rice
½ cup cracked wheat
½ cup chopped onion
2 tablespoons vegetable oil
2 tablespoons butter
*2 cups chicken stock (homemade or
   commercially prepared)*
¼ teaspoon celery salt
*½ cup dried Chinese mushrooms, stems cut off,
   sliced and soaked in warm water for 30
   minutes*
½ cup coarsely chopped pistachios
⅓ cup chopped fresh parsley
½ teaspoon grated lemon rind
2 tablespoons lemon juice
4 scallions, thinly sliced
salt and pepper to taste
2 tablespoons additional butter

In a large, heavy-bottomed pot sauté the mushrooms, rice, cracked wheat and onion in the oil and butter until the onion is golden and the rice begins to color. Add the chicken stock and celery salt. Bring to a boil and then reduce to a simmer. Cover and cook over low heat until all the liquid is absorbed, about 50 minutes. Stir in the Chinese mushrooms and all the remaining ingredients except the butter and fluff with a fork. Dot with the butter, cover and let stand for 3–4 minutes before serving.

Serves 6

PISTACHIO MARZIPAN

My good friend and baker extraordinaire Rose Levy Berenbaum developed this recipe for pistachio marzipan when she wanted to create something new and different for a wedding cake. I like to eat it plain, but you may want to dip yours in chocolate and roll it in chopped pistachios.

> *4 ounces shelled, natural-color, unsalted*
>   *pistachios*
> *12 ounces confectioners' sugar (about 3 cups,*
>   *unsifted)*
> *⅓ cup light corn syrup*
> *2 teaspoons glycerine (available in bakery*
>   *supply or cake decorating shops) or*
>   *unflavored vegetable oil*
> *8 drops green food coloring*

In a food processor fitted with the metal blade, process the pistachios until they form a paste. Add the confectioners' sugar and continue processing for 15 seconds or until well combined. In a small bowl combine the corn syrup, glycerine (or oil) and the food coloring. Stir to blend evenly. Add this mixture to the processor and process until well blended, about 20 seconds. The mixture will appear dry, but a small amount pressed between your fingers should hold together. If the mixture is too dry, add more corn syrup, ¼ teaspoon at a time. Continue processing until the marzipan has a smooth, doughlike consistency. Knead briefly by hand until the color is uniform. Wrap in plastic wrap so it is airtight.

TO DIP IN CHOCOLATE:

> *pistachio marzipan*
> *10 ounces bittersweet chocolate, chopped*
> *1 cup pistachios, chopped*

Break scant teaspoon-sized pieces of the marzipan and roll them into balls. Spread a 12-inch piece of wax paper on a cookie sheet. Melt the chocolate in a small metal bowl set over a pan of gently simmering water. Remove the chocolate from the heat. Place the chopped nuts in a shallow bowl. Dip the marzipan balls, one at a time, in the chocolate. Use a fork or toothpick to lift them out. Place the chocolate-covered balls directly into the chopped pistachios and use the fork to roll them around so that they are coated. Remove the balls to the wax paper to dry.

Makes about 3 dozen candies

CHOCOLATE PISTACHIO ICE CREAM ROLL

This frozen dessert will keep in your freezer until you get the urge to indulge. The sauce can be frozen too.

FOR THE CHOCOLATE ROLL:

8 extra-large eggs, separated and at room
temperature
1 cup granulated sugar
⅓ cup plus 1 tablespoon cocoa (not Dutch
process), sifted
¼ cup flour, sifted
additional cocoa (about ¼ cup)

Preheat the oven to 350 degrees with the rack in the center position. Line an 11 x 17-inch heavy-duty jelly-roll pan with parchment. Or butter the pan, line it with wax paper, butter the paper and dust it with flour.

Beat the egg yolks with ½ cup of the sugar in the large bowl of an electric mixer set on high speed until they are very thick and light in color. On low speed add the cocoa and flour. In a clean bowl with clean beaters, beat the egg whites with the remaining ½ cup of sugar until they hold firm peaks. Fold the 2 mixtures together and spread onto the prepared pan. Bake 12–15 minutes until the top is dry and firm. Cool in the pan. When the cake is cool, sift about ¼ cup of cocoa over the top and cover with 2 long overlapping sheets of plastic wrap. Place a cookie sheet or flat board over the plastic wrap and flip the cake over. Remove the pan and the parchment.

TO ASSEMBLE:

1½ pints best-quality pistachio ice cream
hot fudge sauce (see p. 241)
1 cup chopped, unsalted pistachios for garnish

Place the ice cream in the large bowl of an electric mixer and mix just until soft and spreadable. Spread the ice cream on the cake to within 1 inch of the edges. With 1 long edge of the cake facing you, use the plastic as an aid in rolling up the cake away from you so that you have a long roll. Roll the plastic around the cake and then wrap it in aluminum foil. Freeze for at least 2 hours or until ready to serve.

FOR THE HOT FUDGE SAUCE:

2 cups heavy cream
½ cup dark brown sugar, firmly packed
8 ounces semisweet chocolate, chopped
2 ounces unsweetened chocolate, chopped
3 tablespoons sweet (unsalted) butter, cut into
  small pieces
2–3 tablespoons rum or brandy (optional)

Scald the heavy cream in a 2-quart, heavy-bottomed pan and cook until it is reduced by half. You need a large pan because the cream tends to boil over. Lower the heat and stir in the brown sugar. Continue stirring until it melts. Remove from heat and stir in the chocolates, butter and rum. Stir until the sauce is smooth. Refrigerate until ready to serve. Serve warm or at room temperature.

TO SERVE THE CAKE:

Cut slices on the diagonal, ladle some sauce on top and garnish with the chopped pistachios.

Serves 10

PISTACHIO BROWNIES

½ cup sweet (unsalted) butter
2 ounces unsweetened chocolate
2 extra-large eggs
1 cup granulated sugar
½ cup all-purpose flour, measured after sifting
pinch salt
1 teaspoon almond extract
⅔ cup semisweet chocolate chips
½ cup coarsely chopped, shelled, natural-color
  pistachios

Preheat the oven to 350 degrees with the rack in the center position. Grease and flour an 8- or 9-inch square pan. Melt the butter and chocolate together in a small metal bowl set over gently simmering water. In the bowl of an electric mixer beat the eggs and sugar until the mixture is thick and holds a ribbon when the beater is lifted from the bowl. On low speed, mix in the butter and chocolate. Mix in the flour, salt and almond extract, mixing only until the batter is smooth. Do not overbeat. Stir in the chocolate chips. Pour the batter into the prepared pan and sprinkle the pistachios on top. Bake 25–30 minutes for the 8-inch pan, and no more than 25 minutes for the 9-inch pan. The center, when tested with a toothpick, should be moist, but not gooey. It is easier to cut these when they have cooled completely.

Makes 9 medium or 16 small brownies

Raspberries

My father has a great big, shiny white freezer in his basement. This freezer is filled with raspberries. Here's an idea of how much my father loves raspberries: there is a lock built into the front of his freezer and he has the only key; he keeps this key on his person at all times, except when he is sleeping, and then he keeps it hidden inside the chest next to his bed. Inside the freezer are hundreds of opaque plastic one-pint containers with red lids. On each lid is a piece of tape upon which is written the date the raspberries were frozen. My dad has containers with '78 and '81 on the labels. "Those were great years," he says.

My father has a "relationship" with a woman we call the "raspberry lady." When her crop is ready she calls my dad. He hops into his car, burns rubber all the way out to her farm and, in cash, buys up whatever she has to sell. This journey is made a dozen or so times each summer, so by the end of the season, the trunk of his car is stained with errant berries that have jiggled out of their containers and gotten squashed between the flats.

Each time my father returns from one of his raspberry runs, my mother is pressed into service. She places several dozen plastic containers on the kitchen table. My father lovingly loads each container seven-eighths full with fruit. My mother sprinkles a generous tablespoon of sugar over the tops. The red lids go on, the pieces of tape are applied, the year inscribed. The containers are then whisked to the basement, where they are entombed in the great frosty strongbox. Only one container of berries is not processed this way. This is the container my father eats — so he'll know the quality of that vintage.

When we arrive at my parents' home for a visit, I don't waste any time hinting for some raspberries. Hinting doesn't work; I have to ask outright.

"Hey, Dad, how about some raspberries."

"Oh, you don't like raspberries," he replies. (I don't like raspberries? I would happily trade in one of my children for a couple of pints.)

"Come on, Grandpa," say my children in chorus. (They would happily trade in both their parents for raspberries.) "Unlock the freezer and get some out."

At this point, my mother, who thinks my father's hoarding is ridiculous, usually offers to make a raspberry-blueberry pie if he'll cooperate by providing the main ingredient. My mother's raspberry-blueberry pies are out of this world. We can see that he might be swayed.

With great resignation he'll move toward the basement steps. My mother tries to console him by reminding him that there are enough berries downstairs to make several hundred pies without even making a dent in his supply. Even so, when he returns from the basement he has fetched only half the berries needed to make a pie, and has to be sent back again to get more.

My father once asked me if I wanted him to leave me the grand piano in his will. I said forget the piano. I wanted the freezer — with the raspberries.

❧ Raspberries ❧

SUMMER is raspberry time. Whether you grow your own (it's easy to do!) or buy them at the store, use your nose to tell you if you're picking the winners. The more fragrant the smell, the more wonderful the flavor. Look for firm (not hard) uniformly red berries. If they are dull-looking or have any mold, then they will not taste good. If they are soft and squishy, they are over the hill. It is best not to refrigerate them, and since they begin to lose their flavor immediately after they are picked, try to pick or buy them the day you plan to use them. When I have a bumper crop, I freeze the unwashed berries in pint-sized plastic containers. If you wish, you can spread the berries out on a tray, freeze them that way and then put them in heavy-duty plastic bags after they are frozen solid. The frozen berries are perfect for making sauces or ice cream.

There is a fancy new addition to the already existing dozen or so varieties of raspberries: golden raspberries. They don't look or taste enough like the "real thing" to make them worth the price to this raspberry lover.

QUICK RASPBERRY SAUCE

*2½ cups fresh or previously frozen raspberries
  (unsweetened)
½ cup superfine sugar
¼ cup Framboise (optional)*

Place all the above ingredients in a blender or food processor and puree until smooth. If you find the sauce lacks flavor, try adding a couple of spoonfuls of raspberry preserves and a few drops of lemon juice.

Makes 1½ cups

RASPBERRIES GRATIN

I first had this sublime dish at Maison Robert, the beautiful restaurant in Boston's Old City Hall. The dishes preceding it were unusual and delicious, reflecting the talents of the chef, Pierre Jamet. But the most spectacular dish, as far as I was concerned, was the following raspberry dessert. It is very important to use flavorful raspberries. The sabayon can be made ahead.

FOR THE SABAYON:

*3 extra-large egg yolks
1 tablespoon water
½ cup granulated sugar
½ cup Framboise
1 pint (2 cups) heavy cream*

Combine the egg yolks, water and sugar in a small, heavy-bottomed saucepan. Whisking constantly and vigorously, cook over low heat until the mixture is well combined. Continue cooking only until the mixture is foamy and just begins to thicken. Immediately remove from the heat and strain into a metal bowl. Stir in the liqueur and refrigerate, covered, until cold. Whip the cream until it holds soft peaks and fold it into the cooled mixture.

TO ASSEMBLE:

3 pints (6 cups) flavorful raspberries

Preheat the broiler to high with the rack 3–4 inches from the upper element. Scatter the berries over the bottom of an 8-cup gratin dish with low sides or divide among eight 1-cup individual dishes and place the dish(es) in a roasting pan with low sides or on a heavy-duty baking sheet. Pour the sauce over the berries and broil until the top is browned and bubbling, about 1–2 minutes. Serve immediately.

Serves 8

MERINGUE NESTS WITH RASPBERRIES

The following ice cream dessert is easy to put together at the last minute if you make the meringue nests ahead of time. This recipe can be served with a raspberry sauce (see p. 228 or p. 246).

FOR THE MERINGUE NESTS:

6 extra-large egg whites at room temperature
1 cup granulated sugar

Preheat the oven to 200 degrees with the racks as near the center position as possible. Line 2 heavy-duty baking pans with foil. Beat the egg whites either by hand or in the bowl of an electric mixer, adding the sugar gradually. Continue to beat until the meringue is very shiny and stiff. Place the meringue in a large pastry tube fitted with a large star tip and pipe ten to twelve 4-inch rings (no bottom), then pipe another ring on top of those rings. Bake the nests for half an hour, then let them sit in the turned-off oven with the door closed for another hour. Store them uncovered and unrefrigerated until ready to use. They will keep for up to a week in a dry place.

> *2 pints best-quality vanilla ice cream (or, if*
>   *you can get it, Ben and Jerry's raspberry*
>   *ice cream)*
> *2 pints (4 cups) fresh raspberries*
> *2 cups raspberry sauce (see p. 228 or p. 246)*

Place a meringue nest on a dessert plate. Place a scoop of ice cream on the nest. Top with raspberries. Pass the sauce separately.

Serves 10

$\mathcal{R}$ASPBERRIES AND CREAM

Simply delicious.

> *2 pints fresh raspberries*
> *2 cups heavy cream, chilled*
> *2 tablespoons confectioners' sugar*
> *4 tablespoons Framboise or Kirsch*

Divide the berries among 6 bowls. Whip the cream with the sugar and then add the liqueur. Spoon over the berries.

Serves 6

RASPBERRY-BLACKBERRY SHORTCAKE

6 baking powder biscuits (see recipe below)
1 pint fresh raspberries
1 pint fresh blackberries
1½ cups Quick Raspberry Sauce (see recipe on
p. 246)
1 cup heavy cream, whipped with 2 teaspoons
vanilla extract and 1 tablespoon
confectioners' sugar

Split the biscuits and place the bottom half of each biscuit in one of 6 shallow bowls. Top with berries and then the other half of the biscuit. Spoon on some sauce and then top with a dollop of whipped cream.

Serves 6

QUICK BAKING POWDER BISCUITS

2 cups flour, measured after sifting
1 tablespoon baking powder
4 teaspoons granulated sugar
pinch of salt
½ teaspoon cream of tartar
8 tablespoons butter, very cold and cut into
pieces
⅔ cup milk
1 egg yolk
granulated sugar

Preheat the oven to 400 degrees with the rack in the center position. Line a baking sheet with parchment or line it with foil and butter the foil. Sift the flour together with the baking powder, sugar, salt and cream of tartar into a large mixing bowl. Cut in the butter (this can be done with two butter knives or in a food processor) until the mixture resembles coarse meal. Mix together the milk and egg yolk. Dribble into the dry mixture and stir briefly. Turn out onto a floured board and knead about 10 times. Roll out to a 1-inch thickness. Cut with a cookie cutter into 2½-inch rounds. Place the biscuits about 1 inch apart on the baking sheet, sprinkle lightly with sugar and bake for 15–18 minutes or until golden brown.

Makes 10–12 biscuits

Roquefort

On the small town of Hillsdale, New York, in the rolling Catskill Mountains, just over the Massachusetts border, there is a stately colonial red brick building at the town's major intersection. This lovely building with its well-cared-for exterior and delft blue shutters used to be a way station on the Boston Post Road. Now it houses one of the finest restaurants in the northeast.

The L'Hostellerie Bressane (formerly the Dutch Hearth Inn) is run by Jean and Madeleine Morel, originally from Lyons, France. Jean cooks delicious and elegant meals and Madeleine runs the "front of the house." The interior of the restaurant (which has four bedrooms upstairs for those diners wishing to spend the night) is as beautiful as the exterior. Blue-stenciled whitewashed walls and wide golden oak floorboards that alternate with darker-stained boards give the feeling of comfort and homey elegance. There are working fireplaces in each of the restaurant's dining rooms. Even though it is a three-hour drive from our house near Boston to Hillsdale, we have been known to get into the car and drive there just for dinner, driving back the same night. That's how much we love the place.

One spring weekend David, our friend Kitty Boles and I headed up to Hillsdale and the L'Hostellerie Bressane for a weekend of good food, country air and general relaxation. A Saturday evening at L'Hostellerie Bressane draws elegantly dressed couples from New York City, local patrons from the environs of Hillsdale and in the summer, the Tanglewood crowd from Stockbridge. Arriving in good time, we donned our fancy clothes and headed downstairs to the bar for a leisurely drink before dinner. Kitty, on weekend leave from New York City, was mellowing out; she had threatened to never go back to the city. At nine we went in to dinner.

The evening had cooled, so there were fires in the fireplaces. The brass sconces cast a soft, warm light in which every woman looked beautiful and every man handsome. The tables were set with heavy silverware and crystal glasses. From the kitchen came delicious smells that excited my already rumbling stomach. We had a wonderful table with a great view of the rest of the room. The waiter was a formal gray-haired gentleman in his sixties. He stood very erect and moved with great precision and grace around the dining room. It was clear that he knew what he was doing. We smiled with anticipation as he approached our table with the menus.

The waiter handed the menus around and then asked David if the ladies would like another cocktail before dinner. I rolled my eyes at Kitty. The waiter returned with the wine list, which he automatically gave to David. Perhaps he thought we couldn't read. I frowned at Kitty. Betty Friedan and I were not happy. We perused the menu. David decided to have sweetbreads and chestnuts. Kitty opted for the duck. I chose the lamb. The waiter approached to take our order and of course looked directly at David when he asked what the ladies would like to have for dinner. I opened my mouth to speak and David gave me a swift kick. I closed my mouth and settled for giving the waiter a dirty look. The waiter made one more pass to ask David which wine he had selected and I lost my cool. Before David had another chance to bruise my shin I said, "I'm curious to know why you always ask the man what the ladies will have. Don't you think that we can speak?"

He stood up even straighter (if possible) and said in a heavy French accent, "Madame, the function of women in a fine restaurant is to look beautiful, enjoy the meal and keep silent."

"I think that's a load of bull," I responded diplomatically. The waiter raised one already very arched eyebrow, turned on his heel and left without hearing David say what kind of wine the ladies would like to accompany their meal.

"Well, big mouth, there goes the service," my husband said. I was torn between anger and remorse. I had done Gloria Steinem proud, but I was going to pay for it by starving myself, my husband and my best friend.

Fifteen minutes later the waiter made another pass. He studiously avoided looking in my direction while he took the wine order. Kitty, who had just come back from a year in Paris, began to speak to him in her perfect French. He seemed to soften a bit. As their conversation went on he may even have given her the merest hint of a smile. Kitty seemed to be salvaging the evening. Our food arrived without too much delay and it was dazzling. Between each course the waiter came back to chat with Kitty in French. By the time dessert came he was clearly smitten — putty in her hands. We ordered the delicious praline crepes that are made at the tableside. Kitty, of course, was served first and got the biggest helping. But by that point I had consumed so much wine and good food that I was feeling most forgiving.

Suddenly our waiter came over and asked Kitty, in French, if she would like to see the Roquefort in one of the other dining rooms. At least that's what I thought I heard him say. Equally confused, Kitty said, *"Comment?"* Again he asked if she would like to see the Roquefort in one of the other dining rooms. Kitty looked at us, shrugged her shoulders, pushed back her chair and followed the waiter into another room. When she returned, several minutes later, she looked as if she had seen a ghost. "What's wrong?" we cried. She looked dazed. Her face was drained of color. She moved as if she were in a trance. David got up to take her arm to help her sit down. "Kitty, speak. Say something," we implored.

"Robert Redford is having dinner in the other dining room," Kitty said and slumped into her chair.

Roquefort — Redford. I suddenly got the connection. My all-time number one passion (did I or did I not see *Butch Cassidy and the Sundance Kid* ten times and *The Sting* at least that many?) was only a room away!

"Kitty, what did he look like? Who was he with? Was he short?

Tall? Is his hair bleached? Is he really gorgeous? Did he look at you? What was he eating? Who is he with? Kitty, tell me!"

"I just couldn't believe it was him," she murmured weakly. "I don't remember anything except that I thought I was either going to faint or have a heart attack. I'm still not sure it happened at all." I started to get up to see for myself and instantly felt two iron hands clamp around my shoulders, forcing me back into my chair.

"Lora," said Jean Morel into my ear in his thick accent, "you do not go into zat dining room. Zat poor man deserves to have his dinner in peace wizout all zee women in ziz place trampling in for a look." I sat back down. I did not, however, promise him that I would not do my damnedest to get a glimpse of Robert Redford some other way. We raced through dessert — at least Kitty and I did. David was speechless with amazement at our juvenile conduct, and he frustrated us by taking his sweet time with dessert. Finally he paid the bill and we headed for the bar — the only exit from the restaurant — where we carefully positioned ourselves for "the sighting."

David, who thought that our hysteria was dumb beyond belief, was happy to sit in the bar sipping cognac and watch us make jackasses of ourselves. We were joined at some point by a piano player who, when he heard whom we were lying in wait for, sat down and started to play the music from *The Sting* written by Scott Joplin. The restaurant was emptying out and only one or two tables remained occupied. Our man was at one of those. He was taking a very long time eating his dinner.

One of the waiters (not ours) now off duty asked if I knew how to dance the Charleston. I did, and we took up what little space there was in the bar flapping our hands and kicking our feet to the ragtime tempo. I was facing the dining room when HE came into the bar. My heart stopped, but I kept dancing. Was it really him? Yes! Was he gorgeous? Yes! Was he short? Who cared? Did he pass within two feet of me, look right into my eyes and smile? Yes! Yes! Yes! Did I swoon? Are you crazy? I don't mind making a spectacle of myself, but there are limits. He and his wife and another couple filed through the narrow room and we kept on dancing. After all, I wanted him to think of me in a different class than those hysterical groupies who mob him at every turn screaming uncontrollably.

As soon as they were out the door, Kitty and I rushed over to the window (I, leaving my rather confused dance partner on the floor flapping away by himself) to watch Robert Redford and his wife and their friends climb into their car (green Ford Fairlane station wagon, fake wood siding, automatic V6 engine, new snow tires) and turn left out of the drive. Kitty and I grabbed each other and shrieked uncontrollably. David ordered another cognac.

I was so revved up that I had to share my sighting with the world. It was two A.M. but I knew she wouldn't mind. I raced over to the pay phone in the lobby and dialed.

"Hello?" she said in a sleepy voice.

"Mom! Mom! Wake up! It's me. You'll never guess . . ."

"Are you all right, dear? Is everything okay?" Her voice took on a worried edge and she began to sound awake.

"Yes, yes. Mom, listen. We're in Hillsdale — you know, at the inn? Well, you'll never in a million years guess who we saw here. Somebody fantastic."

"Well, it can't be your father, because he's right here sound asleep. Was it Paul Newman?" Good old Mom, at least she was in the ballpark.

"No, Mom. It was Robert Roquefort, I mean Redford."

"I get it, you mean he's a big cheese . . . ha ha." Even half asleep my mother was a card. "Well dear, it sounds like you've had quite an evening. I hope you haven't forgotten David in all the excitement. Good night."

Sheepishly I looked over to the bar, where my husband had fallen asleep with his head cradled in his arms. In front of him in a neat line were four empty brandy glasses. I gently pulled David's arm to get him headed up to bed, and I tucked into my memory bank an instant photo of that famous smile, and into the safe-deposit box of extraordinary feelings next to my heart went the electric zing of making eye contact with Robert Redford.

⅍ Roquefort ⅍

ROQUEFORT, a sheep's milk cheese, has been called the King of the Blues. Its rich, creamy-smooth texture is moist and firm, yet spreadable. Less salty than the other blue-veined cheeses, the assertive flavor is a result of both the sheep grazing areas (75 percent from the area around Roquefort, 12–15 percent from the French Basque country and 10–12 percent from Corsica) and the natural limestone caves in which the cheese is matured. The sheep's milk procured from areas outside Roquefort is shipped to Roquefort to spend time in these unique caves.

This cheese is a sublime match for big red wines, sherry and port. To make sure you are buying authentic Roquefort cheese, look for a red oval sticker with a sheep in the middle, "Roquefort" above it and "France" below it. Look for firm white cheese with lots of blue veining. The cheese should look moist, but not wet, and not have salt crystals on it. It is a good idea to buy cheese that has been tightly wrapped in plastic so that no air has come in contact with it during storage — this makes the cheese dry out and increases the salt content. The taste is supposed to be tangy and somewhat sharp, but if it stings the back of the tongue, or smells of ammonia, this means the cheese is past its peak. Roquefort will keep for several weeks if well wrapped and refrigerated.

BLUE CHEESE CHEESECAKE

This most unusual appetizer will raise some eyebrows when you serve it. After one bite, your guests' taste buds will salute you! A savory cheesecake is a novel idea, and this particular one with its combination of blue cheese and bacon is a real winner. It makes a superb first course or cocktail buffet dish.

Like all cheesecakes, this is best made in a food processor, but you can make it with a mixer too. If you do make it with a mixer, make sure the cream cheese is at room temperature so that you aren't tempted to overmix it. This will result in air bubbles that will cause the cheesecake to rise in the oven and then fall when cooling, resulting in nasty cracks on the top. *Also, don't use the cream cheese sold by the pound in supermarkets and delis.* It has air whipped into it.

I have used Roquefort, Danish blue and Stilton cheese to make this cake. Any full-bodied blue cheese will do; if you like the way the cheese tastes on a cracker, you'll like the way it tastes in this cheesecake. You can replace the bacon with pieces of cooked ham if you like.

This cheesecake does not freeze well, but will keep, refrigerated and well wrapped, for up to a week.

⅓ cup fine bread crumbs
¼ cup plus 3 tablespoons Parmesan cheese, freshly grated
1 medium onion, finely chopped
3 tablespoons butter
½ pound blue cheese such as Roquefort, Danish blue or Stilton, crumbled
3½ 8-ounce packages best-quality cream cheese at room temperature
4 extra-large eggs
⅓ cup heavy cream
½ pound lean bacon, cooked until very crisp, crumbled
a few drops Tabasco sauce
freshly ground pepper

Preheat the oven to 300 degrees with the rack in the center position. Butter an 8 x 3-inch cheesecake pan. *This is not a springform pan.*

You can find cheesecake pans in gourmet shops and kitchen supply stores. Line the bottom with a circle of parchment or wax paper. Butter the paper. Mix the bread crumbs and Parmesan cheese together and use this mixture to coat the inside of the buttered pan. Shake out the excess crumbs.

Sauté the onion in the 3 tablespoons of butter. Place the blue cheese, cream cheese, eggs and heavy cream in either the work bowl of a food processor fitted with the metal blade or the bowl of an electric mixer. Process or mix at medium speed for 30 seconds or until smooth. Add the onion, bacon, Tabasco and pepper. Process or mix for 10 more seconds or just until the ingredients are incorporated. Scrape the mixture into the prepared pan, smooth the top and bang the pan on the counter a few times to get rid of air bubbles. Place this pan into a roasting pan and place both pans in the oven. Add enough water to the roasting pan to come halfway up the sides of the cheesecake pan. The edges of the 2 pans should not touch.

Bake 1 hour and 40 minutes. Halfway through the baking time, check to make sure there is enough water in the roasting pan. At the end of the baking time, turn off the oven but leave the door closed. At the end of another hour, remove the pans from the oven and let the cake sit. Do not unmold and do not be tempted to refrigerate the cheesecake in the pan to hasten the cooling process. This will make it difficult to remove the cheesecake. To remove, place a sheet of plastic wrap over the top of the pan and then a flat plate over that. Invert the cake onto the plate. You may have to slam the pan a few times to loosen the cake. Remove the parchment or wax paper. Place a flat plate on top (really the bottom) and invert. Remove the plastic wrap.

TO SERVE:

Cut thin wedges with a hot, sharp knife.

Serves about 15 as a first course

TANGLEWOOD SANDWICHES

Years ago when my parents first took me to Tanglewood, the Berkshire home of the Boston Symphony Orchestra, men wore dinner jackets and ladies wore long gowns and white gloves. The most elegant picnics imaginable were laid out on starched linen tablecloths set with silver and crystal. Times, of course, have changed and denim and California wines have taken over the scene. Patchwork quilts have replaced the fancy linen tablecloths and plastic forks and paper plates are more popular than china and silver. The food is still wonderful, though. Our family has its own favorite Tanglewood picnic menu and the star of the show is the following sandwich.

Coat a slice of pumpernickel bread (preferably the kind with Russian caraway on the crust) with a couple of tablespoons of Major Grey's mango chutney and another slice with grainy mustard. Add a couple of leaves of lettuce — we prefer Boston lettuce — and then a fairly thick slab of Roquefort cheese. If your cheese is crumbly, sprinkle on those crumbs and flatten them with a knife. Next comes a choice: either a layer of rare, sliced roast beef, or real turkey breast. NOT TURKEY ROLL! The meat of your choice is topped with several rings of thinly sliced Bermuda onion and the other piece of bread. Wrap each sandwich you make in foil to keep it fresh in transit. These sandwiches mellow considerably if you make them at least an hour ahead. It is best to keep them in a cooler until serving time.

Makes 1 delicious sandwich

$\mathcal{H}$ERBED ROQUEFORT RICE

1 cup long grain rice
4 tablespoons butter
1 cup water
1 cup milk
½ cup white wine
1 chicken bouillon cube
several sprigs of fresh thyme or 1 teaspoon
    dried thyme
6 leaves fresh basil, chopped, or ½ teaspoon
    dried basil
½ teaspoon dried marjoram
½ teaspoon dried chervil
⅔ cup crumbled Roquefort cheese
freshly grated black pepper
salt to taste
½ cup freshly grated Parmesan cheese

Place the rice, butter, water, milk, wine, bouillon cube and herbs in a 2-quart pot. Place a double layer of white paper towels over the top and cover the pot tightly. Set over moderate heat and when the liquid comes to a boil, lower the heat and cook for 20 minutes without removing the cover. Turn the heat off and let the pot sit, covered, for 10 more minutes. Stir in the Roquefort cheese and pepper. Taste for seasoning (you shouldn't need too much more salt because the bouillon and the cheese are both salty). Spoon the rice into a broiler-proof casserole and top with the Parmesan cheese. Place the dish under the broiler until the cheese turns brown and crusty.

To cook the rice in the microwave oven, place the rice, butter, liquids and herbs in a 2-quart glass bowl. Cover lightly with plastic wrap and place a heavy glass plate on top. Microwave for 10 minutes, stir and then microwave 5–6 more minutes. Be careful to lift the edge of the plastic farthest away from you to prevent steam burns. Follow the rest of the above directions to finish the rice under the broiler.

Serves 6–8

BEST ROQUEFORT DRESSING

The ingredients for this dressing come in two parts, creating a creamy Roquefort base with crumbled cheese in it.

PART ONE:

2 tablespoons peanut oil
dash of Worcestershire sauce
1 tablespoon grated Parmesan cheese
¼ teaspoon each: onion salt, garlic powder,
    salt, freshly ground pepper
1 teaspoon granulated sugar
¼ cup red wine vinegar
2 tablespoons fresh lemon juice
1 ounce (2 tablespoons) Roquefort cheese,
    crumbled

PART TWO:

1 cup commercial mayonnaise
½ cup sour cream or plain yogurt
3 ounces (6 tablespoons) Roquefort cheese,
    crumbled

Combine all the ingredients of part one in the work bowl of a food processor and process until smooth. Spoon into a bowl and fold in the ingredients of part two. This dressing will keep 2 weeks stored in a tightly sealed glass jar in the refrigerator.

Makes 2 cups

ROQUEFORT AND RED POTATO SALAD

3 pounds small red potatoes
2 tablespoons chopped fresh dill or 1 teaspoon
 dried dill
1 bunch scallions (both green and white parts),
 sliced into ¼-inch slices
4 sprigs parsley, chopped
¾ cup black or green olives, diced
ingredients for 2 cups Best Roquefort Dressing
 (see p. 261)

Cut the potatoes into quarters and cook them in boiling salted water until just tender. Drain well. Place the potatoes into a large glass bowl and sprinkle with the dill. Pour the mixed ingredients of part one of the Best Roquefort Dressing over the potatoes and toss gently. Chill for 1 hour. Just before serving add the scallions, parsley, olives and the mixed ingredients of part two of the dressing.

Serves 8–10

Saffron

*I*n the fifth grade all the boys got to take woodworking, where they made plaques with their names burned into them or lopsided tree houses. All the girls got to take home ec (it was always called home ec, and it wasn't until I was much older that I figured out that the "ec" was short for economics), where we made cobblers' aprons and baking powder biscuits. My apron was made out of shiny cotton with Scottie dogs on it and looked like something a three-hundred-pound turtle might wear to lay eggs in.

The first biscuits prepared by the class were pretty boring. I guess our teacher thought they were pretty boring too, because she suggested that each of us girls bring something from home to mix into the batter to make them more interesting. She assured us that while the success of any dish depended upon the cook's following the recipe, it was perfectly acceptable to add some touches of our own.

Some of the "touches" we girls brought in were interesting indeed. There were black currants, golden raisins and citron. Poppy seeds, lemon rind, chopped dates and candied ginger. Grated Parmesan cheese, fresh buttermilk and chocolate chips. The Indian girl in our home ec class, whose family was from Bombay, brought the most interesting ingredient of all. It came in a tiny, lacquered-paper, egg-shaped box no bigger than the palm of her hand. The little container was hand-painted with tiny flowers and birds on a deep blue background. We crowded around her with excitement to see what treasure could possibly come in such ornate wrappings. She lifted the lid, and inside the gold-lined box, lying on a tiny piece of silvery paper was, to our great disappointment, what looked like several microscopic pieces of red thread.

"Oh!" said our teacher, her eyes lighting up with pleasure. "You've brought in some saffron." She went on to tell us how rare and valuable real saffron was and that we were in for a treat, as this was a most exotic and unusual spice. She brought a small pan of milk to a simmer, rubbed the strands between her fingers and dropped them into the hot milk. As she stirred, the liquid took on a soft yet intense red-orange color. We sniffed the air, enjoying the strange and fragrant aroma of places and cultures that were a world away.

"You could rub the saffron right into the biscuit dough if you wanted," said our teacher as she poured the hot milk into the dry ingredients, "but I thought it would be more fun to show you how it colored the milk. Besides," she added, "isn't it fun to have orange biscuits?"

It was fun.

By the way, I never wore that apron.

❧ Saffron ❦

THE stigmas of the saffron-bearing *Crocus sativus* (the finest are grown in Spain) add a distinctive golden hue and delicate flavor to the following recipes, as well as to traditional dishes such as paella and bouillabaisse. Harvested in the late fall, the fresh strands are spread out to dry. It takes approximately sixty thousand flowers to make one pound of saffron. The saffron is harvested by hand, which make it easy to see why it is such a costly spice.

Saffron comes in three grades: coupe (the top grade), which is completely red in color with no bits of yellow; superior, containing 90 percent red stigmas (the other 10 percent is made up of the style, another part of the plant that is yellow in color); and the third grade, called selecta, which contains the largest amount of yellow.

While saffron comes in powdered form, it is better to buy the more expensive threads for two reasons: you can see exactly what you are getting, and the threads go a longer way than the powder. Saffron should be heated to release the oils before you use it. The easiest (and safest) way is to line the baking sheet of a toaster oven with foil, place the saffron on it and heat for two to three minutes at a moderate heat (350 degrees). Steeping the threads in warm liquid before using will also release the flavor. Saffron will keep for several months when stored in an airtight container away from heat and direct sunlight. Although the price is high, you only need a very small amount to color or add flavor to a dish. Beware of "bargains"; if the price is low, chances are what you are buying is not real saffron.

SAFFRON SCONES WITH CURRANTS

Scones are an "upper crust" member of the biscuit family. These freeze beautifully.

> ¼ teaspoon saffron threads
> 2 tablespoons plus 1 cup boiling water
> ½ cup dried currants
> 2 cups all-purpose flour, measured after sifting
> 1 tablespoon granulated sugar
> 2 teaspoons baking powder
> ½ teaspoon salt
> ½ teaspoon baking soda
> 5 tablespoons cold, sweet (unsalted) butter
> 1 egg, separated
> 1 cup sour cream or plain yogurt
> 1 tablespoon sugar combined with ¼ teaspoon
>   cinnamon

Preheat the oven to 400 degrees with the rack in the center position. Line a baking sheet with parchment, or lightly grease and flour the baking sheet. Place the saffron in a small bowl or measuring cup and pour the 2 tablespoons of boiling water over it. Let stand while assembling the other ingredients. Pour the additional 1 cup of boiling water over the currants and let them soak for 5 minutes. Drain well and discard the water.

Place the flour, sugar, baking powder, salt and baking soda in the work bowl of a food processor and blend for 15 seconds. Cut the butter into small pieces and add to the processor. Blend by turning the machine on and off several times until the mixture looks like coarse meal. Empty the mixture into a medium-sized bowl. Stir in the currants. Beat the egg yolk slightly with the saffron and the water and the sour cream or yogurt. Make a well in the dry mixture and add the wet mixture all at once, stirring with a fork or your hand until a dough is formed. Turn out onto a floured board and knead 10–12 times to make a smooth dough. Pat into a 9-inch round. Cut out three 4-inch circles and gently stack the trimmings to make one more 4-inch circle. Transfer the circles to the baking sheet and cut through the circles to quarter them, but *do not separate them*. Brush with the egg white and sprinkle with the cinnamon sugar. Bake for 15–20 minutes or until an even golden brown.

Makes 16 scones

SPICED CHICKEN WITH SAFFRON RICE

FOR THE CHICKEN:

1 broiling chicken, quartered
2 cups plain yogurt
1 large onion, finely diced
¼ cup soy sauce
1 teaspoon dry mustard
1 teaspoon ground ginger
½ teaspoon turmeric
½ teaspoon cardamom
1 teaspoon ground coriander or ½ cup chopped
  fresh coriander (cilantro)
1 teaspoon salt

Preheat the oven to 350 degrees with the rack in the lower third but not the lowest position. Arrange the chicken pieces in 1 layer in a shallow roasting pan. Combine all the other ingredients in a small bowl, mix well and spread over the chicken. Bake for 50 minutes. While the chicken is cooking prepare the rice.

FOR THE RICE:

4 tablespoons butter
1 medium onion, finely chopped
1 cup long grain rice
1 cup dry white wine
1 cup water
1 chicken bouillon cube
¼ teaspoon saffron threads
1 bay leaf

Melt the butter in a 2-quart pot and sauté the onion until it is translucent. Add the rice and cook it until it becomes pale gold in color. Add the other ingredients. Place a double thickness of white paper towels over the top of the pot and then cover the pot as tightly as possible. Cook over low heat for 20 minutes and then turn off the heat and let the rice sit for another 20 minutes, covered. Remove the bay leaf before serving.

Serves 4

SCALLOPS WITH SAFFRON CREAM SAUCE

1½ pounds scallops (if you use the larger sea
scallops, pull off the small hard muscle and
quarter the scallops)
4 tablespoons butter
4 shallots, peeled and minced
⅔ cup dry white wine
1 cup heavy cream
4 threads saffron
salt and white pepper to taste

Rinse the scallops and remove the small tough muscle. Heat the butter in a large, heavy skillet, add the scallops and cook them over high heat, shaking the pan briskly back and forth to keep the scallops moving. Cook the scallops for 3–4 minutes; overcooking makes them tough. Remove the scallops to a warm serving dish and add the shallots and wine to the skillet. Cook over very high heat until the wine is reduced to a glaze. Whisk in the cream and saffron and cook for 2 minutes over very high heat, scraping the pan to loosen the bits stuck on the bottom. Add the salt and white pepper to taste and pour over the scallops. This dish is delicious served with buttered spaghetti squash.

Serves 6

CARROT SOUP WITH SAFFRON CREAM

This soup can be served hot or cold. It freezes beautifully.

> 3 large potatoes, peeled and cut into 2-inch
>   cubes
> 3 pounds carrots, peeled and sliced
> 6 cups chicken stock (canned or homemade)
> 3 tablespoons butter
> 3 medium-sized onions, chopped
> 2 teaspoons dried thyme
> 1 teaspoon celery salt
> 2 teaspoons Worcestershire sauce
> 2–3 dashes Tabasco sauce
> salt and pepper to taste
> 1–2 cups light cream or milk
> saffron cream and fresh chives for garnish

Cook the potatoes and carrots together with the stock in a large covered pot until they are very tender, about 40 minutes. Cool slightly. In a heavy skillet set over medium heat, melt the butter. Lower the heat, add the onions and cook, stirring occasionally, until they are translucent, but not brown. Stir in the thyme. In a food processor or blender, puree the cooked potatoes and carrots, along with the stock, about 2 cups at a time. Add the onions to the last batch to be pureed and combine all the puree in the stockpot. Add the seasonings. Stir in as much cream as necessary to give desired consistency.

Garnish with the following saffron cream and fresh chives.

FOR THE SAFFRON CREAM:

> 1 heaping teaspoon saffron threads
> ½ teaspoon granulated sugar
> ½ teaspoon salt
> freshly ground pepper
> 2 teaspoons boiling water
> 2 tablespoons sour cream
> 1 cup heavy cream, whipped
> ¾ cup plain yogurt

Toast the saffron threads according to the directions on p. 265. With a mortar and pestle, grind the saffron, sugar, salt and pepper to a fine powder. Add the boiling water and stir to incorporate every bit of saffron. Blend in the sour cream. Use a rubber scraper to scoop out the saffron mixture and fold it into the whipped cream. Fold in the yogurt. Cover and chill until serving time.

Serves 8

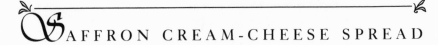

SAFFRON CREAM-CHEESE SPREAD

Use this on date nut bread to make unusual tea sandwiches.

> *¼ teaspoon saffron threads, toasted (see p. 265)*
> *and then crushed but not powdered*
> *2 teaspoons Grand Marnier*
> *1 8-ounce package cream cheese, at room*
> *temperature*
> *finely grated rind of 1 orange*
> *2 teaspoons honey*

Sprinkle saffron over the Grand Marnier in a small cup, stir and set aside. Beat the cream cheese either by hand or in a food processor. Add the orange rind and honey. Add the Grand Marnier/saffron mixture and stir well. Refrigerate for several hours before using. Bring to room temperature before spreading.

Makes 1 cup

Smoked Salmon

hen Julia Child came to dinner I envied my other guests — they had to concern themselves only with what to wear and what to say. I had to worry about what to cook. I got so much advice from family and friends that in the end I made my favorite dishes and that was that. It was spring and warm enough for cold soup, so the first course was cold borscht. The main course was supplied by a wonderful business friend of David's who for a few weeks each year rents part of a river in Iceland and catches magnificent salmon. He presented one to us a week before the dinner. I defrosted it and filleted it, then made an unusual kind of gravlax by rubbing the fillets with cognac, coarse salt, white pepper and sugar. I packed the fillets in green peppercorns, wrapped it all well in foil and placed heavy weights on it for five days.

The day of the dinner things went smoothly, probably because I had been smart enough to make dishes I had made many times before. The last thing I needed was a surprise. We had just moved and I guess our new neighbors were pretty impressed that Julia was coming to dinner. Some of them were sort of hanging out on their porches watching for her arrival. I know this because as her car pulled into the driveway I heard the little boy across the street scream at the top of his lungs, "Hey, Mom! She's here. That lady's here!" Subtle welcome.

I was going to grill the gravlax just before I served it. This is the way it is prepared at the Four Seasons restaurant in New York, and it gives the fish an outstanding taste while allowing you to serve what is usually a cold first course as a hot entree. The salmon, already cured by the action of the salt and sugar, is generously brushed with melted butter and lime juice. It is then placed under the broiler for a few minutes, until the top is bubbly and turns crispy brown. The fish is cooked only on one side, so the inside is very tender. The combination of textures is sublimely delicate and the taste is perfection. I made a honey-mustard sauce to go with it.

Since there was to be a pause between courses and since my two oldest sons (then eight and ten years old) were dying to get into the act, I let them "entertain" the guests while I cooked. They wrapped themselves up in large white aprons (which went several times around their waists and fell to the tops of their sneakers), donned their Groucho Marx glasses — the kind with the bushy eyebrows and big nose — and with great ceremony brought their course to the table. Lying on a silver tray, garnished with radish roses and sprigs of parsley, was a rubber chicken. Barely controlling their giggles, they marched around to Julia's chair and told her that this was a dish they had created just for her. It was called *Pollo al Dente*. Very seriously, Julia hoisted the bird up by its feet, looked it up and down and then pronounced in her marvelous one-of-a-kind voice, "My goodness, you can certainly stretch this dish to feed a crowd." The boys collapsed with laughter and the guests grinned in amusement. Everyone loved the salmon and nobody asked for a taste of *Pollo al Dente*.

❧ Smoked Salmon ❧

THERE are so many different types of smoked salmon that the consumer can easily be confused. First of all, the "smoking" referred to usually means that the fish has been cured, rather than cooked, at an extremely low temperature (around 88 degrees) for several hours. The wood used is alder (popular in this country) or oak and juniper (popular in Europe). During this curing process, salt (and sometimes a little sugar) is applied to the fish. This method results in the most sought-after and expensive variety of smoked salmon, called lox, Scottish smoked salmon or Nova Scotia–style (simply, Nova). This fish is perishable and must be kept refrigerated. Atlantic salmon is commonly used for this product because of its high natural oil content and buttery texture.

When choosing smoked salmon, look for a brand with all-natural ingredients, not prefrozen and not presliced. The color can vary from light yellow to dark orange with all shades of pink in between. Avoid fish that is gray-looking or dried out. Whole fillets are available by mail order and are sold in gourmet shops. If you are buying smoked salmon by the slice, ask that it be hand-sliced, not machine-sliced. The taste should be fresh and slightly salty, the texture smooth and buttery and there should be no oily, rancid aftertaste. Sliced smoked salmon keeps for two to three days after it has been purchased, while whole fillets will keep slightly longer. If you must freeze smoked salmon, it is best to use it as an ingredient to be cooked in one of the following recipes after it has been defrosted, since freezing will cause the salmon to lose some of its marvelous texture.

The best success I've had with making home-cured salmon was with the recipe for Grilled Gravlax with Mustard Sauce that appears on p. 275. While the fish is not smoked, the texture and flavor are infinitely better, I think, than with poached or broiled salmon.

$\mathcal{T}$O SERVE SMOKED SALMON

Gwen Cohen, of Beverly, Massachusetts, is a true visionary as far as cooking goes and looks like a beautiful high-fashion model. This outgoing and creative woman has married into a family of smoked fish experts. Her husband, Sidney, imports smoked salmon. Gwen, with her usual passion for presenting food in such a way that the inherent quality and flavor shine through, gave me her thoughts on serving smoked salmon.

She finds that the tradition of piling chopped onions and capers on top of a delicate piece of smoked salmon thoroughly masks its delicious flavor. Gwen prefers to hand-slice Scotch salmon (see note below) and serve it on top of very thin white bread. Here is the method she uses.

> *slices of either homemade white bread or*
>   *Pepperidge Farm Thin Sliced White*
> *best-quality sweet (unsalted) butter at room*
>   *temperature*
> *hand-sliced smoked salmon*
> *lemon wedges for garnish*

Lightly toast the bread. While it is still warm from the toaster, roll it lightly with a rolling pin to make it even thinner. Cut the crusts off the bread and cut it into 2-inch strips. When the strips are cool, coat them with the sweet butter. Place a slice of smoked salmon on each piece of toast. Garnish the platter with lemon wedges.

When serving the oilier Norwegian salmon, use medium pumpernickel bread (the German kind that comes foil-wrapped has too strong a taste). Slice the bread thinly, coat each piece with a thin layer of cream cheese and top it with a slice of salmon. Gwen passes the following sauce separately.

$\mathcal{G}$WEN COHEN'S DILL-MUSTARD SAUCE

1½ cups sweet mustard
2 teaspoons white prepared horseradish
1 cup fresh dill, rinsed well, dried and finely
chopped
white vinegar
salt
freshly ground pepper

Combine the mustard and horseradish and mix until they are incorporated. Stir in the dill and thin to the desired consistency with a few teaspoons of vinegar. Season with salt and freshly ground pepper.

To slice smoked salmon by hand, use a very sharp, very thin, long knife. Hold the knife almost parallel to the top of the fish so that you are "skimming" instead of cutting. Start at the narrow end and discard the first slice (discard it right into your mouth). Continue slicing, making the pieces paper-thin. Arrange the slices overlapping on a platter and serve immediately.

$\mathcal{G}$RILLED GRAVLAX WITH MUSTARD SAUCE

This is the recipe for curing your own salmon. It's not the same as smoking, but the results are sublime. Start this dish at least four days before you plan to serve it.

FOR THE GRAVLAX:

2 large salmon fillets, skinned (about 4–5
pounds total weight)
¼ cup brandy or cognac
¼ cup coarse (Kosher) salt
¼ cup granulated sugar
1 teaspoon white pepper
4 large bunches of fresh dill, rinsed and dried
1 small can green peppercorns, drained of their
brine

Run your fingers over the salmon and use a tweezer to pull out any bones you might feel. Sprinkle the flesh and skin sides of the fish with the brandy or cognac. Rub it in lightly with your hands. Combine the salt, sugar and pepper in a small dish and gently rub about 2 teaspoons into each side of the fish fillets. You will not need all the mixture. Discard the rest. Lay several large overlapping sheets of heavy-duty foil on your counter. Spread 1 of the bunches of dill on the foil and place 1 of the fillets, skin side down, on it. Rub half the peppercorns over the fish. Spread 2 bunches of the dill over this fillet. Sprinkle the rest of the peppercorns over the dill and place the second fillet, skin side up, on top of the first. Spread the remaining bunch of dill over the skin side of the top fillet. (You'll have a salmon sandwich of sorts, with dill and peppercorns in the middle, then fish, then more dill on the top and bottom.) Fold the foil around the fish, securing it into a neat package. Add 2 other layers of foil and seal it tightly. Place the package in a roasting pan or jelly-roll pan (make sure the pan has sides, because the fish might leak). Place the fish in the refrigerator and weight it by placing a cookie sheet with several heavy cans (or other objects) on top. Turn the fish over every day for not less than 4 and not more than 5 days.

This sauce should be made before broiling the gravlax. It will keep refrigerated for up to a week.

FOR THE MUSTARD SAUCE:

⅓ cup grainy mustard
⅓ cup dark brown sugar, firmly packed
1½ cups crème fraîche (either commercial or
*   made by following the recipe on p. 107)*
freshly squeezed lemon or lime juice

Place the mustard and brown sugar in a small saucepan and whisk over moderate heat until smooth. On low heat add the crème fraîche and stir until incorporated. Add the lemon or lime juice to taste. Heat the sauce before spooning over the fish.

TO BROIL THE GRAVLAX:

½ pound sweet (unsalted) butter
juice of 3 limes or 2 lemons

Set the broiler on high with the rack as close to the broiler unit as possible. Unwrap the gravlax and remove the dill and green peppercorns. Gently run the fish under cool water briefly, to remove the salt mixture. Dry well. Cut the fillets (leave the skin on — it keeps the fish from falling apart) into 8 serving pieces and place them on a greased heavy-duty baking sheet. Make sure the baking sheet is broiler-proof and won't warp under the heat. (A good dish for this is a shallow Corning baking dish.) Melt the butter and lime or lemon juice in a small saucepan. Brush the fish generously with the butter mixture and broil for 3–5 minutes, brushing again frequently with the melted butter. Cook the fish on only one side. Remember that the fish is really "cooked" already by the action of the salt and sugar. This cooking is only to heat it and get the top crusty. If you cook it too long, it will get dry and lose the wonderful gravlax quality and flavor.

Serves 6–8

HERBED CREPES WITH SMOKED SALMON

Looking for something smashing to serve as a first course? Look no further because here it is — herbed crepes wrapped around smoked salmon, served with butter and crème fraîche. The crepes can be made the day before.

FOR THE CREPES:

2 cups milk
½ teaspoon salt
5 tablespoons clarified butter (see technique on
    p. 25)
1¼ cups all-purpose flour
3 extra-large eggs
½ cup beer
1 teaspoon dried thyme
1 teaspoon dried chervil
1 teaspoon dried tarragon

Place the milk in a blender or food processor with the motor off. Add the salt, the butter and then the flour. Add the eggs and process or blend until the flour starts to incorporate into the milk. Slowly add the beer and continue to process only until the batter is smooth. It should be the consistency of medium cream. Blend in the herbs. Cover the batter and refrigerate it for at least 2 hours or overnight.

When you are ready to make the crepes, thin the batter if necessary with a little milk. Spread about a tablespoon of butter in a crepe pan (Teflon is wonderful for this) and set it over high heat. Swirl the butter around to coat the bottom and sides of the pan and discard the excess. Ladle in enough crepe batter to just cover the bottom. Quickly swirl the batter around to cover halfway up the sides of the pan. Cook for about 1 minute over high heat on the first side, then use a fork to help flip the crepe over. Cook for another 30 seconds. The crepes should be very thin and have brown spots on the first side. It may take one or two times before you get the hang of it. Don't bother regreasing the pan unless the crepes start to stick. Stack the cooked crepes between pieces of wax paper and refrigerate until ready to assemble.

Makes about thirty 6-inch crepes

TO ASSEMBLE:

24 herbed crepes
10 ounces hand-sliced Nova Scotia or Scotch salmon
1 cup crème fraîche (commercial or made from the recipe on p. 107)
8 tablespoons sweet (unsalted) butter, melted and hot
3 tablespoons red caviar for garnish (optional)

Spread the crepes on a cookie sheet and warm them in a 200-degree oven for a few moments. Or warm them in the wax paper in the microwave oven. Spread each crepe with about a tablespoon of crème fraîche and then divide the smoked salmon among the crepes, laying it down the middle, unfolded. Fold the ends of each crepe over the salmon and place them, seam side down, on 8 warmed plates. Dribble the hot butter over the crepes and garnish with a spoonful of the red caviar. Serve immediately.

Serves 8

Tenderloin

$\mathcal{O}$nce upon a time, a long time ago, there was a land where people thought exercise was something for men in basic training, and raw fish was something that cats ate out of garbage cans. The evils of mixing cholesterol and triglycerides had yet to be discovered and beef was the meat of choice. Every young bride worth her salt aspired to knocking the socks off her dinner guests, after slaving away for days in her kitchen, by offering up the ultimate in gustatory overload: beef Wellington. Hand in hand with this quest went a serious attitude toward home entertaining that took second place only to presidential inaugurations and brain surgery. Boy, did I learn my lesson.

My introduction to beef Wellington had come via the *New York*

Times Magazine. There it was proclaimed to be the ne plus ultra of haute cuisine. I didn't know what either of those French idioms meant, but I was heavy into the hostess role and loved a challenge. If Craig Claiborne said that this beef Wellington was the dish to make, I was game. I thought that New Year's Eve would be an appropriate time to serve something this fancy, so along about November I sent out invitations. Three of the four chosen couples accepted with great delight and anticipation. The fourth couple presented a problem. The wife's sister and brother-in-law were coming for the holidays. They would feel funny accepting a dinner invitation and leaving their relatives behind. Would it be okay? they asked. Of course! What's one more couple? No problem. Bring them along. It wasn't a problem until I realized that no matter how I stretched that old piece of tenderloin (which rivaled a semester's college tuition in cost), I wasn't going to be able to feed twelve people with it. I thought about serving three appetizers made with bread and heavy drinks like piña coladas to fill up the crowd so they wouldn't mind a tiny serving of the main course, but vetoed that plan. Why should everyone have to carbohydrate-load because of this "bonus" couple?

Even for a practiced cook, classic beef Wellington is a time-consuming and technically difficult dish to execute. You have to know how to pick out a good tenderloin and trim it (or really trust your butcher), how to work with pastry, how to make the duxelles, or mushroom mixture, that goes on top of the beef, how to cook the beef so it is still rare without leaving the pastry underdone. You have to make the whole thing look beautiful while you are reeling from the price of the truffles for the sauce. The sauce itself (I made an espagnole sauce) takes the right kind of kitchen equipment and several days' preparation, not to mention a palate trained enough to know if it tastes the way it should. In other words this classic dish is a classic pain to make — and expensive! And now I had to make two. Also, this was only one of the dishes I was making for this party. I had to worry about an appetizer, several different kinds of vegetables, a starch, and of course two or three desserts. I had to make sure our apartment was clean and devoid of Legos and Lincoln Logs. I had to make do with china and silver for ten people. I reluctantly set two places with our everyday chipped pottery plates and disposal-scarred stainless, angry at the thought of all our other guests getting to use the good stuff and David and me — the ones who went through the wedding and all to get it — using the crumby stuff.

By the time New Year's Eve rolled around I was exhausted and not a little resentful at my own generosity. Our table wasn't really big enough for twelve, but you couldn't serve this meal buffet-style, so all the place settings were crammed next to one another. There was so little room between the chairs that people would have to eat with their arms pressed up against their sides. We got the kids to sleep early and raced to get dressed, meanwhile having the prerequisite pre-dinner-party fight. She: "I'm doing all the work and you're not helping one bit. I would think after all these years you could have figured out that those ironed embroidered towels in the bathroom were for the guests — not for wiping down the kids." He: "This dinner party was not my idea. You're the one who invited all those people. I'd rather have take-out Chinese food." At that point I would have too.

Three of the couples arrived on time. We served drinks and chatted while waiting for the other couple and their relatives. Timing was crucial to this meal. In order to get the beef to the table still hot yet allow it its "resting" period, the rest of the courses had to go on schedule. The fact that two couples were late was already beginning to screw up the works. I was not happy. They finally called to say they'd been held up and we should start without them. This was not my idea of how things should go. This was not an open house. It was a formal dinner party to which all the other guests had managed to make it on time. We started on the soup. I turned the oven temperature down on the beef. Salad was supposed to come after the main course (we were trying to be continental), but I served it right after the soup since the other couples hadn't arrived yet.

As soon as we started on the salad the doorbell rang. David answered it. There were my friends and the sister and brother-in-law *and* their brand-new baby. Baby! They brought their baby to my dinner party? They were invited secondhand and had the nerve to bring their kid? I couldn't believe it. "Hope you don't mind that we brought little Adrianna. We've never ever left her — she goes everywhere with us. She's really good — won't make a peep. Can I put her down on this nice soft white couch? She hardly ever spits up." Of course all the other guests had to get up from the dinner table to take a look at the baby, lying there, getting ready to throw up on my white couch — the one I waited until my kids didn't throw up anymore to buy. I sounded like a cross between a camp counselor and a drill sergeant as I strongly urged everyone back to the table.

The beef Wellingtons smelled done, but since I'd fooled around with the oven temperature so often, I couldn't be sure. I took them out and started heating the vegetables. For once David remembered to clear the plates from the previous course. I cut into the beef after it had rested and it was perfect. The trick then was to get it onto the plates with the vegetables and rice, sauce it and get it out while it was still hot. I was going a million miles an hour and everything looked as if it was going to be fine. We whipped the plates onto the table and everyone oohed and aahed in delight. I got to sit down for the first time that evening. Just as we picked up our forks, little Adrianna, the baby who never cried or spit up, started screaming.

Several things happened at once. My blood pressure rose to a dangerous level. Mother, father, aunt and uncle jumped up and raced over to the couch. My kids woke up and came into the dining room demanding both to know what was going on and to have something to eat and drink. Everyone put down his fork — except David, the smart one, who knew that even under ideal conditions he would never be served beef Wellington in this house again. The aunt and uncle sort of drifted back to the table while the anxious parents hovered over the screaming kid. They began to fight about the best course of action — feeding versus diaper change. Mother was all for feeding, Dad wanted to try the diaper route. Mom, on the verge of tears, won. She brought the baby, its face purple with angst, with her to the table. "Hope you don't mind my nursing her here," she says. "I wouldn't want to miss a minute of this wonderful meal." How could she have known whether or not it was wonderful?

Before I go on with this tale, I should tell those of you who had their children in the seventies and eighties that before the La Leche League and Gloria S. said it was okay, no one nursed her baby at the dining room table or anywhere else where there were people who were not either your mother or your husband. This young mother was not only avant-garde, but the ballsiest chick I had ever met.

Not only that, but she was a knockout. She was wearing a sort of Greek revival evening gown (long, flowing pleats) that was held up by two thin straps. She shrugged off one of the straps, and most of the top half of the dress fell onto her lap. Lucky for her it wasn't during the energy crisis. She would have frozen to death because she wasn't wearing anything under the dress. The dinner guests sat in shocked silence trying to figure out where to direct their eyes while she spent a few minutes jiggling about and getting comfortable before she finally picked up the kid and plugged her in. David and every other man at the table had completely forgotten about their beef Wellington growing cold and congealed on the plates in front of them. Even the other wives had a hard time making small talk with this spectacle going on. The aunt and uncle (our ex-friends) were squirming with embarrassment. I was speechless with fury and amazement. I had to fight back the urge to dump my plate full of food on her head. Instead I cut the meat up and let my boys eat it in front of the TV while they watched the ball go down in Times Square.

It was a long time before I could laugh about what was, in retrospect, a really hilarious scenario. I was simply being paid back for taking the food part of the evening so deadly seriously. And of course I resented being upstaged by a baby and her showstopping mom. I am happy to report that ten years later I nursed my new baby at the table (although I didn't feel the need to expose the entire upper half of my body). While beef Wellington has not become a staple in our house, I do make other wonderful (and much simpler) dishes with tenderloin. And we do have Chinese food on New Year's Eve.

⊱ Tenderloin ⊰

THIS extremely tender, somewhat bland cut of meat runs through the short loin (next to the ribs) and the sirloin. Wedge-shaped, it runs about five inches across at the large end to two inches at the narrow end. An entire fillet, roasted whole, will feed about eight people, while steaks trimmed from the fillet serve closer to six.

There is virtually no difference between prime and choice tenderloin, except that the price of the prime is higher. If you buy a tenderloin from your butcher, you should ask him to trim it for you. He will remove the runner and trim the end piece, or tail. Ask him to grind this meat up — it makes terrific steak tartar or hamburger. Ask him to remove the silver skin and trim the fat. This cut of meat is well marbled internally, so you won't need extra fat around the outside. The finished weight of a trimmed tenderloin will be about 50 percent less than what you started out with. If you buy a tenderloin in a supermarket, it usually comes in a heavy, vacuum-sealed plastic bag called Cryovac. These tenderloins are untrimmed. Pick out one that is firm, not soft and floppy. It is hard to judge by the color, since the blood will look dark in the plastic but will lighten up when exposed to oxygen. The meat (when you get it home and smell it) should have no odor. The fat should be creamy white, not yellow. Before attempting to trim your own meat, it's well worth the investment to buy a tenderloin from a butcher and watch him trim it.

CARPACCIO 21 FEDERAL STREET

The two tenderloin recipes below are creations of my friend Bob Kinkead, who is the shining talent behind the dishes served at 21 Federal Street, the hot place to eat on Nantucket Island. The first is a variation of the Italian dish in which the beef is served raw. The other recipe calls for grilling the tenderloin.

FOR THE MEAT:

*12 ounces tenderloin, cut into ¼-inch slices
across the grain. You can do this yourself
with a very sharp, thin knife, or ask your
butcher to do it for you.*

Place the slices between 2 sheets of plastic wrap and use a mallet or the side of a large chef's knife to pound the pieces until the beef is ⅛ inch thick and the fibers have broken down (you'll be able to see this).

FOR THE MAYONNAISE:

*1 extra-large egg plus 1 egg yolk
2 tablespoons lemon juice
⅓ cup Dijon mustard
½ cup corn oil mixed with ½ cup olive oil
1 tablespoon brandy or cognac
salt and pepper to taste*

Place the egg, egg yolk and 1 tablespoon of the lemon juice and 1 teaspoon of the mustard in the work bowl of a food processor fitted with a steel blade. Process for 15 seconds, then very slowly, in a thin stream, dribble in the oil until the mixture begins to emulsify. Add all the oil, the rest of the lemon juice and mustard, and then the brandy or cognac. Add more lemon juice if you wish and season with salt and pepper.

olive oil
capers
4 large mushrooms, sliced very thin, for
*   garnish*
freshly ground pepper
French bread

Divide the tenderloin (overlapping the slices) among 4 plates. Drizzle with olive oil and sprinkle with a few capers. Put a dab of the mayonnaise on the side of each plate and garnish with the mushroom slices. Pass the pepper grinder and bread.

Serves 4 as an appetizer or 2–3 as a main course

ℬOB KINKEAD'S GRILLED TENDERLOIN WITH PANCETTA

To be authentic, this dish should be cooked on a grill. You can try it under the broiler but the dish will lack that wonderful charcoal flavor. The meat is accompanied by a relish made from grilled onions.

FOR THE MEAT:

6 6-ounce tenderloin fillets, trimmed
6 strips of pancetta (Italian bacon)
1 cup olive oil
4 cloves garlic
1 tablespoon dried thyme
1 tablespoon dried rosemary
1 tablespoon dried oregano
1 teaspoon salt
½ teaspoon freshly ground pepper

Around the outside rim of each fillet wrap a strip of pancetta and secure it with a toothpick. Place the olive oil in a shallow, oblong metal pan or dish. Crush the garlic cloves with the flat side of a chef's knife and add them to the oil. Add all the herbs and the salt and pepper. Add the meat, turning to coat all sides. Refrigerate in the marinade for 2 hours. Meanwhile prepare the onion relish.

FOR THE ONION RELISH:

2 large Spanish onions, peeled and cut into
   1-inch slices
2 cloves garlic, peeled
¼ cup sherry vinegar or red wine vinegar
¼ cup olive oil
salt
freshly ground pepper

Grill the onions until they are charred on the outside. Place the slices in the work bowl of a food processor fitted with the metal blade. Add the garlic and process for 15 seconds. It should *not* be a smooth puree. Add the vinegar and olive oil and process only until the ingredients are incorporated. Season with salt and pepper to taste.

Grill the meat (it should be quite rare inside) and serve it with the onion relish. Another nice accompaniment to this dish is grilled potatoes. These are made simply by cutting peeled Idaho potatoes into 2-inch slices, parboiling them for about 10 minutes, drying them well, brushing them with olive oil and grilling them with a sprig of fresh rosemary (if available) on top.

Serves 6

INDIVIDUAL BEEF WELLINGTONS

This is a wildly simplified version of the classic dish. It allows the host or hostess to get in a game of tennis, not to mention a shower and perhaps even a nap, the day of the dinner party and still make a splash with the main course. Instead of wrapping the whole tenderloin in puff pastry, the uncooked meat is sliced into serving portions, briefly sautéed in a skillet, and then placed on a rectangle of puff pastry and topped with duxelles (mushroom puree), a slice of canned foie gras, and the espagnole sauce. The sauce (which does take time) and the duxelles can be made well ahead and frozen until needed.

FOR THE ESPAGNOLE SAUCE:

4 tablespoons vegetable oil
½ cup lean bacon, diced
1 large onion, diced
3 carrots, sliced
5 tablespoons all-purpose flour
4 cups brown beef stock (see recipe below)
2 cups dry red wine
1 bay leaf
1 teaspoon dried thyme
6 black peppercorns
½ cup fresh parsley, chopped
2 tomatoes, chopped
2 tablespoons tomato paste
2–3 tablespoons Madeira
salt and pepper to taste

In a heavy-bottomed, 2-quart pan, heat the oil and add the bacon, onion and carrots. Cook over moderate heat, stirring occasionally, until the vegetables wilt and are lightly browned. Add the flour and stir constantly until the mixture is a rich brown color. Heat the stock and whisk it gradually into the flour mixture. Add the wine, bay leaf, thyme, peppercorns, parsley, tomatoes and tomato paste. Bring to a boil, stirring constantly, then lower the heat and let the sauce cook, barely simmering, uncovered, for 3 hours or until it is reduced almost by half. Every 20 minutes or so skim the top with a large metal spoon. Add the Madeira during the last half hour of cooking. Strain the sauce and correct the seasoning with salt and pepper.

3 pounds veal bones
3 pounds beef bones
⅓ cup vegetable oil
2 large onions, quartered
4 large carrots, sliced (unpeeled, but washed well)
3 stalks celery, sliced, with leaves left on
2 bay leaves
1 teaspoon whole black peppercorns
2 tablespoons tomato paste
4–5 quarts cold water

Preheat the oven to 450 degrees with the rack in the center position. Place the bones in a large roasting pan — in a single layer if possible — and rub them with some of the oil, reserving the remainder of it for the vegetables. Roast the bones for about 20–30 minutes, stirring occasionally. Coat the vegetables with the remaining oil (using more if necessary) and add them to the roasting pan. Roast about 20 more minutes or until the vegetables are well browned, but not burned (this will give the stock a bitter taste). Place the bones and the vegetables in a large stockpot, leaving as much fat as possible in the roasting pan. Discard the fat. Scrape the browned bits in the roasting pan into the stockpot. Add the rest of the ingredients, including the water, and bring the stock to a simmer. Simmer the stock very slowly (you can do this overnight), skimming occasionally at first, for at least 5 hours. Chill the stock well and skim off all the fat. Taste the stock. If the flavor is not strong enough, cook for another hour or so uncovered. Strain the stock and reduce it by simmering it until you have 2 quarts. Do not add salt! The stock can be kept refrigerated for 2 days and frozen for several months.

FOR THE DUXELLES:

2 pounds clean white mushrooms
3 shallots
3 tablespoons butter
2 cups heavy cream
salt and pepper to taste

Chop the mushrooms in the work bowl of a food processor fitted with the metal blade until they are in fine pieces. Chop the shallots (by hand is best, since the pieces get lost in the processor). Melt the butter in a very large, heavy-bottomed skillet and add the shallots. Cook over moderate heat for about 5 minutes. Stir in the mushrooms and the cream and cook over moderate heat for about 30 minutes or until the mixture forms a thickish paste. Add salt and pepper to taste. This can be made up to 5 days ahead and kept refrigerated. It also freezes well.

TO ASSEMBLE:

6 6-ounce fillet steaks
2–3 tablespoons vegetable oil
3 large cloves garlic, peeled
salt and pepper
6 4-inch squares of cooked puff pastry (see last
  paragraph)
6 ½-inch slices canned foie gras (available in
  gourmet shops or gourmet sections of large
  department stores)
1½ cups warm duxelles
1½ cups warm sauce
6 slices fresh or canned black truffle for garnish

Place a very heavy-duty sauté pan over high heat and let it get very hot. Rub the steaks with the oil and then smash the garlic with the side of a chef's knife and rub the garlic over both sides of the meat. Cook the meat over high heat for about 3 minutes on each side for very rare and slightly longer if you wish it more well done. Sprinkle lightly with salt and pepper. Place a square of pastry on each plate and place a fillet on top. Place a slice of foie gras on top and then about ¼ cup of duxelles. Ladle on some sauce and top with the slice of truffle. Serve at once. A good accompaniment to this dish is *haricots verts* (thin French green beans).

The commercial puff pastry sold in the freezer section of some groceries and gourmet shops is a real time saver. Use a sharp knife to cut the pastry into 4-inch squares that are ⅛ inch thick and chill it well before you bake it. Follow the baking directions on the package. The pastry should be baked the day you plan to serve the beef Wellington and stored uncovered at room temperature.

$\mathscr{S}$TEAK TARTAR

The first time I ever saw someone eat steak tartar was on my honeymoon. Near starvation as a result of our dismal command of menu French, David and I sat in a street café on the main plaza in the lovely town of Bruges in Belgium. We had been subsisting on onion soup, pommes frites and French bread, since these were the only things that were familiar on menus. We were not into our adventuresome food mode as yet and we were scared that we'd end up with eel or tripe if we selected at random. The waiter brought the now unappetizingly familiar tureen of onion soup while we debated about whether to take a chance and try something else.

At the next table was a Hercule Poirot type, complete with waxed curling mustache and great round middle. He wore a dark pinstriped suit with a pearl gray vest that had yards of gold watch chain draped across it. The waiter brought out a silver dome-covered dish and set it in front of him. Next he wheeled out a cart on which was an assortment of little china crocks and a wire basket piled with smooth brown eggs. With great ceremony the waiter lifted the dome to reveal — a mound of chopped meat? David and I exchanged looks. I glanced at the cart to see if I could see where the waiter was planning to cook the meat. No burner in sight. The waiter used two oversized soup spoons to make a well in the center of the mound of meat. Into the well he broke two eggs. Our untasted soup was growing cold in front of us. The waiter then spooned capers, anchovies, chopped onions and some condiments from the little crocks onto the plate next to the meat. Then he used the spoons to mash up all that stuff into the meat. The rotund diner sat at somewhat disinterested attention while this was going on, as if he witnessed this spectacle every day of his life. When the waiter was finished, the diner gave him a discreet nod, tucked his oversized linen napkin into his collar and dug in. It took years before we could be convinced to try it, but when we did, steak tartar became an instant hit with us — so much more interesting than onion soup!

1 pound tenderloin, well trimmed and all
  silver skin removed
4 eggs
1 medium onion, minced
⅓ cup fresh parsley, chopped
4 anchovy fillets, drained of oil
4 tablespoons capers
4 slices lemon
cognac
Tabasco sauce
Worcestershire sauce
Dijon mustard
salt and freshly ground pepper

Have your butcher grind the meat twice. If you grind it yourself, use a meat grinder, not a food processor. Divide the meat among 4 chilled plates. Make a well in the center of each and crack an egg into each well. Garnish each plate with the onion, parsley, anchovy, capers and a lemon slice. Bring the plates to the table and pass the sauces and condiments separately. Let your guests season their meat as they wish.

Serves 4–6

Tuna

As a child I was a terrible eater. Tuna fish, lamb chops and candy were about it. I ate tuna fish every single day for lunch — and I do mean every single day. My idea of a gastronomic high was a tuna salad sandwich made of a small can of Bumble Bee solid white-meat tuna, finely mashed, with a diced stalk of celery, and a healthy glob of Hellmann's Mayonnaise. The outside (the bread part) had to be white bread, preferably Wonder Bread, but my mother's fresh challah was more than acceptable. The only variation on this theme that I would accept was when we went to Sage-Allen's, a department store in downtown Hartford. In the store's cafeteria I would eat my tuna sandwich on light rye bread with lettuce. We're talking about a childhood and adolescence in which tuna ranked right up there with SAT's and a date to the prom.

Years later, after I had learned to eat real food, I found myself working in the kitchen of a restaurant where fishermen would bring the catch of the day right to the chef for approval. One day a young guy came in with a heavyweight, clear plastic bag in which he carried a big chunk of something black, blue and red. On his face he wore a pleased-as-punch look. On my counter, where I was carefully making dozens of radish roses, he upended his bag. This hunk of bluish/maroon slid out.

"Yuck," I said. "Get that gross thing off my counter."

"Sweetie, this here is bluefin tuna. You won't find a better cut or better quality anywhere. Caught it myself and shipped the rest over to Japan, where I'll get me enough to spend the long, cold winter on some nice, warm island."

I was alternately disbelieving and horrified. How could this be tuna? Tuna came in a can and it wasn't blue — it was white, and it never looked like raw beef, it looked like cooked chicken. As a matter of fact my mother used to pass it off as chicken in her American chop suey. I wrinkled up my nose and told him I didn't believe it was tuna.

He cut off a little slice. "Here," he said, shoving it toward my face, "take a bite. It's really delicious!"

"You want me to eat it raw? Are you crazy? That's disgusting."

"That's how they eat it in Japan. Call it sashimi. The stuff's great, I'm telling you. You're passing up a treat."

Some treat. This guy wanted me to eat raw fish that looked like bloody beef. I'd sooner eat my hat. He moved on to the chef, who seemed delighted with the fish and was more than eager to try a bite.

That winter I was invited to a fancy food-and-wine dinner that cost, as my husband was quick to point out, as much as summer camp for one child. At the table I found myself surrounded by a lot of food professionals who sounded as if they knew what they were talking about — culinarily. The courses came and went and everyone but me seemed to know all there was to know about them. Even if I could have got a word in edgewise, I had nothing to say but mmm, mmm good. Then, after a brief lull in the service, the waiter approached our table with a serving platter with blue-red rectangles on it. "Bluefin tuna," he announced. Please remember that this was long before there was a sushi bar on every corner in New York City and raw fish had replaced celery as a diet food.

He placed the dish in the center of the table and left. No one made a grab for the fish, although there was a lot of murmuring about the fact that it was raw fish. I saw my opportunity and went for it. I blithely reached my fork toward the center of the table and, just as if I did this every day of my life, speared a piece of fish and said cheerily, "Oh what great luck! I just love sashimi, it's so Japanese, and tuna is my favorite." I said a quick prayer and stuck it into my mouth. Boy, was I surprised. While it wasn't the old tuna that I was used to, it was certainly delicious. It had a light taste, not fishy at all, a tiny bit metallic and very subtle. The texture was very slightly oily, but delicate too. And I had scored big points with this crowd. I could tell by the way they were looking at me that they were impressed with my bravery at not only eating, but actually enjoying raw fish. Reluctantly they dug in, and while most liked it too, some were lukewarm, which left more for us instant converts.

When a Japanese restaurant opened up in our neighborhood, I was the first one in line for sashimi. Now I have lunch there at least once a week, if not more often. Tuna fish sandwiches are still a favorite food for me, but now that my horizon has been expanded, I have to find room for both versions.

☙ Tuna ❧

THE two kinds of fresh tuna readily available, bluefin and yellowfin, provide two kinds of cuts: the deep red toro, or fatty type, prized by the Japanese and savvy sashimi lovers in this country; and the leaner, pinker cut more suitable for grilling or broiling. Until recently Americans have shied away from the fattier cuts, but now, with new and very positive information about the value of fish oil, this may change.

Both species are highly migratory and are fished in all the major oceans of the world year-round. They run in size from 150 pounds (yellowfin) to well over 1,000 pounds (giant bluefin). The paler, less oily yellowfin is the more prevalent and is at its best in this country at the end of the summer feeding season.

Tuna can be found all year long in many fish markets. Look for moist, firm-textured, glossy cuts with the blood spot well trimmed. Avoid fish with iridescent coloring, which indicates the fish is dry. Also avoid, if possible, the cuts made lengthwise along the spine, since this meat is dark, coarse and of somewhat inferior quality. As with all fish, there should be no smell whatsoever. The fish should be used as soon as possible, and while it can be frozen, the texture will change and the flesh will not be as firm.

TUNA SASHIMI WITH ORIENTAL SAUCE

FOR THE SAUCE:

½ cup red wine vinegar
½ cup dry sherry
½ cup water
⅓ cup fresh ginger, peeled and very finely
   julienned
4 large cloves garlic, minced
3 tablespoons soy sauce
1 tablespoon grainy mustard (like Pommery)
⅔ cup olive oil
toasted sesame seeds for garnish (see note)

Place the vinegar, sherry, water, ginger and garlic in a skillet. Simmer over moderate heat until the liquid is reduced to half a cup and the ginger and garlic are soft. Stir in the soy sauce and mustard. Off the heat, whisk in the olive oil.

Makes about 1⅓ cups

FOR THE SASHIMI:

1 pound tuna (preferably toro, or belly cut)

Use a very sharp knife to slice the fish into pieces 1½ inches long, ½ inch wide and ¼ inch thick.

TO SERVE:

Arrange the slices overlapping on a plate and pour a few tablespoons of the above sauce on it. Garnish with the toasted sesame seeds.

Serves 4–6 as an appetizer

NOTE: To toast sesame seeds, place them in a large dry skillet (Teflon works well here). Shake the skillet back and forth over high heat, tossing the seeds around or stirring them with a wooden spoon so they won't burn. Continue until they are golden brown.

GRILLED TUNA WITH CORIANDER SAUCE

FOR THE FISH:

3 pounds fresh tuna (ask for a lean cut)
1½ sticks (6 ounces) very soft butter

Cut the tuna into 4-ounce steaks and grill or barbecue, basting frequently with the butter. Cook only about 4 minutes on each side. Do not overcook. Pass the following sauce separately.

FOR THE SAUCE:

1½ cups fresh coriander (also called cilantro or
Chinese parsley)
juice of 4 limes
¾ cup vegetable oil
1 small chile pepper (or 1 teaspoon Chipotle
pepper if possible)
½–1 teaspoon salt

Place the coriander in the work bowl of a food processor and chop. Add the lime juice and process for a few seconds. Slowly add the oil, then add the chile pepper and the salt.

Serves 8

TUNA EN BROCHETTE

½ pound lean bacon, thickly sliced
1½ pounds fresh tuna steaks, cut into 1½-inch
  cubes
3–4 small zucchini, cut into ¾-inch slices
12 large mushroom caps
12 onion slices, cut ¾ inch thick
12 cherry tomatoes
⅓ cup melted butter
2 teaspoons lemon juice
pinch of freshly ground pepper
2 teaspoons soy sauce
2 teaspoons fresh parsley, chopped

Partially cook the bacon to render some of the fat. This is easily done in a microwave oven by layering the pieces of bacon between sheets of paper toweling. Cut the bacon strips in half the short way and wrap a piece around each cube of tuna. Beginning with pieces of zucchini on each skewer (stick the skewers through the side, not the middle, of the slice), alternate tuna with mushrooms, onion slices and tomatoes and then end with a few pieces of zucchini (which help to anchor the filled skewers). Combine the remaining ingredients and brush over the tuna and vegetables. Grill 3 inches from the coals for about 2–3 minutes on each side. Do not overcook —the tuna should stay moist and tender.

Serves 6

Vanilla Beans

Remember "Gilligan's Island"? Where those goofy characters were marooned on a Hollywood set with palm trees and had adventures that were rewarded with canned laughter? Well, I knew that there was more to life in the South Pacific than that. When I was twelve I read and reread James A. Michener's *Tales of the South Pacific* until my copy fell apart. I watched Mary Martin and Rossano Brazzi gaze, in larger-than-life Technicolor, toward Bali Ha'i during at least ten matinees, and on Monday evenings I sailed with Adam Troy from island to island in the green-blue sea (my imagination supplied the colors). Ah, yes, I was going to grow up (sixteen was old enough in Polynesia), marry Gardner McKay and spend the rest of my life throwing orchids into active volcanos in order to save hundreds of grateful and adoring natives. Who is more fickle — a television network or an adolescent girl? When my romancing sailor was canceled I moved on to Mannix.

Last year, however, I had a Tahitian déjà vu when I received a present from a friend who had just come back from the South Pacific. She brought me fresh vanilla beans. Even before I had opened the package, the room was filled with their exotic perfume. Moist, full and round and so heavenly sweet-smelling, those soft, long mahogany-colored strips bore no resemblance to the scrawny, dried-up variety I was accustomed to. Since the aroma lasted a long time, I didn't have to rush to use them for anything but smelling. That's how wonderful they were! I just kept them next to my desk and every once in a while I would pick one up and inhale deeply. Visions of Adam Troy and his long white sailboat floated into view. Outside my window the January day was gray and bleak and outrageously cold. The fragrance of vanilla transported me over frigid continents toward the azure waters of the South Seas. Ah, yes, I could marry Gardner McKay and grow vanilla beans on Tahiti, and then throw perfectly cooked vanilla sauce into the grumbling volcanos, saving hundreds of grateful natives.

❧ Vanilla Beans ☙

VANILLA beans come from the pods of a climbing vine in the orchid family. Some varieties of this vine are native to Central America, Mexico and Madagascar. Makers of vanilla extract prefer these widely available beans for their product, since they are less expensive than the hand-picked and processed ones from vines grown by Tahitians.

The soil and climate of the growing area profoundly affect the flavor of the vanilla, so if it is extraordinary aroma and flavor that you are after, then the vanilla beans from Tahiti are what you should use. Until recently their secret was known only to the French, to whom the bulk of the crop was exported, but now they are available by mail order (see resource list). They really are a world apart from their competitors. Tahitian beans are pleasantly moist and squooshy, unlike ordinary vanilla beans, which are dry and harder to use. Vanilla beans are used by infusing their flavor into other ingredients: sugar, sauces, milk, ice creams. A whole bean stored in sugar in a closed container will flavor that sugar for all its baking and confectionary uses. Beans can be used to sweeten beverages — hot and cold. The aroma is long-lasting, and the beans can be rinsed, dried and used over and over again until the flavor gradually fades.

HOMEMADE VANILLA EXTRACT

This makes a lovely present.

> *1 Tahitian vanilla bean*
> *2 cups best-quality cognac*

Use a sharp knife to split the bean lengthwise. Pour the cognac into a clean glass jar with a screw-on lid (a pint-sized canning jar is good for this) and add the bean. Screw on the top. Put the jar in a cool, dark place for about 4 weeks. I leave the bean in the jar and pour more cognac in when the vanilla extract gets low.

Makes 1 pint

WHITE CHOCOLATE VANILLA SAUCE

Try this velvety-smooth sauce on baked apples or fresh berries.

> *1½ cups heavy cream*
> *1 vanilla bean, split lengthwise*
> *9 ounces white chocolate (I use Tobler*
> *Narcisse), broken into pieces*

Heat the cream in a small saucepan, add the split vanilla bean and simmer until the cream reduces to 1 cup. Remove the bean, rinse it and reserve it for another use. Stir in the chocolate, whisking until it is incorporated. If the mixture is not smooth, it is because the milk solids in the chocolate have not dissolved. Process the sauce in a blender or food processor for a few seconds. This sauce will keep refrigerated for 2 weeks or you can freeze it. Heat slightly to thin before serving.

Makes 2 cups

Ultimate Vanilla Milk Shake (or Frappe, Depending Upon Where You Live)

1 cup whole milk
1 fresh vanilla bean, split lengthwise
1 cup best-quality vanilla ice cream
whipped cream for garnish (optional)

The day before you plan to make the milk shake, scald the milk in a small saucepan with the vanilla bean. Let the milk cool in the refrigerator with the bean in it. The next day wash off the bean and reserve it for another use. Place the milk and ice cream in a blender and blend for 30 seconds. Top with whipped cream.

Serves 1

Kahlúa

4 cups water
1 pound light brown sugar (2¼ cups, lightly packed)
1¾ cups granulated sugar
¾ cup freeze-dried instant coffee
1 vanilla bean or 2 tablespoons vanilla extract
3¼ cups vodka

In a large saucepan combine the water and both sugars. Cook over low heat, stirring until the sugars are dissolved. Raise the heat and boil for 5 minutes without stirring. Lower the heat and add the coffee, stirring to dissolve. Remove from heat. Slit the vanilla bean lengthwise and add it (or the vanilla extract) along with the vodka. Pour into a clean glass jar. Seal and shake once a day for 3 weeks. Strain before using.

Makes about 2 quarts

White Asparagus

As in most families, for us, certain holidays are associated with special foods. In my mother-in-law's home, spring is heralded during the Passover Seder with tender, bright green stalks of asparagus, briefly steamed and served with melted butter. After months of drab and boring winter vegetables, the delicate green color and crunchy fresh taste of the tender asparagus are a welcome change signaling that it won't be long before there will be crocuses in the garden and buds on the maple trees. My mother-in-law's Seder table was the first place I had ever eaten asparagus and it was love at first taste. But even as much as I love it, and although it comes on the market earlier and earlier each year, I always wait until the first Seder to eat it. This is tradition.

One early springtime not so long ago found our family in the Provence area of France. We had rented a house in a hill town called Roussillon, which was about an hour's drive northwest of Avignon. The three-storied stucco house was painted with the same ochre clay that gave such a distinctive hue to the steep hill our town was perched on. Most days found us in our town simply living a country life, practicing our French and temporarily adopted life-style. We shopped in the local markets and went to the neighboring vineyard with our gallon jugs to get wine straight from the barrel. The produce was exceptionally fresh and beautiful, the chickens range-fed, plump and tasty, and the olives that made our oil were grown nearby. Our bread was delivered fresh twice a day to Madame Albertini's *boulangerie*. Even the simplest meal was a joy to prepare and delicious to eat.

It was in this house in our French village that we had a very special Passover Seder. While it wasn't possible for the usual assortment of grandparents and aunts and uncles to be with us, friends came from Switzerland to share this special time and were joined by other American friends traveling in France. I left the organizing of the Seder service to David and the boys and with great relish took on the planning of the meal and getting the house ready. During the seven days of Passover, the festival that commemorates the Jews' exodus from Egypt, leavened products are not consumed or even allowed in the house. So, all breads (except for the traditional unleavened matzoh), cookies, crackers and the like are removed, as are noodles, rice and cereals. In very traditional homes (not mine), the dishes, pots and pans and cutlery, as well as all other food preparation utensils used during the rest of the year, are put away and replaced with cookware used only for Passover.

The day before the first Seder (there are two, one the first night and one the second), long shopping list in hand, we went off to the market. Not only did I need food for the meal itself, but also symbolic food items that went on the Seder plate. Among them were bitter herbs (parsley), horseradish, lamb shank, apples, nuts and sweet wine to make the mixture called *charoseth*, which symbolizes the mortar the Jewish slaves used in laying bricks. In most parts of America, where even grocery stores stock up on matzoh and macaroons Kosher for Passover, preparing for the holiday is no problem. But in this rural section of France it was not the one-stop shopping I was used to — but a delight just the same. For the meal itself I bought the traditional paschal lamb. Finding chicken liver for the chopped liver was no problem, nor was locating a fowl for the chicken soup. From the olive man we bought Niçoise olives, tiny black salty morsels, to nibble on before dinner and from the nut man, shelled walnuts for the *charoseth* and almonds to grind for the flourless chocolate torte. We bought Brazil nuts and hazelnuts in their shells for the kids to crack and eat as snacks. My husband, once a confirmed anchovy hater, now reformed, dragged me over to the cart of salted fish displayed in various barrels and trays to buy the once-dreaded and now-beloved little fish to mash up with tuna and capers for an appetizer spread. The last stop was the fruit and vegetable stalls. I bought giant heads of garlic to bake and tiny eggplants and red and green peppers to be gently sautéed in olive oil to accompany the lamb. It was hard to choose between the twenty or so different kinds of lettuce and salad greens displayed there in every color green imaginable, from bright yellow green to deep purple green. I bought bunches of carrots, sweet parsnips and flat-leaf parsley for the chicken soup. The kids picked out small golden apples for the *charoseth* and dried apricots, figs, apples and plump, sweet raisins for the compote. A small bag of Moroccan dates completed our purchases. As we were paying, one of the children wandered around to the far end of a cart. "Mom and Dad!" he called. "Come here and look at this weird asparagus." I had completely forgotten to look for our traditional vegetable amid this magnificent cornucopia of produce, and was delighted that it was available. I made room in my shopping basket as I went toward my son, but when I saw what he was pointing to I hesitated.

"Oh, Jonathan, that's white asparagus, we can't afford it."

Jonathan, who had figured out the conversion rate of francs and dollars, said, "Mom, I don't think four dollars a kilo is so much, although this stuff looks really mutant. Maybe they'll give you a break on the price."

Less than two dollars a pound for white asparagus was a terrific price. The one or two times I had seen it in the States it had cost close to ten dollars a pound. The only kind I had ever tasted was the oversalted, overcooked, canned variety that usually made its appearance as a garnish on a ladies' luncheon salad between the tomato rose and the slice of hard-boiled egg. I explained to the kids that this kind of asparagus was grown underground and was white because the sun didn't have a chance to turn the chlorophyll green. I also explained, as I was picking out the nice, firm, plump stalks with faint rosy tips, that this was a real delicacy even though they thought it looked like a pale version of what they were used to. As is my habit when faced with a bargain, I bought far more than we could ever eat at one sitting, but I figured it would make once-in-a-lifetime great leftovers. Since our guests were bringing the sweet wine and the matzoh for the Seder, all our shopping was done. We loaded our bundles into the car and headed for home.

The next day our work began at dawn. The boys scoured the house for *chametz* (food not Kosher for Passover), set the long refectory table in the dining room, which grew as a natural extension of the homey kitchen, with its view of the valley below. They gathered together all the candlesticks and thick candles — colored and white, whole and half burned — that they could find, since they were determined that this meal be illuminated without the aid of electricity. I sent them out to gather sprigs of rosemary and bunches of thyme and mustard to season the lamb. From the terrace garden they picked tarragon for the salad dressing.

I had made the soup, the cake and the compote the night before, leaving the chopped liver, the lamb and vegetables for that day. I placed four of the giant heads of garlic, still in their skins, in a pottery dish with a stick of sweet butter and stuck it in a very low oven to bake for several hours, until the garlic turned soft and its buttery-sweet insides could be squeezed out in a paste that would thicken the lamb sauce. The rest of the garlic was cut into slivers and stuck into slits, made with a small, sharp knife, into the lamb itself. The lamb, set in a shallow, enameled roasting dish, was then rubbed with olive oil, sprinkled with coarse salt and ground pepper, topped with the fresh herbs and surrounded with the tiny eggplants and slices of pepper. I washed the lettuce for the salad, made the dressing, skimmed the fat off the soup and strained off the chicken and vegetables. I placed the chicken livers on a baking sheet covered with heavy brown paper, sprinkled them with lots of coarse ground pepper and some salt and baked them in the oven until the outsides were crisp and the insides pink and tender. The liver was chopped in a wooden bowl with a wooden-handled chopper just like my grandmother once used; minced onion and chopped hard-boiled egg were added along with some of the fat from the chicken soup. David, the official taster, pronounced it the best he'd ever had, which is exactly what he had said the year before and the year before that. The other guests had arrived and had joined our family. Fortifying themselves with olives, they tried to construct a service without the help of Passover *Haggadoth*, the small books that are used during the service.

I had saved the asparagus for last because I wanted the rest of the work done so I could concentrate my energy on creating a spectacular dish with them. They looked so beautiful simply lying in the torn-open brown paper bag. The thick stems were pearly, almost iridescent white, and the tiny pinkish leaves at the tips lay flat and tight against the stalks. To see how long they would take to cook I made a test run. I peeled one stalk, cut a bit off the end and placed it in simmering water. After ten minutes I tested it with the tip of a knife. It was tender, but not mushy. With thoughts of elaborate sauces swimming in my head I cut up the stalk and tasted it. The green version, which I thought captured the taste of springtime, paled in comparison. This amazing flavor was the sweet smell of April, new grass pushing through the snow. It was a robin on the lawn and the warm spring sun on your face. The texture, crisp and firm, was the new shoots of daffodils, the bounce of defrosted earth. Why in heaven's name was I thinking of how to add to or improve something already perfect? I quickly peeled the rest of the stalks, tied them in several bunches with string and set them upright in simmering water to steam. After they were cooked I would serve them just the way my mother-in-law did, with melted butter. We started the Seder.

The table looked beautiful with its mix-and-match pottery dishes, woven placemats, napkins in wooden rings and home-fashioned Seder plate. A pewter vase held a huge bunch of red tulips, the first of the season, and a hand-carved wooden plate covered with a white linen napkin displayed the thick octagonal sheets of Syrian matzoh. Although the traditional role of the mother during the Seder, or any holiday meal for that matter, is to continuously jump up and down and race between the kitchen and dining room table, I managed to relax for a moment to take in the sight of my family and friends, so far from home, sitting together observing a holiday that has for thousands of generations been sustained and carried on by people just like us. I watched my then youngest son ask the Four Questions ("Dad, do you want them in French or Hebrew?") and saw how the gentle candlelight softly illuminated the faces around the table, casting long shadows into the corners of the room and into the kitchen with its aromas that promised great things to come.

❧ White Asparagus ❧

WHITE asparagus is grown under sandy soil in France, Spain, Belgium, Germany, Chile and, more recently, Taiwan. While the most obvious difference between white and green asparagus is the former's lack of the familiar green coloring (which is caused in the green variety by exposure to the sunlight that provides chlorophyll necessary for photosynthesis), the differences go beyond that. White asparagus, while it has a tough, stringy outer skin that must be peeled up to the tip before cooking, has a sweeter, more distinctive taste than the green variety. It also grows to a larger size both in length and diameter. White asparagus is much more popular in Europe than it is in this country, two explanations being the cost of exporting the vegetable as well as its short shelf life. Additionally, this delicate vegetable must be treated by hand through every step, from planting to harvesting and packing, which increases the cost over that of the familiar green variety.

White asparagus is also available in tins. That product is very different from the fresh variety, however. Usually soggy and oversalted, the vegetable tastes bland and has virtually none of its inherent flavor left after the canning process. White asparagus from Chile is making appearances in supermarkets across this country, starting in the early spring and lasting into early summer. If you are lucky enough to find some, check the ends and tips for mold or rot — they should not be soft or mushy. Look for firm white stalks with faint pink or maroon markings near the flat leaves. Try to use the asparagus right away. (It's probably been some days since it was picked, so you don't want to hold it even longer.)

WHITE ASPARAGUS

fresh white asparagus
sweet (unsalted) butter, melted
freshly ground white pepper

Cut the bottom one quarter or one third off the bottoms of the asparagus, depending upon how woody the stems are, and peel the stalks with a sharp knife or vegetable peeler to within half an inch of the tip. In a lidded skillet large enough to hold all the asparagus, bring about 2 cups of water to a boil (there should be enough water to cover the asparagus). Add a teaspoon of salt to the water and place the asparagus in the skillet. Cover and when the water begins to simmer turn the heat down slightly and let the asparagus simmer for 10–12 minutes or until a sharp knife pierces the stalks easily. Remove from the water and drain on paper towels. Place a few stalks on each plate, drizzle with butter and season with pepper.

WHITE ASPARAGUS WITH RED PEPPER PUREE

This dish makes a simple yet strikingly elegant presentation. Serve it as a first course.

FOR THE RED PEPPER PUREE:

3 large red bell peppers (about 1½ pounds)
2 cloves garlic
2 tablespoons fresh basil or 1 tablespoon dried
  basil
¼ cup olive oil
1 tablespoon red wine vinegar
salt and pepper

Set the broiler on "High" with the rack in the highest position. Line a heavy-duty baking sheet with foil. Cut the peppers in half from stem to base, remove the seeds and inner membrane and flatten them with your hand (they will rip — that's okay). Put the peppers on the baking sheet and place under the broiler. Let the peppers roast about 5 minutes, until they get good and black. Use tongs to change their positions so that most of the surface is charred. Immediately place the peppers in a heavy-duty plastic bag and seal the top. Let the peppers cool and then use your fingers to slip off the skins.

Cut the peppers into chunks and place them in the work bowl of a food processor. Process until the pieces are finely chopped. Add all the other ingredients and puree. Correct the seasoning.

Makes 1½ cups

TO ASSEMBLE:

*16 stalks of white asparagus, cooked and at
room temperature*

Place 3 or 4 stalks of white asparagus on each of 4 plates. Spoon some sauce over each plate.

Serves 4

White Truffles

The first time I felt extravagant enough to buy a fresh white truffle (as opposed to the kind that comes in a jar), I spent so much time agonizing about what to do with it after I bought it that before I ever got around to using it, it had gone bad. I was left with a lot of aromatic rice in which I had stored the damn thing.

My second run-in with fresh truffles came during a trip to Italy. My husband and I had spent two whirlwind weeks eating our way across the country and we found ourselves in Florence in the Piazza Michelangelo about to eat our last dinner before returning to the States. The restaurant, situated high above the magic city, had glass walls to show off the spectacular view. I was a bit melancholy at the thought of having to return to real life after having such a wonderful time on vacation. David was in the throes of his we-spent-so-much-money-on-this-trip-how-are-we-ever-going-to-pay-off-American-Express syndrome. He had visions of our bill, too large to fit in the mailbox, being hand delivered by two strong men.

The waiter approached and I told him that this was our very last meal in Italy and we wanted something delicious and memorable to eat. The waiter rubbed his hands together with glee and said he had just the thing. Anticipating yet another second-mortgage meal, David rolled his eyes in a way that reminded me of the lemons and oranges on a slot machine. I truly expected to see dollar bills roll up next.

We started with roasted red peppers dressed simply with olive oil and fresh oregano. Next the waiter brought out two large oval plates piled high with pasta that looked as if it had been tossed with melted butter. Hell, I could make this at home. What was so special about it? The waiter put the dishes down in front of us and went back into the kitchen. He came back with a small dish covered with a silver dome. With a smile and a flourish he removed the dome and revealed a rather lumpy, dirty-white, irregularly shaped baseball.

My eyes lit up. "Oh boy! A white truffle," I said softly, with great reverence.

"Oh, boy. Instant bankruptcy," said David, turning as white as the truffle. He looked as if he was about to slide underneath the table.

To his immense relief the waiter took a truffle peeler from his pocket and proceeded to shave a few slices of white truffle on top of our steaming pasta. We didn't have to buy the whole thing. A sprinkling of Parmesan cheese completed the dish and we dug in with gusto.

The truffle had a dark, mysterious taste, musky and woodslike. It smelled like the damp earth in a forest in spring, pungent and smoky. It was a powerful flavor that stayed in our mouths even after we swallowed.

"I think it tastes sexy," I said. "I know what I want for dessert."

"Leave it to you," said my husband, not totally disapproving, "to find the most expensive aphrodisiac in the world."

❧ White Truffles ❧

IF you ever have the great fortune to find yourself in Northern Italy during the fall, make a special trip to Alba for the white truffle festival. This area is the source for most of the world's white truffles and during the festival you can have your fill.

Truffles cannot be cultivated, so this rare and perishable fungus is costly and sometimes hard to find fresh in this country. Fortunately, there are a few good mail-order sources listed in the back of this book.

The intensely deep and woodsy smell of just the smallest slice of white truffle enhances and adds dimension to sauces and a uniquely unmistakable flavor to dishes. If even it's only once in a lifetime that you can justify the purchase of this delicacy you should make the most of it. Store the truffle in a plastic container full of rice for a day. The rice will absorb the truffle's aroma and when you cook up the rice (a risotto, perhaps) it will have a wonderful taste.

Use the truffle within a day or so after purchase. Avoid letting moisture collect on it, for it will get moldy. Wrap it airtight (or store it in rice, as mentioned above) so it won't dry out and begin to shrivel and lose its strong flavor. Use every bit of it, from the outer peeling to enhance sauces (remove it with a very small, sharp knife), to little "scrapes" to add to omelets.

Select firm, solid truffles with no mold or soft spots. They should not be shriveled and should have a powerful, distinctive aroma — they will not smell "pretty." Remember, while they are wildly expensive, one small white truffle goes a long way in the flavor department.

SCRAMBLED EGGS WITH WHITE TRUFFLES

If you have any money left over after you buy the truffle, get a good bottle of champagne — it's really the only thing to serve with this dish.

1 fresh white truffle
12 extra-large eggs
⅔ cup heavy cream
1 teaspoon salt
freshly ground white pepper
1 stick sweet (unsalted) butter

Slice the truffle with a small, sharp knife (or truffle peeler) and set aside. Crack the eggs into a large glass bowl and whisk briefly. Strain through a fine-mesh strainer. Stir in the heavy cream, salt and pepper. In a large skillet, melt the butter over moderate heat and when it is hot (don't let it brown) add the eggs. Stir continuously until the eggs have just begun to set. Divide the eggs among 4–6 hot plates and sprinkle with the truffle slices. Serve with toasted egg bread such as challah or brioche.

Serves 4–6

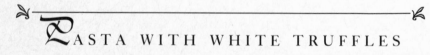

PASTA WITH WHITE TRUFFLES

1 fresh white truffle
4 tablespoons butter
1 pound fresh or dried egg pasta
½ cup heavy cream
freshly ground white pepper and salt to taste

Slice the truffle thinly with a small, sharp knife or truffle peeler. Melt the butter in a small sauté pan or skillet and toss the truffle in it for about 1 minute. Cook the pasta just until it is al dente and drain it well. Toss with heavy cream and the truffle butter. Season to taste with the white pepper and salt. Divide among 4 bowls and serve immediately.

Serves 4

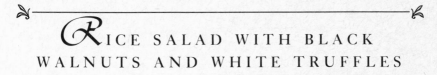

RICE SALAD WITH BLACK WALNUTS AND WHITE TRUFFLES

This dish is full of indulgent ingredients. If you are looking to economize, use white rice (but not the instant cooking kind) in place of the wild rice. If you are unable to find black walnuts, substitute regular walnuts or pecans.

FOR THE RICE:

1 fresh white truffle
1 cup wild rice
3 tablespoons butter
2 shallots, minced
2½ cups chicken stock (either homemade or canned)
½ teaspoon dried thyme
1 tablespoon butter
½ cup black walnut meats, broken into pieces
½ cup very finely minced celery

Place the truffle and the rice in a refrigerated, tightly covered plastic container for 2 or 3 days. This way the rice will pick up the intense flavor of the truffle. Just before preparing the dish, remove the truffle and reserve. In a two-quart pan, melt the 3 tablespoons of butter and sauté the shallots until they are soft, then combine them with the rice (if you are using wild rice, rinse it by placing it in a strainer and running water over it for a minute), stock and thyme. Cover the pan and bring the stock to a simmer. Cook the rice for 35–40 minutes or until it is soft, but still crunchy. Drain off the excess liquid. Sauté the nuts in a small skillet in the 1 tablespoon of butter for a few minutes, then add them to the rice. Mix in the celery. Peel the truffle, or simply scrub the outside, and use a sharp knife or peeler to make shavings. Mix the shavings into the rice and chill while you prepare the dressing.

FOR THE DRESSING:

⅔ cup vegetable oil, or ⅓ cup walnut oil and
⅓ cup vegetable oil
2 teaspoons dried mustard
½ teaspoon dried thyme
½ teaspoon dried tarragon
½ teaspoon salt
pinch of sugar
¼ cup red wine vinegar
ground pepper to taste

Place the oil in a bowl with the mustard, thyme, tarragon, salt and sugar. Whisk in the vinegar and season with the pepper.

TO ASSEMBLE:

3 medium-sized endives
1 bunch watercress
2 ripe, flavorful tomatoes, sliced

Add only enough dressing to the rice to moisten it. You will not need to use it all. Slice the endives into ½-inch pieces. Place some watercress and some slices of endive on one side of each of six chilled salad plates. Place a scoop of rice salad in the center. Place several slices of tomato on the other side.

Serves 6

Mail Order Resource List

ost of these fine establishments will be delighted to send you their catalogue or price list. With these in hand, mail-order shopping for your indulgences will be a snap. Some of the items are seasonal, so it makes sense to call ahead before you send in your order.

❧ APRICOTS ❦

Barnard Nut Company
113 N.W. Thirty-sixth Street
Miami, FL 33127
(305) 576-0704
Dried apricots

Sahadi Importing Company, Inc.
187–189 Atlantic Avenue
Brooklyn, NY 11201
(718) 624-4550
(718) 624-5762
Dried apricots

Paprikas Weiss Importer
1546 Second Avenue
New York, NY 10028
(212) 288-6117
Apricot lekvar

❧ CAVIAR ❦

Petrossian, Inc.
182 West Fifty-eighth Street
New York, NY 10019
(212) 245-2217

Boyajian, Inc.
P.O. Box 26
Belmont, MA 02178
(617) 423-9333
(617) 423-9334

Caviarteria, Inc.
29 East Sixtieth Street
New York, NY 10022
1-800-422-8427
In New York (212) 759-7410

❧ CHESTNUTS ❦

Assouline and Ting, Inc.
926 West Allegheny Avenue
Philadelphia, PA 19133
(215) 225-8600
Canned chestnut puree, whole
  roasted chestnuts

Caviarteria, Inc.
29 East Sixtieth Street
New York, NY 10022
1-800-422-8427
In New York (212) 759-7410
Marrons glacés

❧ CHILES ❦

The El Paso Chile Company
100 Ruhlin Court
El Paso, TX 79922
(915) 544-3434

The Mexican Kitchen
P.O. Box 213
Brownsville, TX 78520-0213
(512) 544-6028

The Spice House
2621 North Hackett Avenue
Milwaukee, WI 53211
(414) 272-0977

⤜ CHOCOLATE ⤛

Assouline and Ting, Inc.
926 West Allegheny Avenue
Philadelphia, PA 19133
(215) 225-8600

S. E. Rykoff and Company
P.O. Box 21467
Los Angeles, CA 90021
1-800-443-0100

⤜ COFFEE ⤛

Gillies
160 Bleecker Street
New York, NY 10012
(212) 261-2130

⤜ DUCK ⤛

**Night Bird Game and Poultry
Company**
907 Harrison Street
San Francisco, CA 94107
(415) 543-6508

Pietrus Foods, Inc.
Sleepy Eye, MN 56085
(507) 794-3411

Gourmet Specialties, Inc.
333 Henry Street
Stamford, CT 06902
1-800-222-8427
In Connecticut (203) 325-8981

⤜ FIGS ⤛

Barnard Nut Company
113 N.W. Thirty-sixth Street
Miami, FL 33127
(305) 576-0704
Dried figs

Farnsworth's Gourmet
P.O. Box 298
Carlisle, MA 01741
(617) 369-2066
Dried figs

❧ FRAISES DES BOIS ❧

White Flower Farm
Litchfield 9089, CT 06759-0050
(617) 496-9600
Fraises des bois plants

❧ TEXAS RUBY RED GRAPEFRUIT ❧

Frank Lewis's Alamo Fruits
North Tower Road
Alamo, TX 78516
(512) 787-5971
In Texas 1-800-531-7470

Alex's Flamingo Groves
236 North Federal Highway
Dania, FL 33004
1-800-327-3767
In Florida 1-800-654-4347

❧ SMITHFIELD HAM ❧

The Smithfield Ham and Products Company, Inc.
P.O. Box 487
Smithfield, VA 23430
(804) 357-2121

❧ HAZELNUTS ❧

Barnard Nut Company
113 N.W. Thirty-sixth Street
Miami, FL 33127
(305) 576-0704

Westnut
P.O. Box 125
Dundee, OR 97115
(513) 538-2161

❧ LAMB ❧

Omaha Steaks International
P.O. Box 3300
Omaha, NE 68103
1-800-228-9055
In Nebraska (402) 391-3660

Glen Echo Farms
Box 21 B
Wendell, NH 03783
(603) 863-6780

❧ LOBSTER ❧

Legal Sea Foods Mail Order Department
33 Everett Street
Allston, MA 02134
1-800-343-5804
In Massachusetts (617)
254-7000

Down East Seafood Express
Box 138
Brooksville, ME 04617
1-800-556-2326

❧ MACADAMIA NUTS ❧

Barnard Nut Company
113 N.W. Thirty-sixth Street
Miami, FL 33127
(305) 576-0704

Hawaiian Plantations
1311 Kalakaua Avenue
Honolulu, HI 96826
1-800-955-8888
1-800-367-2177

Mauna Loa Macadamia Nuts
S.R. Box 3
Volcano Highway
Hilo, HI 96702
1-800-367-8047

❧ MANGOS ❧

S. E. Rykoff and Company
P.O. Box 21467
Los Angeles, CA 90021
1-800-443-0100
Mango puree

The Postilion
615 Old Pioneer Road
Fond du Lac, WI 54935
(414) 922-4170
The Postilion Imperial Mango
Chutney

❧ MASCARPONE ❧

Assouline and Ting, Inc.
926 West Allegheny Avenue
Philadelphia, PA 19133
(215) 225-8600

**To order Savoiardi biscuits for
*tirami su:***
J. Pace & Sons, Inc.
42 Cross Street
Boston, MA 02113
(617) 227-9673

❧ DRIED MUSHROOMS ❧

Woodland Pantry Forest Foods, Inc.
355 North Ashland Avenue
Chicago, IL 60607
(312) 421-3676

Festive Foods
20 Carrollton Road
Sterling, VA 22170
(703) 450-4504

Gourmet Specialties, Inc.
333 Henry Street
Stamford, CT 06902
1-800-222-8427
In Connecticut (203) 325-8981

❧ OYSTERS ❧

**Legal Sea Foods Mail Order
    Department**
33 Everett Street
Allston, MA 02134
1-800-343-5804
In Massachusetts (617)
    254-7000

York Harbor Export, Inc.
P.O. Box 737
Varell Lane
York Harbor, ME 03911
(207) 363-7206

❧ PEACHES ❧

Harry and David
Bear Creek Orchards
Medford, OR 97501
(503) 776-2400

❧ ROYAL RIVIERA PEARS ❧

Harry and David
Bear Creek Orchards
Medford, OR 97501
(503) 776-2400

❧ PISTACHIOS ❧

Barnard Nut Company
113 N.W. Thirty-sixth Street
Miami, FL 33127
(305) 576-0704

S. E. Rykoff and Company
P.O. Box 21467
Los Angeles, CA 90021
1-800-443-0100

❧ RASPBERRIES ❧

Walter K. Morss and Company
RFD 3
Bradford, MA 01830
(617) 352-2633
Raspberry plants

❧ ROQUEFORT ❧

Assouline and Ting, Inc.
926 West Allegheny Avenue
Philadelphia, PA 19133
(215) 225-8600

❧ SAFFRON ❧

Saffron Imports
70 Manchester Street
San Francisco, CA 94110
(415) 648-8990

The Spice House
2621 North Hackett Avenue
Milwaukee, WI 53211
(414) 272-0977

❧ SMOKED SALMON ❧

Petrossian, Inc.
182 West Fifty-eighth Street
New York, NY 10019
(212) 245-2217

Gourmet Specialties, Inc.
333 Henry Street
Stamford, CT 06902
1-800-222-8427
In Connecticut (203) 325-8981

Caviarteria, Inc.
29 East Sixtieth Street
New York, NY 10022
1-800-422-8427
In New York (212) 759-7410

❧ TENDERLOIN ❦

Omaha Steaks International
P.O. Box 3300
Omaha, NE 68103
1-800-228-9055
In Nebraska (402) 391-3660

❧ VANILLA BEANS ❦

Tahitian Imports
P.O. Box 67A54
Los Angeles, CA 90067
(213) 655-4895

Saffron Imports
70 Manchester Street
San Francisco, CA 94110
(415) 648-8990

Festive Foods
20 Carrollton Road
Sterling, VA 22170
(703) 450-4504

❧ WHITE ASPARAGUS ❦

Assouline and Ting, Inc.
962 West Allegheny Avenue
Philadelphia, PA 19133
(215) 225-8600

❧ WHITE TRUFFLES ❦

Urbani Truffles USA
415 West Twenty-fourth
   Street, Suite 2H
New York, NY 10011
(212) 620-0099
(212) 255-8520

Index